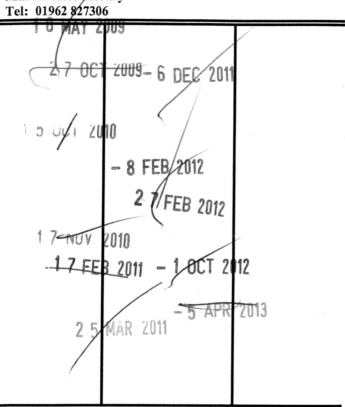

For information about the activities of Augusto Boal and the centres of the Theatre of the Oppressed in Paris and Rio de Janeiro (workshops, courses and conventions), please send a self-addressed envelope and two International Reply Coupons to:

C.T.O. – BOAL
Rua Francisco Otaviano 185/41
CEP 22080, Ipanema, Arpoador
Rio de Janeiro, RJ
Brazil

GAMES FOR ACTORS AND NON-ACTORS

Translated by
Adrian Jackson

Augusto Boal

London and New York

First published in 1992
by Routledge
11 New Fetter Lane, London EC4P 4EE

Simultaneously published in the USA and Canada
by Routledge
29 West 35th Street, New York, NY 10001

Reprinted 1993, 1994

© 1992 Original text: Augusto Boal
© 1992 Introduction and translation: Adrian Jackson

Filmset by Selwood Systems, Midsomer Norton
Printed and bound in Great Britain by
Butler & Tanner Ltd, Frome and London

British Library Cataloguing in Publication Data
Boal, Augusto
Games for actors and non-actors.
I. Title   II. [Jeux pour acteurs et non-acteurs English]
792

Library of Congress Cataloging in Publication Data
Boal, Augusto.
[Jeux pour acteurs et non-acteurs. English]
Games for actors and non-actors/Augusto Boal; translated by
Adrian Jackson.
p.   cm.
Translation of: Jeux pour acteurs et non-acteurs.
Includes bibliographical references and index.
1. Acting.   2. Games.   I. Title.
PN2061.B49413   1992
792'.028—dc20   91–43612

ISBN 0–415–06154–7   ISBN 0–415–06155–5 (pbk)

This book is dedicated to
Adrian Jackson, for his creative translation;
Helena Reckitt and Talia Rodgers, for their enthusiasm and help;
Edla Van Steen and Sábato Magaldi, forever friends;
Blanca Laksman and Leonardo Thumin, for having invented Cecilia!

CONTENTS

CONTENTS

CONTENTS

CONTENTS

CONTENTS

TRANSLATOR'S INTRODUCTION

This is a conflation of two books, *Stop! C'est magique* (Paris: Hachette, 1980) and *Jeux pour acteurs et non-acteurs* (Paris: La Découverte, 1989), with liberal additions and alterations as Boal has added examples of his latest ever-developing practice. As the title suggests, the exercises and games detailed are mostly suitable both for trained and untrained performers – it is fundamental to Boal's work that anyone can act and that theatrical performance should not be solely the province of professionals. The dual meaning of the word 'act', to perform and to take action, is also at the heart of the work.

Three main categories of the Theatre of the Oppressed are discussed in this book – Image Theatre, Invisible Theatre and Forum Theatre. However, there is a continuous overlap and interplay between all these forms, and the choice of the particular form simply depends on the situation in which the work is being made and the goal of the theatrical event.

Image Theatre is a series of exercises and games designed to uncover essential truths about societies and cultures without resort, in the first instance, to spoken language – though this may be added in the various 'dynamisations' of the images. The participants in Image Theatre make still images of their lives, feelings, experiences, oppressions; groups suggest titles or themes, and then individuals 'sculpt' three-dimensional images under these titles, using their own and others' bodies as the 'clay'. However, the image work never remains static – as with all of the Theatre of the Oppressed, the frozen image is simply the starting point for or prelude to the action, which is revealed in the dynamisation process, the bringing to life of the images and the discovery of whatever direction or intention is innate in them.

At its simplest, the idea underlying this is that 'a picture paints a thousand words'; that our over-reliance on words can confuse or obfuscate central issues, rather than clarifying them; that images can be closer to our true feelings, even our subconscious feelings, than words, since the process of 'thinking with our hands' can short-circuit the censorship of the brain, the 'cops in the head' placed there by society or personal experience. The polysemy of images is a vital factor in this work; a group of individuals will perceive a whole range of different, but often intriguingly related, meanings within a single image, often seeing things which the sculptors had no idea were there. Images work across language and culture barriers and, as Boal shows, frequently reveal unexpected universalities. Also, working with images, sculpting rather than talking, can be more democratic, as it does not privilege more verbally articulate people. Image Theatre can be used in the preparation of Invisible Theatre or Forum Theatre, and is central to the more recent therapeutic work, the subject of Boal's next book, *Méthode Boal de théâtre et de thérapie – l'arc-en-ciel du désir* (see p. 191).

Invisible Theatre is public theatre which involves the public as participants in the action without their knowing it. They are the 'spect-actors', the active spectators, of a piece of theatre, but while it is happening, and usually even after the event, they do not know that this is theatre rather than 'real life'; of course it is also 'real life', because it is actually happening, the people are real, the incidents are real, the reactions are real. This is theatre which does not take place in a theatre building or other obvious theatrical context, with an audience which does not know it is an audience. Several actors rehearse a scene which they then play in an appropriate public space; the scene usually involves an unexpected subversion of 'normal' behaviour within that particular society. In reaction to the incidents in the scene, the public becomes involved in an argument, usually aided by a couple of *agent provocateur* actors mingling with the public and expressing extreme and opposite reactions to the events of the scene.

For example, in Brazil, a man in Boal's group went to a shop with street frontage, with a woman friend, and started trying on women's dresses; another actor, as part of the gathering crowd, expressed loud indignation at this 'perversion', while a third actor took the cross-dresser's part – why shouldn't he wear women's clothes if he wants to ... in no time at all a crowd is involved in heated discussion. Invisible Theatre is a way of using theatre to stimulate debate, getting people to question issues in a public forum. It might be compared to 'agit-prop' street theatre, with the essential difference that the audience is free to take up any position it wants, and has no feeling of being preached at. It asks questions without dictating the answers. This again is fundamental to the Theatre of the Oppressed – it is never didactic to its audience, it involves a process of learning together rather than one-way teaching; it assumes that there is as much likelihood of the audience knowing the answers as the performers.

Forum Theatre is a theatrical game in which a problem is shown in an unsolved form, to which the audience, again spect-actors, is invited to suggest and enact solutions. The problem is always the symptom of an oppression, and generally involves visible oppressors and a protagonist who is oppressed. In its purest form, both actors and spect-actors will be people who are victims of the oppression under consideration; that is why they are able to offer alternative solutions, because they themselves are personally acquainted with the oppression. After one showing of the scene, which is known as 'the model' (it can be a full-length play), it is shown again slightly speeded up, and follows exactly the same course until a member of the audience shouts 'Stop!', takes the place of the protagonist and tries to defeat the oppressors.

The game is a form of contest between spect-actors trying to bring the play to a different end (in which the cycle of oppression is broken) and actors ostensibly making every possible effort to bring it to its original end (in which the oppressed is beaten and the oppressors are triumphant). The proceedings are presided over by a figure called the 'joker' (see pp. xxiv and 232), whose function is to ensure the smooth running of the game and teach the audience the rules; however, like all the participants in Forum Theatre, the joker can be replaced if the spect-actors do not think he or she is doing a fair job, and virtually any of the 'rules' of the game can be changed if the audience wants. Many different solutions are enacted in the course of a single forum – the result is a pooling of knowledge, tactics and experience, and at the same time what Boal calls a 'rehearsal for reality'.

This is a very simplified description of Forum Theatre – and, as befits a form of theatre which is now over twenty years old, there are many different manifestations of it in operation all over the world. It is used in schools, factories, day centres, community centres, with tenants' groups, homeless people, disabled people, people in ethnic minorities, etc. – anywhere where there is a community which shares an oppression. Its aim again is to stimulate debate (in the form of action, not just words), to show alternatives, to enable people 'to become the protagonists of their own lives'.

Having used Forum Theatre myself with a variety of different communities in Britain, I can testify to its efficacy, both as a way of using theatre to make sense of life and as a means of giving people the strength and confidence to overcome their oppressions. It is also great fun, giving rise to many different kinds of hilarity – laughter of recognition at the tricks of the oppressors, laughter at the ingenuity of spect-actors' ruses, triumphant laughter at the defeat of oppression. Initially one might have thought that the traditionally 'reserved' British might be the last people to get up on a stage and intervene in a theatrical action; however, if the model is right, if it is true to life, and is sufficiently effective at making the audience angry about the treatment of the protagonist, then up on stage they will come, especially when a first brave spect-actor has broken the ice. The phrase 'true to life' should not, however, be taken as an indication that Boal favours realism as a style for Forum Theatre; as detailed in the following pages, he sees truth as being utterly distinct from realism – theatrical truth, as shown in Theatre of the Oppressed work, need bear no relation to literal realism; if the oppressed see their oppressors as monsters, then it is monsters that we should show, even if this means developing a visual style more akin to expression-ism than realism.

Boal's work pursues a dogged course with endless energy and relentless optimism. He himself zooms around the world, from Africa to Canada to Europe to Rio, teaching his methods and techniques and, to all appearances, seeming on every occasion to take as much joy in seeing a group work for the first time with an exercise he must have done some thousands of times before. (One of the problems of translating the book has been actually discovering where Boal is in the world at any particular time, coupled with the vagaries of the international postal system.) When you take in this frenetic globe-trotting, you start to understand that his ambitions for the Theatre of the Oppressed as a world-changing practice are no mere quixotism.

This is not to suggest any stasis in Boal's practice – while remain-ing true to the fundamental principles of the Theatre of the Oppressed, first set down some twenty years ago, Boal continues to invent new exercises and adapt old ones with the vigour of a 20-year-old; magpie-like, he raids traditional games in whatever country he finds them, changes them if necessary to suit his particular goals, and then brings them back to his Paris and Rio centres like a hunter bringing back trophies. It is this element of joy and enthusiasm, coupled with an immense and warm humanity, which I fear no translation could entirely convey.

When watching him work, one is struck by his constant awareness and analysis of everything that is going on in the room. Impatience is rare, and emerges only when it is clear that the questioner has not listened to the answer or is not prepared to apply his or her own intellect to the work, or is looking for something more akin to paternal acceptance than knowledge of theatre and how it can help us understand and challenge the world we live in.

In his working practice as a teacher of the Theatre of the Oppressed, he eschews labels, carefully dodging questions which might pin down his current ideology or pigeon-hole it in a category of, say, 'Marxist', or 'Brechtian', or whatever; such limiting categorisations are inimical to the whole spirit of the Theatre of the Oppressed, involving as they do the mechanisation of actions and reactions, and eliminating the possibility of change or individuality – in almost every case, the Theatre of the Oppressed moves from the individual to the general, rather than vice versa. Whatever Boal's current political views, they never infringe on this work, beyond the basic philosophy of being in sympathy with the oppressed in any situation and the belief in humanity's ability to change. This does not mean that Boal does not involve himself in direct political action, sometimes using theatre – in the recent Brazilian elections he campaigned actively for Lula, the candidate of the Partido dos Trabajadores (the Workers' Party), who came very close to winning. Boal also directs 'straight' plays in 'straight' theatres, and sees Theatre of the Oppressed as just one of the many forms of theatre, not the only one, but one which can live happily alongside the others. But the Theatre of the Oppressed is the Theatre of the Oppressed, its own animal, nothing else.

Certain points of translation may need highlighting. First of all, gender – with so many thousands of references to people, whose gender is irrelevant to the context, the constant use of 'he or she' (or the other way round) would simply have taken up space and interrupted the flow. 'S/he' was an option, but it is unsayable and there is no equivalent for the possessive pronoun; where possible I have pluralised, but in many instances this would have made things difficult to understand. So, where the subject-matter is not particular to one gender, I have used he and she in, I hope, roughly equal quantities; if there are passages where one predominates this may be to do with having reordered various games and exercises, or it may be simple oversight. The word 'actor' is always used as applying to both sexes.

'Joker' presented another problem, as in English it can conjure up visions of Batman's enemy. The word 'joker' refers to the joker in a pack or cards, and has no link with the idea of playing jokes. The joker figure is, in various different contexts and combinations, the director, referee, facilitator and workshop leader; in the context of Forum Theatre, the joker is the person who acts as intermediary between audience and performers, and is attached to no one party – just as the joker in a pack of cards belongs to no one suit but floats between them. Any translation of the word would have been reductive, and in any case the word is now in such common parlance among Theatre of the Oppressed practitioners (who also use the verb 'to joke' to describe the joker's function) that it is really too late to change it – apart from the fact that it is a good word.

'Spect-actor' is a Boal coinage to describe a member of the audience who takes part in the action in any way; the spect-actor is an active spectator, as opposed to the passivity normally associated with the role of audience member. 'Magic' as in 'Stop – that's magic' refers to interventions in Forum Theatre which move from reality to the realms of magic or fantasy – for instance, a spect-actor who takes the place of a penniless protagonist and suddenly finds a thousand pounds in the road; this is probably magic, but, as in all cases, it is up to the audience to decide. I have used the word 'forum' (with no capital letter) to describe the part of an evening of Forum Theatre in which the audience, the spect-actors, start to intervene in the action, on the second showing. 'Debate' and 'discussion' almost never refer to sedentary verbal exchanges of ideas, but to views expressed in theatrical form, as interventions, rather than what Boal calls 'radio forum'. Other words are explained in context when necessary.

The Theatre of the Oppressed is about acting rather than talking, questioning rather than giving answers, analysing rather than accepting. This is a book for all those who are interested in theatre as a force for change.

Adrian Jackson
November 1991

PREFACE:
THE FABLE OF XUA-XUA, THE PRE-HUMAN WOMAN WHO DISCOVERED THEATRE

The word 'theatre' is so rich in different meanings, some complementary, some contradictory, that we never know what we mean when we talk about theatre. Which theatre do we mean?

First of all, theatre is a place: a building, any kind of construction specifically designed to house shows, plays, theatrical presentations. In this context the word 'theatre' takes in all the paraphernalia of theatrical production – sets, lights, costumes, etc. – and all the agents of that production, the actors, playwrights, directors, designers and so on.

Theatre is the setting for major events, comic or tragic, which we are obliged to observe at a distance, as paralysed spectators: the theatre of crime, the theatre of war, the theatre of the play of our passions.

We can also use the word 'theatre' in reference to the great social occasions: the inauguration of a monument, the launching of a ship, the coronation of a monarch, a military parade, a mass, a ball. The word 'rite' can be used to designate these manifestations of theatre.

Theatre can also be the repetitive acts of daily life. We perform the play of breakfast, the scene of going to work, the act of working, the epilogue of supper, the epic of Sunday lunch with the family, etc.; like actors in a long run of a successful show, repeating the same lines to the same partners, executing the same movements, at the same times, thousands of times over. Life can become a series of mechanisations, as rigid and as lifeless as the movements of a machine. This type of theatre, encrusted in our lives, can be called 'profane ritual(s)'.

Phrases like 'over-dramatising', 'making a scene', 'playing it up' – or in French '*faire du théâtre*' – are used to describe situations where people are manipulating or exaggerating or distorting the truth. In this context, theatre and lies are synonymous.

But in its most archaic sense, theatre is the capacity possessed by human beings – and not by animals – to observe themselves in action. Humans are capable of seeing themselves in the act of seeing, of thinking their emotions, of being moved by their thoughts. They can see themselves here and imagine themselves there; they can see themselves today and imagine themselves tomorrow.

This is why humans are able to identify (themselves and others) and not merely to recognise. A cat recognises its master, who gives it food and strokes it, but cannot identify him as a teacher, a professional person, a lover. To identify is to be able not only to trecognise within the same repetitive context but also to extrapolate to other contexts; to see beyond what the eye sees, to hear beyond what the ear hears, to feel beyond what touches the skin, to think beyond what words mean. I can identify a friend by a single gesture, a painter by his style, a politician by the policies he supports. Even in the absence of the subject, I can identify his mark, his traces, his actions, his merits.

An ancient Chinese fable, dating from ten thousand years before Christ, tells the story of Xua-Xua (pronounced 'Shwa-Shwa'), the pre-human woman who made the extraordinary discovery of theatre. According to this old tale,* it was a woman – not a man! – who made this discovery. Men only embezzled this wonderful art and, at various times through the ages, excluded women as actors and even as spectators. In some societies men even appropriated and acted women's roles – for instance, in Shakespearean times young boys (men not yet adult, not yet mature) played fully grown queens! In Greek theatre women were not even allowed to be passive spectators.... Because theatre is such a strong and powerful art, men invented new ways of using what was essentially women's discovery. Women discovered the art, and men invented its artifices – buildings, plays, acting.

Xua-Xua lived hundreds of thousands of years ago, when pre-women and pre-men wandered from mountain to valley, from land to sea, killing other animals to feed themselves, eating leaves and fruits from trees, drinking water from rivers, protecting themselves inside caverns among the rocks. These times were long before the

---

* This story was told to me by the last living direct descendant of Xua-Xua, who has since died. *A.B.*

arrival of Neanderthal and Cro-Magnon, long before *Homo sapiens* and *Homo habilis*, who were already almost human in their physical appearance, in the weight of their brains, and in their cruelty.

These pre-human beings lived in hordes, the better to defend themselves. Xua-Xua – who of course had no such name, nor any other, as no verbal language had yet been invented, not even the 'proto-mundo', the primal language – Xua-Xua was the most beautiful female in her horde, and Li-Peng was the strongest of the males. Naturally they were attracted to one another; they liked swimming together, climbing trees and mountains together, they liked to smell and lick one another, to touch, to embrace, to have sex together. It was good to be with one another. Together.

They were happy, as happy as two pre-human people could be.

One day, Xua-Xua felt her body becoming different. Her belly was growing, and growing. And, as her belly grew, she became shy and started to avoid Li-Peng who couldn't understand what was happening; his Xua-Xua was no longer the same Xua-Xua, neither physically nor in her moods. They kept their distance from one another. Xua-Xua liked to stay alone, watching her belly; Li-Peng went off in pursuit of other females, but could find no one like his original female.

Xua-Xua felt her belly moving; when she was on the point of falling asleep, her belly would shift from right to left, from left to right. As time went by, her belly grew bigger and bigger, and moved more and more. Like a well-behaved member of the audience, Li-Peng simply looked on from afar, very sad and very afraid. He just watched without acting, spectator to her incomprehensible actions.

In his mother's womb, Lig-Lig-Le – this was the name of the child, even though he had no name because no language had yet been invented, but this is an old Chinese fable where all liberties are licensed and welcomed! – was growing bigger and bigger, but he could not determine the extent and limits of his body. Did his body stop at his skin? At the amniotic fluid in which he was floating? Did Lig-Lig-Le end at the limits of his mother's surrounding body? Was that the world? He, his mother and the world were one single unity, he was they and they were he. This is why, even today, when we immerse our naked bodies in the water of a bathtub, the swimming pool, or the sea, we feel again those primal sensations and we merge our bodies with the whole world, Mother Earth.

This confusion of body and world could occur because Lig-Lig-Le's senses were not yet fully activated; he still couldn't see because his eyes were closed, he couldn't smell because there was no atmosphere in that tiny, cramped space, and he couldn't breathe; he couldn't taste because he was fed through the umbilical cord and not through his mouth. He couldn't feel because his skin was always touching the same liquid at the same temperature, and there was nothing to compare it with. All feeling is comparing: we sense a sound because we can hear silence, we smell a perfume because we can smell bad odours.

Hearing was the first sense to make a clear appearance. Lig-Lig-Le was concretely stimulated by his ears. He heard continuous rhythms, periodical sounds and aleatory noises – his mother's heartbeat and his own, blood running fast, gastric sounds and external voices. His first clear sensations were acoustic and he had to organise those sounds, to orchestrate them; that is why music is the most archaic art, the most deeply rooted – it comes from the womb. It helps to organise the world but not to understand it; it is a pre-human art, created before birth.

The other arts come after, when other senses are revealed. One month after birth the baby starts to see, at first only shapes, then with more precision. But what can we see, we adults? We see a continuous flow of images in movement. That's why we need the plastic arts to fix images, to immobilise them, which is impossible in daily life. Photography, cinema, impressionism come later to immobilise movement itself. Those arts see reality from the outside; dance, by contrast, penetrates movement and organises it, using sounds to support this organisation. These are the three artistic senses – hearing and sight, the main ones, and, between the actors – and occasionally from actor to audience – touch. The other two – taste and smell – are concerned with practical aspects of animal life.

One bright, sunny day, Xua-Xua gave birth to a child, on the banks of the river. Still Li-Peng watched, from behind a tree, taking no action, frightened.

This was pure magic. Xua-Xua looked at her child but could not understand. That tiny little body was part of her body; it had been inside her, now it was outside her, but undoubtedly it was she. Mother and child were one and the same; the evidence was that the small body (part of her) wanted to come back, to join up with the big body, by sucking her breast. So she could rest assured, she was both, both bodies were she. Without doubt. From afar Li-Peng, the good spectator, observed.

Lig-Lig-Le grew up, learned to walk on his own two feet, to feed on things other than the milk from the mother-body. And in the same measure he became more independent, sometimes he would not obey the big body. Xua-Xua was terrified – it was like telling one's hands to pray and instead they start to box, or telling one's legs to sit and they walk away. A rebellion was taking place, led by a small part of her – a small but dear part of her body. And she would look at herself-mother and herself-baby; both of them were she, but one of her was playing tricks, being naughty, disobeying. Li-Peng merely watched them (watching her-big and her-small). He kept his distance, just looking.

One day, Xua-Xua was sleeping. Li-Peng was curious, because he could not understand the relation between Xua-Xua and her son, and he wanted to try to establish his own relation with the boy. So when the boy awoke before his mother, Li-Peng attracted his attention, and the two of them went off together. From the start Li-Peng knew that he and the boy were two different bodies, the boy was 'the other' and not himself, not Li.

Li-Peng taught Lig-Lig-Le how to hunt and fish, and the boy was happy. When Xua-Xua awoke and looked for her small body and could not find it, she was unhappy. She cried and cried – because she had lost part of herself – and shouted and shouted, hoping her cries would be heard, but Li-Peng and the little boy had gone away.

However, since they belonged to the same horde, a few days later Xua-Xua saw them both, father and child. She wanted to get her baby-body back, but he refused, for he was also happy with his father, who taught him things his mother didn't know.

Xua-Xua had to accept that the small body, even though it had been born inside her – it was she! – was also somebody else, with his own needs and desires. The refusal of Lig-Lig-Le to obey his mother made her aware that they were two, not one; she did not want to stay with Li-Peng, Lig-Lig-Le wanted to – each had made their own choice! Each had an opinion. Each had their own feelings. They were different people.

This recognition forced her to identify herself: who was she? Who was her child? Who was Li-Peng? Where were they? What would happen next time, if her belly swelled again? Did she like Li-Peng as much now as she had done before? Would she try other males, as he had tried other females? Would all males be as predatory as Li-Peng? And what about she herself? Would she stay the same? What would happen tomorrow? Xua-Xua looked for answers by looking at herself.

In this moment, theatre was discovered. The moment when Xua-Xua gave up trying to recover her baby and keep him all for herself, accepted that he was somebody else, and looked at herself, emptied of part of herself. At that moment she was at one and the same time, Actor and Spectator. She was Spect-Actor. In discovering theatre, the being became human.

This is theatre – the art of looking at ourselves.

The Theatre of the Oppressed is *theatre* in this most archaic application of the word. In this usage, all human beings are Actors (they act!) and Spectators (they observe!). They are Spect-Actors.

This book is a systematisation of exercises (physical monologues), games (physical dialogues) and techniques of Image Theatre, designed to be used both by Actors (those who make acting their profession or craft) and Non-Actors (that is, everybody). Everybody acts. Everyone is an Actor.

The theatrical language is the most essential human language. Everything that actors do, we do throughout our lives, always and everywhere. Actors talk, move, dress to suit the setting, express ideas, reveal passions – just as we all do in our daily lives. The only difference is that actors are conscious that they are using the language of theatre, and are thus better able to turn it to their advantage, whereas the woman and man in the street do not know that they are speaking theatre, just as Molière's Monsieur Jourdain (Le Bourgeois Gentilhomme) was unaware that he spoke prose.

Many of the games, exercises and techniques in this book are original, having been completely invented; others were taken from well-known games and modified, the better to serve our purposes, i.e. the development in everyone of the capacity to express themselves through theatre. As some of the titles indicate, the exercises have a wide range of origins. Some of the games are as old as Breughel (*v.* the painting *Children's Games*).

As the most important element of theatre is the human body, this book is concerned with physical movements, distances, volumes, relations. None of the exercises or games should be done with violence, nor should any cause pain; all should be done with pleasure and understanding. Nothing should ever be done in a competitive manner – we try to be better than ourselves, not better than others.

This book is not a recipe book. To clarify the intentions of the Theatre of the Oppressed (even though I stress that this book can be used equally by professional and amateur actors, by teachers and therapists, in political or social research) I have included in it an introduction narrating many experiments undertaken during the first few years of my time in Europe, from 1976 onwards.* I have also included a theoretical explanation of my method, and some information about work I did at the Arena Theatre of São Paulo in Brazil, where I worked at the beginning of my career.

This is the most up-to-date edition in any language of this book. I hope it will be useful and entertaining; theatre should be happiness, it should help us learn about ourselves and our times. We should know the world we live in, the better to change it.

Theatre is a form of knowledge; it should and can also be a means of transforming society. Theatre can help us build our future, rather than just waiting for it.

---

* Part of this introduction was written at the same time as most of the book which follows – this should be borne in mind when reading, as the state of our world then was quite different to the world which we see now. *A.B.*

1

THE THEATRE OF THE OPPRESSED IN EUROPE

INTRODUCTION

In the pages which follow, I am going to give a brief account of some experiments carried out recently in a number of European countries. All these experiments were done in precarious conditions, with little time; two weeks in Portugal, a week in Paris, two in Stockholm, and five days in Godrano, a small Sicilian village near Palermo.

In all of these places I was able only to explain the mechanics of the different techniques, without ever being in a position to carry out an in-depth analysis. Everywhere I tried to follow the same basic scheme.

First came two days' work integrating the group, with exercises and games, and discussions on the political and economic situation in Latin America, and on the nature of the popular theatre which exists in some of our countries. These two preliminary days were necessary because the groups with which I was working were heterogeneous; in Paris, the actors came from several troupes (Aquarium, La Grande Cuillère, Carmagnole, La Tempête); in Stockholm, they were actors and spectators at the Scandinavian Skeppsholm Festival (Swedes, Norwegians, Danes, immigrants); in Portugal, people from all backgrounds; and only in Godrano actors who were all from the same group, i.e. the inhabitants of the village.

Even if they had all been homogenous groups, I believe that this introduction would still have been necessary; actors must always work on their bodies to get to know them better and to make them more expressive. The first two days' exercises are those I describe in the second section of this book. When, afterwards, we worked with the public, we would begin by asking them to do the same exercises, in order not only to warm them up and help them shed their inhibitions, but also to establish a form of theatrical communion with them.

During the following two days, exercises and games would be linked together and we would prepare Invisible and Forum Theatre scenes.

On the fifth day came the showing of the Invisible Theatre scenes and on the sixth day the Forum Theatre presentation.

Contact with the audience in the Forum Theatre sessions was always established following the same format: physical warm-up and disinhibition of the spect-actors by means of games and exercises, then Image Theatre work, and finally the Forum Theatre piece itself. The themes to be treated were always suggested by the group or by the spect-actors; I myself never imposed, or even proposed, anything by way of subject-matter – if the intention is to create a theatre which liberates, then it is vital to let those concerned put forward their own themes. And, as the preparation time was short, we never managed to write whole plays, just short scenarios.

IMAGES OF TRANSITION – THE BEGINNINGS OF IMAGE THEATRE

The technique is very simple.

First the spect-actors are asked to make a group of statues, i.e. one image, which shows in a visual form a collective perspective on a given theme. For example, in France the subject was unemployment; in Portugal, the family; in Sweden, male/female sexual oppression. One after another, the spect-actors show their images. A first group statue sculpted by a spect-actor is exhibited; if the watching group, collectively or as individuals, does not agree with the image presented a second spect-actor remakes it, differently; if the audience still only partially agrees with it, other spect-actors can modify the original statue, or complete it, or build another, completely different statue. The goal is to arrive at an image which represents a consensus among the participants. When, finally, everyone is in agreement, we will have arrived at the *Real Image* (that is, the image of reality, the world as it is), which is always the representation of an oppression.

The spect-actors are then asked to construct the *Ideal Image* (the image of ideality, the world as it could be), in which the oppression will have disappeared – the representation of the desired society, in which existing problems will have been overcome.

We return then to the *Real Image* and the debate begins. Each spect-actor, one by one, has the right to modify the Real Image, in order to show in a visual form how it may be possible to move away from our actual reality and create the reality we desire; they must show the *Image of the Possible Transition.*

The spect-actors must express themselves rapidly (so that they don't think with words and then try to translate their words into concrete representations); the aim is for the spect-actors to think with their own images, to speak with their hands, like sculptors. Then the 'statues' themselves are asked to change the oppressive reality, in slow motion or in a series of freeze-frames. Each 'statue' (actor) must act like a character in role, and not display his or her own personal character traits.

Examples of Image Theatre

1 Love-making

In Sweden, a young girl of 18 showed as a representation of oppression a woman lying on her back, legs apart, with a man on top of her, in the most conventional love-making position. I asked the spect-actors to make the *Ideal Image*. A man approached and reversed the positions: the woman on top, the man underneath. But the young woman protested and made her own image: man and woman sitting facing each other, their legs intertwined; this was her representation of two human beings, of two 'subjects', two free people, making love.

2 The family

In Portugal, someone depicted a family in an inland province: a man sitting at the end of a table, a woman standing next to him, serving him a plate of food, and several people sitting round the table. A young man from Lisbon made almost the same image again, except that now all those who were seated sat on one side of the table, the left-hand side, leaving the right-hand side empty, and everyone – apart from the head of the family – was gazing at a fixed point: the television. The same theme in the United States had been shown in the following way: a central character seated in an armchair, the other characters sitting on an arm of the chair, or on the floor, or lying flat on their stomachs, all with plate in hand, all watching the television,

3

the table banished to a corner of the room, serving only as a place to dump the food. In France, a similar picture had been created, with the difference that the characters were not together, but each in their own space; one stretched out on the ground, almost asleep, watching the television, another leaning against the door craning his neck to see better, etc. The whole gamut of representations corresponded to the whole gamut of 'families'; the father as boss, the television as centre, the other members of the family integrated or not, etc. After the presentation of such images, we always ask the audience to build the *Ideal Image*.

3 Immigrants

In Sweden, an immigrant suggested a representation of immigrants. The different expressions of this theme were: a man with outstretched arms asking for help, another man working like a dog, a young black woman lying on the ground, wretched – expressions of despair. I then asked seven Swedes to show with their bodies how they saw themselves in relation to the immigrants. The seven struck attitudes of solidarity: arms open, embraces, a hand stretched out to signify the offer of help. I immediately asked the immigrants to come back and asked both parties to try to incorporate one another into their images, first as immobile statues, then in slow-motion sequences. It was extraordinary how, in spite of their enormous and clearly visible efforts, none of them made physical contact with each other – the requests for help and the offers of help did not connect, they remained apart. I let the exercise go on, and the audience saw clearly that the proffered help was pure fiction. This became even more evident when I insisted on prolonging the exercise even further; then the amazed audience was able to register the fact that not one outstretched arm came near the young black woman on the floor who was asking for help.

Thus, we were able to see the *desire* to help, and not the *act*.

Later, one of the Swedish participants declared that he had felt willing to help and that he had demonstrated this by his stance. He had not, however, shown the desire to reach out his hand to the young black girl. He explained later that only at the end had he understood that if his willingness was real, then the young woman was also real – at least within the authenticity, within the reality of the exercise – because the exercise was true, was real, and within this reality he had done nothing. In other words he realised that if his desire had

4

been real, he would really have helped the young black woman, who was really there.

4 Old age

In Sweden again, someone proposed that we treat the subject of old age; the young people then depicted unproductive, contemplative old people, awaiting death, soliciting help to cross the road, holding up the traffic, etc. Afterwards, when I asked these same young people to enter into contact with the old people they had presented, and show the *Ideal Image*, all of them, at first, showed themselves feeding an old person, or helping one cross the road, or bathing one, etc. Scenes in which all, to a greater or lesser extent, acted as nurses; scenes in which the old people were always just as unproductive and useless as before. I asked them to try to take up the original *Real Image* again, and, in slow motion, show an *Image of the Possible Transition*. Slowly, very slowly in fact, this attitude changed: one person, then another, and finally all the young people, started to show old people engaged in activities which were productive or creative, or at least not merely contemplative; for example, looking after children, reading a book, painting a picture, teaching, etc.

5 Unemployment

In France, unemployment was the topic proposed. Generally speaking, all the scenes were very similar: a never-ending queue leading up to a young woman typing. Near her, other people working. All the people in the queue had long faces. In Denmark, I saw the same theme illustrated in almost the same way, except that the people queuing were smiling and distributing political pamphlets; it seems that in Denmark the Social Security system is more generous and the unemployed can get up to 90 per cent of their salary – they take advantage of this to engage in a variety of activities, including politics. In Portugal, the same theme had been more comprehensively dealt with: the same queue, the same young woman, but in addition, by her side, a figure composed of three men holding up three women in a sort of pyramid, crowned with arms holding a loaf of bread. In the activated version of this image, the loaf of bread was given to a policeman, who in turn gave it to a man reclining some distance away from the bread production process, lying on his back, eating; this man gave the policeman some crumbs from the loaf he had received, the policeman kept half of these for himself, and gave the other half to the human pyramid which had produced it. Opposite, in the line, men and women awaited their turn to join the pyramid, to start working, to get half the crumbs of the loaf. (For more examples of Image Theatre, see pp. 164–201.)

FIRST EXPERIENCES WITH INVISIBLE THEATRE

One point must be clearly understood: Invisible Theatre is theatre; it must have a text with a scripted core, which will inevitably be modified, according to the circumstances, to suit the interventions of the spect-actors.

The chosen subject must be an issue of burning importance, something known to be a matter of profound and genuine concern for the future spect-actors. From that starting point, a small play is constructed. The actors must play their parts as if they were playing in a traditional theatre, for a traditional audience. How-ever, when the play is ready, it will be performed in a place which is not a theatre and for an audience which is not an audience. In the course of our European experiences, we did shows in the Paris Métro, in ferry-boats, in the restaurants and streets of Stockholm, and even on a stage, in a theatre where a conference was taking place.

I repeat again: in the Invisible Theatre, the actors must perform just like real actors; that is, they must live.

Examples of Invisible Theatre

1 Sexual harassment

This invisible play was performed three times in the Métro in Paris, on the Vincennes–Neuilly line. Our chosen theatre was always the last carriage before the first-class section, in the middle of the train.

1st action

The group (apart from two actors) got on at the first stop; the scene-setting took place at the second. Two female actors remained standing near the central doors; one actor, the Female Victim, sat down, with the Tunisian on the next-door seat, the Mother and Son a little further away, and the other actors scattered around the carriage. Through two stations, nothing abnormal took place; they all read the papers or engaged in minimal conversation with the other passengers, etc.

6

2nd action

At the third station, another actor, the Male Aggressor, got on board. He sat down opposite the Female Victim, or, if the seat was taken, stood beside her. After a little while, he started nudging his leg against the young woman's, and she immediately began to protest. The Aggressor said he hadn't done anything, it was an accident. On no occasion did a single passenger ever defend the young woman. After a short interval, the Aggressor returned to his task, and this time didn't stop at leaning his leg against the young woman's, but openly placed his hand on her thigh. The latter became indignant, but no one backed her up. She got up and crossed to the other side of the compartment, where she remained standing. The Tunisian grasped the opportunity to stick up for ... the Aggressor. That concluded the second action.

3rd action

At the fifth station, the Male Victim got on, a very handsome young actor, the best-looking man in our group (– we were no James Deans!). He had barely entered before the two women by the doors, the Feminist and her Female Friend, started airing various opinions on this young man's good looks. After a bit, the Feminist addressed the Male Victim, asking him the time. He answered. She asked him which station he was getting off at. He objected:

> Look, what's with the questions? Have I asked you anything, have I asked you what station you are getting off at?

> If you had asked me, I would have told you: I'm getting off at République, and if you'd like to get off at the same place, we could 'get off' together.

As she spoke she caressed him, under the outraged stares of the passengers (who must have had some difficulty believing this unusual scene). The young man tried to escape her clutches, but she hung on to him:

> Are you aware that you're a very handsome man? Do you know, I have this terrible urge to kiss you ...

The young man tried to flee, but he was hemmed in between the Feminist and her Friend, who were loudly asserting their right to kiss him. And this time the passengers did make a stand ... against the women.

Several passengers had already intervened directly in the action. The Male Aggressor had leapt to the defence of the Male Victim. The Female Victim had taken sides with the Feminist, explaining that when she herself had been assaulted a few moments earlier, no one had defended her, and that if a man had the right to assault a woman, a woman must also have the right to lay hands on a man she found attractive.

4th action

The Female Victim, the Feminist and her Friend together tried to attack the Male Aggressor, threatening to strip him naked as a punishment, but he disappeared. The other actors stayed in the carriage to listen to what the passengers said, and also to direct the conversations gently on to the barbarity of sexual harassment on the Paris Métro or anywhere else for that matter.

In order to be sure that the whole carriage would know what was going on, the Mother asked her Son what it was all about. The boy watched, and delivered a vocal commentary (in such a way that everyone could hear) thus 'broadcasting' the action unfolding further away.

In the course of these scenes, there were some delicious episodes. For example, the old lady who exclaimed:

She's absolutely right – that young man really is rather handsome.

Or the man who vehemently defended the male's 'right':

It's the law of nature; that's the way men are, and there's no getting away from it.

For him, male advances were a law of nature, but the same gestures made by a woman were an aberration. Worse still, another man added that when a woman is sexually assaulted, it is because she has 'done something – it's always the woman's fault!'

One of the two men defending this strange theory was sitting right next to his wife at the time. The Tunisian didn't waste this opportunity:

D'you think so? Do you think that men have the right to touch up women in the Métro?

Yes, I do – they provoke us!

Then if you'll excuse me, that's exactly what I was about to do to your wife.

And he made as if to caress her.

We were within a hair's-breadth of a fight! The Tunisian had to make his excuses and get off before the intended stop.

At one of the 'performances' of this piece, there was such a great commotion that the Métro stopped at the next station and all the passengers came to watch. But the actors in the spotlight (the first Aggressor, the Female Victim, the Feminist and her Friend) hadn't bargained for the tube train stopping, they had only prepared their script as far as the station – thus they had to improvise for a good five minutes, without any preconceived plan, with the spect-actors/passengers urging the women to go ahead and strip the Aggressor ...

In this scene, the theme of the piece was clear enough: neither men nor women have the right to sexually harass anyone. However, for this piece to have a political dimension, fifty groups would have to play it five hundred times! In such circumstances, perhaps abuses of this kind would cease or at least become less frequent, and perhaps the aggressors might worry about the possibility of becoming victims of aggression themselves.

2 Queen Silvia's baby

During the Skeppsholm Festival in Stockholm, I worked with several mixed groups of actors and spect-actors. I told them all about the Parisian experience, and they wanted to do some Invisible Theatre in the Métro themselves. We prepared a number of scenes, and chose 10 July 1977 as our 'opening day', a day on which several plays were to be performed in the festival.

But the news spread quickly; though we were rehearsing in 'work-shop groups' (each being limited to thirty people), a number of people knew what we were planning. The result was that the next morning, the *Svenska Dagbladet*, one of the leading Swedish newspapers, published my photograph with an enormous headline announcing the 'première' of the Invisible Theatre in the Stockholm Métro, and advising passengers not to let themselves be caught unawares by this new form of theatre.

We decided to change 'theatres'. Stockholm (Stock-holm, island of piles) is an archipelago – fourteen islands in the centre, and more than 24,000 in all. The ferry-boats are an important and efficient means of transport. So we decided to perform in a ferry-boat.

It was around this time that Queen Silvia's baby was due to be born. The group told me that there was a general feeling of discontent about the cost of the renovation of the hospital where 'the prince' – it turned out to be a princess – was to be born; four doctors had been assigned full-time to watching and attending the royal confinement! The Swedish National Health Service may well be one of the best in the world, but many Swedes still complain of shortcomings in that area.

1st action

A young Pregnant Woman (complete with false belly) chats to a Female Friend and tells of her great admiration for Queen Silvia and her anxious wait for the birth of the heir to the throne. An actor, in the guise of a Random Passenger, doesn't agree and says so. Various details about the costs come out, the salaries, the advantages of the royal family, republic versus royalty, medicine and socialism, etc.

2nd action

The young Pregnant Woman feels the onset of labour pains. Immediately an actor playing the part of a Doctor appears and offers his services to help her. She refuses his help:

So where have you suddenly appeared from, Doctor?

I'm on my way back from the hospital. I have been working there all night. I have already attended five births today, and as far as I'm concerned, one more birth is no big deal –

That's precisely why I don't want your help. When I had my first child the doctor who looked after me was so tired that he ended up doing an unnecessary Caesarean on me, just because he wanted to finish as quickly as possible and didn't want to wait around. [I should say in passing that this had really happened to the 'pregnant' actress.] This time I want the person who takes care of me to be one of the Queen's four doctors – you know,

10

the lot who have been waiting around there for the past several weeks, they'll be well rested by now. Who'll take me there? I want someone to take me to one of the Queen's four doctors.

The scene carried on, and the actors argued with the passengers about the Swedish hospital system, which was the subject of the piece. At least half of the passengers joined in the discussion; the other half followed the debate attentively.

3rd action

On the Djugarden–Slussen line, the journey takes seven minutes, which was exactly the duration of the 'show'. By the time the boat docked, the crew had already warned the hospital by radio, and there was an ambulance waiting for our Pregnant Woman. As the actors had foreseen this eventuality, we also had a car at our disposal and the young woman refused the ambulance and set off in the company of her friends while the discussion continued on the quayside.

3 Racism I: the Greek

This piece was played in two different restaurants, both open-air establishments. The theme, put forward by the actors, was obviously of enormous importance in Sweden, where there is considerable prejudice against foreigners. 'Dog's Eye' is an epithet applied to anyone whose eyes are not blue (in a country where the majority of the indigenous population do have blue eyes).

1st action

The Wife and the Husband are seated together at a table, loudly engaged in argument. She tells him off for being too fond of (other) women, for not helping with the household chores, not taking enough interest in their son, etc. He tries to assert his 'man's rights'.

2nd action

A young woman, the Husband's Mistress, comes in and sits down at another table. The Husband leaves his Wife on her own, in spite of her protests, and goes to sit with his mistress. An amorous dialogue ensues.

11

3rd action

Enter a young Greek man, who looks for a place to sit. The Wife invites him to sit next to her. To his astonishment, the Wife tries to seduce him.

4th action

The Husband sees that his Wife has company, he returns to her side and tries to get rid of the Greek. He attacks him on grounds of nationality. The Wife insists on the Greek staying with her. The waiter is forced to intervene, because the Husband asks him to throw the Greek out of the restaurant, and the Wife asks him to throw her Husband out. General argument. The Husband's rage is based not on the fact that his Wife is with another man, but that this man is ... a Greek. And he proclaims this fact to the assembled company.

On the two occasions on which this scene was performed, the public's participation was full-blooded. The second time, I was sitting next to a Swedish journalist covering the story. At a table some distance away were some of her friends. According to her, they were all self-proclaimed anti-racists. And now this racist scene was being played out in front of them, it was happening right there and then. And yet the only ones who didn't want to join in were these friends of the journalist. They were the exception – the argument was intense. Racism was not the only topic under discussion, but also a married woman's right to get her own back on her husband.

4 Racism II: the black woman

This piece was performed on a ferry-boat.

1st action

The group once again took the Slussen boat, but this time in the opposite direction, towards Djugarden, which is the zoological garden. The boat was packed. This was the most explosive of the Skeppsholm shows, the most violent show and also the one which provoked the most spirited reactions.

As the first move, a Black Woman actor takes a seat positioning herself strategically in a visible spot. An Italian man, a male Office

Worker and a female Drunkard all sit or stand a little distance away.
The Drunkard (an excellent actor) was one of the first people on
board. Can of beer in hand, she solemnly greets every passenger who
enters. She chats amiably to some, provokes others and generally
outrages most with her behaviour.

2nd action

The boat leaves. After a few moments, the Italian approaches the
young Black Woman and asks her what she's doing there; she, a
black girl, is sitting, and he, a white man, is standing. Violent
argument about racial rights. The angry Black Woman gets up and
the Italian sits; he starts reading an Italian newspaper. The Drunkard,
who has witnessed the scene along with everyone else, approaches
the Italian.

3rd action

The Drunkard insists that the Italian get up and give her his place.

> You said that this was a land for whites – fair enough, this is a
> land for whites, white Swedes; and you're Italian. Get out of
> that seat.

Further discussion on countries of origin, races and the rights of man.
Finally the Italian leaves.

4th action

The Office Worker approaches the Drunkard. He insists that she get
up and give him her place, because Swedish she may be, but she is
also drunk and unproductive, and, in his book, the priority for seated
accommodation is not solely a question of race and nationality but
also of class: he is white, Swedish *and* a white-collar worker. General
revolt.

The cumulative effect was extraordinary. A crowd of people
defended the Drunkard, all arguing at once, for and against relative
differences in rights for different nationalities, races or classes.

5th action

An actor pretends to convince the young Black Woman to return to her place. She refuses the 'charity'. Different actors seated around the place stand up to argue against prejudice, and each cites a reason: 'I am standing up because I am Brazilian!' 'I am standing because I am Indian!' 'I am standing because I am poor', etc.

The result was incredible and wonderful. Quite apart from the effectiveness of the discussion, it was amazing to see so many empty seats, vacated in token of protest, in spite of the fact that the boat was crowded and everyone was cramped.

After the show, the actor who took the role of the Office Worker, a professional with a long career behind him, told me that he had never been so nervous at an opening night, he had never been so terrified. But he also acknowledged that he had rarely been so glad to take part in a show.

5 Picnic in the streets of Stockholm

I have lived in São Paulo in Brazil for fifteen years. There the streets are right on top of each other, which means that people who live on the third floor sometimes have car exhaust pipes level with their windows; those who live on the first or second floor see cars moving around above them. That's why for me Stockholm is a nice city. But it's not the same for the people who live there. They say that the city was planned for cars and not for pedestrians. So they chose this as their theme and mounted the following play.

1st action

A Family (Father, Mother, Son, Daughter) set out a table, complete with flowers, cups, a Thermos of tea, biscuits, etc., right in the middle of the pavement, and they start having tea. Three car-loads of actors park nearby and watch.

2nd action

Two actors take the role of Passers-by; they grumble, saying that the pavement was made for people to walk on and not for people to set up tables and have tea on. The Family, after a short discussion, gives in.

14

Since we can't have tea on the pavement, which is intended for pedestrians, let's have it in the middle of the road.

3rd action

The three cars move off together and the Family signal them to stop; the three cars stop. They block the road, bringing the traffic to a complete standstill. The Family set out their table, flowers, cups, Thermos flask and biscuits, in the middle of the road, and take tea, with an utterly British imperturbability. The actors in the three cars act like normal drivers and remonstrate with the Family; as far as they're concerned the road was made for cars and not as a place for families to have tea.

4th action

A sort of contest develops between the Family and the Drivers, both parties trying to convince the spect-actors to support their cause.

In a matter of minutes, the road was chock-a-block with buses, taxis, cars, mopeds, all hooting their horns. The actors tried to persuade them to take tea with them. Some accepted. Others got annoyed:

Why don't you go and have tea at home?

Because we haven't got such a nice car as you. Because we haven't got time; we only have an hour's break from work, we work in Stockholm and live in Salsjöbaden, which is nearly an hour from here! Because ... etc.

The arguments raged. The actors were fired with enthusiasm and went on to improvise well beyond the bounds of their prepared text. As a result of the marvellous response from the spect-actors, the improvisation went on a further quarter of an hour, which is a very long time for this kind of theatrical event and in circumstances such as these. The arguments came thick and fast ... right up until the arrival of the police.

An unrehearsed action: the Police

Invisible Theatre almost always comes up against an important problem; safety. Invisible Theatre offers scenes of fiction. But without the mitigating effects of the rites of conventional theatre, this fiction becomes reality. *Invisible Theatre is not realism; it is reality.*

And everything that happens, happens in reality: a young woman kissing a boy in the Métro in Paris, an expectant mother feeling labour pains in a Stockholm ferry-boat, a black girl driven from her seat, a Greek man arguing with a Swedish husband over his wife, a family taking tea in the middle of the road – all this is reality, even though it has been rehearsed.

The family was a real family, the tea and toast were real tea and real toast – and the police who turned up were also real. They arrived with two cars and a police van. The Stockholm police have installed a network of television cameras, so that the strategic points of the town are continually under the surveillance of these invisible eyes. And the Invisible Theatre had been seen by these invisible cameras connected to the police's invisible headquarters ...

Had the scene run its intended course, the protagonists of the play would by this time have packed their bags and departed peacefully, 'with the Lord's blessing'. But as a result of the enthusiasm of both actors and spect-actors (who even went as far as forming a circle and dancing to the rhythm of the bus and taxi horns) the police had time to make their spectacular entry. The sergeant wanted to arrest 'the actors'; but how could he work out who was an actor and who wasn't? So he decided that everyone touching any part of the set (sitting on a chair, holding a cup of tea, or even eating a piece of cake) was an actor. Several actors were arrested – including a few charming ladies who were just passing by – and had their records checked over the radio. As they were not on a wanted list, they were immediately freed again.

One should never explain to the public that Invisible Theatre is theatre, lest it lose its impact. However, in this particular case, we had no option but to explain to the police. But I have a feeling that they still didn't really understand ...

6 The audience's children

For my last lecture at the festival, there were some 700 adults and at least 50 unruly children. In Sweden there is an incredibly tolerant attitude towards children; they're allowed to do whatever they like. In the course of the performances, there were occasions when they got on to the stage and, during a musical, even spoke into the microphone; nothing ever happened to them, not even the smallest reprimand.

In this last lecture, my task was to explain what Invisible Theatre was, and to describe the pieces we had done. But the actors had a better idea; they prepared an Invisible Theatre scene about children. The result was fantastic.

1st action

The actors were scattered throughout the audience. We arranged that when I was going to talk about Invisible Theatre, I would give a signal by putting my hands on my head. The moment came, I put my hands on my head. One of the actors stood up and proposed in Swedish (the conference was being held in English) that the children be removed from the room because not a single word of what I was saying could be heard, and this was annoying for the other people present.

2nd action

A female actor defended the children and their right to participate in the conference even if they couldn't understand it. A male actor tried to eject a child from the room, another caught hold of the child and tried to stop him being ejected. From various parts of the room chunks of prepared dialogue were delivered, blending in with the audience's spontaneous interventions. I asked in English what was happening. Here once again was a situation which was explosive, a situation which involved the participation of everyone in the theatre.

3rd action

At another signal given by me, all the actors got on stage at the same time, and I invited them to take a bow to the audience, just like in a conventional theatre. It was only at this moment that the audience realised that they had been involved in an Invisible Theatre scene. And it was then that they understood what Invisible Theatre is. There was no need to say any more ...

FORUM THEATRE

In Invisible Theatre the spectator is transformed into a protagonist in the action, a spect-actor, without ever being aware of it. He is the protagonist of the reality he sees, because he is unaware of its fictitious origin.

That is why it is essential to go further, and make the audience participants in a dramatic action, but in complete consciousness of the reason. And in order to encourage them to participate, they need to be 'warmed up' beforehand with exercises and games; the statue-making Image Theatre game is an essential tool in emboldening the spectator.

Before coming to Europe, I had done a lot of Forum Theatre, in a number of Latin American countries, but always in 'workshop' situations, never as a 'performance'. Here in Europe, at the time of writing, I have already done several Forum Theatre sessions as performances.* In Latin America, the audience was generally small and homogeneous, the spect-actors almost always being the workers from one factory, the residents of a particular neighbourhood, the congregation of a church, the students of a university, etc. Here, besides that kind of 'workshop' forum, I have also done shows for hundreds of people who didn't know each other at all. This is a new type of Forum Theatre, which I began to develop here, with some very positive results.

Also, most of the Forum Theatre pieces I did in Latin America had a 'realistic' style. Here in Europe I have also done 'symbolist' scenes, as was the case in Portugal for a work about agrarian reform (see p. 22).

The rules of the game

Forum Theatre is a sort of fight or game, and like all forms of game or fight there are rules. They can be modified, but they still exist, to ensure that all the players are involved in the same enterprise, and to facilitate the generation of serious and fruitful discussion.

Dramaturgy

1 The text must clearly delineate the nature of each character, it must identify them precisely, so that the spect-actors can easily recognise each one's ideology.

2 The original solutions proposed by the protagonist must contain at the very least one political or social error, which will be analysed

---

* Now in 1991, I have been involved in several hundred such performances, in dozens of countries; most recently, the Theatre of the Oppressed Encounter at Massy in Paris (March–April 1991) brought together more than twenty Theatre of the Oppressed groups, practising the method in seventeen countries. *A.B.*

during the forum session. These errors must be clearly expressed and carefully rehearsed, in well-defined situations. This is because Forum Theatre is not propaganda theatre, it is not the old didactic theatre. It is pedagogical in the sense that we all learn together, actors and audience. The play – or 'model' – must present a mistake, a failure, so that the spect-actors will be spurred into finding solutions and inventing new ways of confronting oppression. We pose good questions, but the audience must supply good answers.

3 The piece can be of any genre (realism, symbolism, expressionism, etc.) except 'surrealism' or the irrational; the style doesn't matter, as long as the objective is to discuss concrete situations (through the medium of theatre).

Staging

1 The actors must have physical styles of playing which successfully articulate their characters' ideology, work, social function, profession, etc. It is important that there is a logic to the characters' evolution, and that they *do things*, or else the audience will be inclined to take their seats and do the 'forum' without the theatre – by speech alone (without action) like a radio forum.

2 Every show must find the most suitable means of 'expression' for its particular subject-matter; preferably this should be found by common consent with the public, either in the course of the presentation or by prior research.

3 Each character must be presented 'visually', in such a way as to be recognisable independently of their spoken script; also the costumes must be easy for the spect-actors to get in and out of, with the minimum of fuss.

The performance game

The performance is an artistic and intellectual game played between actor and spect-actor.

1 To start off with, the show is performed as if it were a conventional play. A certain image of the world is presented.

2 The spect-actors are asked if they agree with the solutions advanced by the protagonist; they will probably say no. The audience is then told that the play is going to be done a second

time, exactly as it was done the first time. The actors will try to bring the piece to the same end as before, and the spectators are to try to change it, showing that new solutions are possible and valid. In other words, the actors stand for a particular *vision of the world* and consequently will try to maintain that world as it is and ensure that things go exactly the same way ... at least until a spect-actor intervenes and changes the vision of the world *as it is* into a world *as it could be*. It is vital to generate a degree of tension among the spect-actors – if no one changes the world it will stay as it is, if no one changes the play it will come to the same end as before.

3 The audience is informed that the first step is to take the protagonist's place whenever he or she is making a mistake, in order to try to bring about a better solution. All they have to do is approach the playing area and shout 'Stop!' Then, immediately, the actors must stop where they are without changing position. With the minimum delay, the spect-actor must say where he or she wants the scene taken from, indicating the relevant phrase, moment, or movement (whichever is easiest). The actors then start the scene again from the prescribed point, with the spectactor as protagonist.

4 The actor who has been replaced doesn't immediately retire from the game; he or she stays on the sidelines as a sort of coach or supporter, to encourage the spect-actors and correct them if they start to go wrong. For example, in Portugal a peasant who was replacing the actor playing the part of the Boss started shouting 'Long live socialism!' The replaced actor had to explain to her that, generally speaking, bosses aren't great fans of socialism ...

5 From the moment at which the spect-actor replaces the protagonist and begins to put forward a new solution, all the other actors transform themselves into agents of oppression, or, if they already were agents of oppression, they intensify their oppression, to show the spect-actor how difficult it is to change reality. The game is spect-actors – trying to find a new solution, trying to change the world – against actors – trying to hold them back, to force them to accept the world as it is. But of course the aim of the forum is not to win, but to learn and to train. The spect-actors, by acting out their ideas, train for 'real life' action; and actors and audience alike, by playing, learn the possible consequences of their actions. They learn the arsenal of the oppressors and the possible tactics and strategies of the oppressed.

6 If the spect-actor gives in, he or she drops out of the game, the actor takes up the role again, and the piece rapidly heads back towards the already known ending. Another spect-actor can then approach the stage, shout 'Stop!' and say where he or she wants the play taken from, and the play will start again from that point. A new solution will be tried out.

7 At some point the spect-actor may eventually manage to break the oppression imposed by the actors. The actors must give in – one after another or all together. From this moment on, the spect-actors are invited to replace anyone they like, to show new forms of oppression which perhaps the actors are unaware of. This then becomes the game of spect-actor/protagonist against spect-actor/oppressor. Thus the oppression is subjected to the scrutiny of the spect-actors, who discuss (through their actions) ways of fighting it. All the actors, from off stage, carry on their work as coaches and supporters, each actor continuing to help and urge on his or her spect-actor.

8 One of the actors must also exercise the auxiliary function of joker, the wild card, leader of the game. It is up to him or her to explain the rules of the game, to correct errors made, and to encourage both parties not to stop playing. Indeed, the effect of the forum is all the more powerful if it is made entirely clear to the audience that if they don't change the world, no one will change it for them, and everything will inevitably turn out exactly the same – which is the last thing we would want to happen.

9 The knowledge which results from this investigation will, of necessity, be the best that that particular human social group can attain at that particular moment in time. The joker is not the president of a conference, he or she is not the custodian of the truth; the joker's job is simply to try to ensure that those who know a little more get the chance to explain it, and that those who dare a little, dare a little more, and show what they are capable of.

10 The 'forum' over, it is proposed that a 'model of action for the future' be constructed, this model first to be played out by the spect-actors.

Examples of Forum Theatre

1 Agrarian reform seen from a public bench

In Portugal, just after 25 April 1974, the people took agrarian reform into their own hands. They didn't wait for a law to be passed, they simply occupied the unproductive land and made it productive. At the time of writing, the government intends to institute an agrarian law which will challenge the popular conquests on that front, returning areas of land to their former owners (who made no use of them).

1st action

The scene takes place on two benches in a garden. A man, the Landowner, is lying stretched out across both benches, taking his ease. Enter seven men and women singing 'Grandula Vila Morena' by Jose Afonso, the Eurovision Song Contest tune used as the signal for the start of the military action which ousted the 50-year-old fascist Salazar–Caetano dictatorship. The seven men and women evict the great Landowner from one of the two benches in which he is ensconced; in spite of his removal, they are none the less cramped on their one bench, because there are many of them.

2nd action

They get down to work, miming the tasks of cultivation, while singing other popular songs. They start to discuss the need to push their conquest of public benches further. They take exception to the unproductiveness of the Landowner who has stayed put, with one bench all to himself, but opinions are divided: some want to turf him out, while others think that they've done enough already, that enough ground has been gained.

3rd action

A Policeman comes along, bearing an order that they vacate 20 cm of the collective bench ('the law of return'). They break into factions; some are for giving way, others are not, since to make a concession now would signify a victory for the forces of reaction, which would then gradually try to regain more ground. Eventually they give in.

4th action

The Landowner, protected by the Policeman, sits himself down on the vacated end of the bench. The seven others crowd in on the remaining section. The Landowner opens up a big umbrella, obscuring the light from the others. The seven protest. The Policeman declares that the Landowner is entitled to do what he is doing, since though the ground may be taken, the air is not. The seven are divided: some want to fight, others are happy with the little they've obtained and want peace at any price.

5th action

The Policeman insists on the need to erect a wall dividing the collective bench into two parts, this wall to be built on 'land' which doesn't belong to anyone; evidently the intention is that it will be built on the part of the bench occupied by the seven, not on the former owner's side. More discussions, more divisions, more concessions. One of the seven abandons the struggle, a second also goes, then a third and a fourth.

6th action

The Policeman announces that the occupation is pointless since the majority of the occupants have abandoned the occupied land. Consequently, the last three are thrown out and the former owner reassumes his rights over both public benches.

The forum

This scene was performed at Porto and at Vila Nova de Gaia. On the day of the first performance, there were more than a thousand people on the square in the open air. The 'model' was performed, then the 'forum' began. On the second showing, a number of spect-actors enacted their vision of how to resist the Landowner's counter-attack. But the best moment was when a woman in the audience protested. On the simple stage, there were some male spect-actors arguing among themselves – in role – about the best tactics to use; finally they decided that they were all of one mind and that the forum had been useful. At this point the woman in the audience said:

There you go, talking about oppression – that's all very well;

the only people on the stage are men from the audience, who don't seem in the slightest oppressed by the actors, who were their deadly enemies a moment ago. And meanwhile, here in the audience, it's us women who continue to be oppressed since we are just as inactive as before, sitting here, watching the men act!

One of the male spectators then invited several women to give vent to their feelings in the different roles. They agreed to do so, allowing only one man to remain on stage, the man who played the Policeman. As the woman said:

Since the Policeman is the number one oppressor, that part can certainly be played by a man.

2 The people judge a secret policeman

The special secret police force active during the regime of Salazar and Caetano (the *Pides*) was extremely brutal and repressive. This model showed the moment when a character recognises one of his torturers in a market-place, and tries to arrest him. The opinions of the onlookers in the scene are divided; some believe that popular justice should still be meted out by the old institutions. Thus the moment a Soldier appears, they are tempted to obey him and to recognise in him the incarnation of 'authority' – the first mistake. Then, when the Soldier has examined the situation and looked over a 'safe-conduct' document issued to the Secret Policeman by the military authorities, it is decided to let him go, even if the man was a former torturer – the second mistake, since no safe-conduct document could count for more than, or replace, the will of the people.

The forum

In one of the versions of this scene we presented our vision of a 'people's tribunal'. The spect-actors of the forum soon showed us how far off the mark we were; in a people's tribunal you don't find the same characters as in bourgeois judicial cases. For example, the defence lawyer does not exist, there is a jury made up of people who hear the evidence and then judge, accuse, or impose a penalty. At Vila Nova de Gaia, the audience was particularly worked up. Their in-role jury got so angry with the spect-actor representing the Secret

Policeman that they even went as far as physically attacking him. The poor spect-actor had to go to the doctor to get two stitches on his forehead. Forum Theatre can sometimes be violent; this must be avoided at all costs – the physical security of all participants must be ensured.

3 Leader at work, slave in the home

In Paris, during a strike by the employees in the electronic accounting department of a bank, we did a Forum Theatre show about a woman who was a leading trade unionist at her work, but a slave in her own home.

1st action

Too much work. A rush of customers. As soon as the bank closes, the Trade Unionist tries to organise her comrades, makes telephone calls here, there and everywhere, fixes up appointments, arranges meetings, etc. Everyone follows her advice.

2nd action

Enter (outside) the Trade Unionist's Husband. He hoots his horn. She resists for a moment or two, but ends up abandoning her colleagues and going home with her Husband.

3rd action

At her place. She takes care of everything for her husband, who is getting ready for his after-work pastimes and who thus can't be bothered with any household chores. She bathes her child, who is playing up and needs continual attention. The scene ends on that note – this woman is entirely a slave to her family.

The forum

Many women took part in the forum, replacing the protagonist and trying to break the oppression. At the same time, the woman's colleagues at the bank also changed themselves into oppressors and made her give in to her husband. And even if she had still wanted to carry on with her work, in spite of her husband, in spite of her colleagues, her office manager arrived and virtually threw her out. This continued until a woman spect-actor proposed the best possible form of resistance – not to let the Husband in! Thereupon, the Actor-Husband gave up and was replaced by other spect-actors who applied other forms of pressure: telephoning, emotional blackmail, lying, etc.

During the scene in the house, a curious thing happened: the Spect-actor Trade Unionist was so wrapped up in her work, that she paid no attention either to her daughter or her husband. The little daughter in her bath, having previously cried 'Mummy, Mummy, Mummy ...', now began to cry 'Daddy, Daddy, Daddy ...' and it was the Husband who eventually went to deal with the child and did the housework!

4 The return to work at the Crédit Lyonnais

The same day, and for the same audience, we presented another scene during which there were sequences showing a return to work after a strike. The scene was centred on the portrait of a strike-breaker. In the version played by the actors, the Strike-breaker was completely isolated, total ostracism: no one wanted to talk to him, he was maltreated by everyone.

When the forum commenced, two things struck us. First of all, the spect-actors, who really did work at the bank, refuted our vision of it; they completely redirected the scene, showing us that what we had presented as a 'bank' was more like a sub-post office.

Second, the spect-actors immediately did the opposite of what we had done; instead of abandoning and isolating the Strike-breaker, on the contrary they tried every way to persuade him to stand with them and to adopt the position of collective responsibility.

5 The nuclear power station

In Sweden, the controversy over nuclear energy and the construction of power stations was very much a live issue. Some even said that the main reason for the gunning down of Prime Minister Olof Palme was his having affirmed that he would pursue a policy of nuclear gearing-up. His opponents said the opposite – and afterwards, they did it anyway ...

1st action

Eva is in her office, at work. The scene shows friends, the Boss, day-to-day problems, the process of finding new projects to work on, the daily grind of a hard life.

2nd action

Eva is at home; her husband is out of work, their daughters are spendthrifts, they need money. A Female Friend drops round, they go out. They go straight to a demonstration against the construction of atomic power stations.

3rd action

Back at the office. The Boss comes in whooping with joy: a new project has been accepted! Everyone celebrates the news! Champagne is consumed! Joy unbounded ... till the Boss explains what this new project is about – the development of a refrigeration system for a nuclear power station. Eva is torn; she needs work, she wants to support her fellow workers, but this situation poses a moral problem for her. She gives all the reasons she can for not accepting this new project, and her colleagues give their opposing reasons. Finally Eva gives in and accepts the job!

The forum

In this piece it was clear that the protagonist was going to have to commit an error and not be heroic. The audience almost cried when Eva gave in. And the effect of this was an extraordinary intensification of the fight – the game of actors/oppressors against spect-actors/oppressed – when it came to finding reasons for Eva to say no. Each time a spect-actor gave in and saw that she was beaten, the piece rapidly retraced its path towards Eva's 'Yes'. Passions in the audience ran high again till someone shouted 'Stop!'; then the scene stopped and the new spect-actor tried a new solution starting from the first action, or the second, or even the third. Everything was analysed: the husband's unemployment, the daughters' mania for consumption, Eva's indecision. Sometimes the analysis was purely 'psychological', then another actor would come in and try to show the political side of the problem.

Should we be for or against nuclear power stations? Can one be against scientific progress? Can the word 'progress' be applied to science when it leads us to the discovery of nuclear weapons?

And on the question of the disposal of 'nuclear waste': surely it could be satisfactorily disposed of in a social system whose central value was the human being rather than the profit motive.

I have already twice had the opportunity to take part in pieces of this kind. The first time was in the USA, where an analogous piece had been written about the inhabitants of a town which was producing the napalm used in Vietnam. In the end, in the American example, the inhabitants accepted the factory, reaching the conclusion that it would be economically ruinous to close it. ... Ruinous for whom? The second time was in Lisbon, again with a similar model: there is a refinery there which is causing a noticeable increase in the occurrence of lung cancer ... but it is important for the economy. Here again, the residents gave way and resigned themselves to living with pollution, rather than living without jobs.

In this example, the function of Forum Theatre is quite clear: it is the other side of Ibsen's *An Enemy of the People*, whose leading character, Stockman, faced with an identical situation, takes an heroic stance.

Who exactly is taking an heroic stance? The character, the fiction. What I want is for the spect-actor to take an heroic stance, not the character. I think it is perfectly clear: if Stockman is a hero and prefers to stand alone, not compromising his moral principles, that can serve as an example. But this is cathartic – Stockman has an heroic attitude and demands of me that I sympathise with his heroic attitude. He drains me of my desire to behave like a hero myself.

In Forum Theatre, the reverse mechanism is at work. The character gives in and I am called upon to correct him, to show him a possible right, to rectify his action. And in so doing within the fiction of the play, I am preparing myself to do it in reality as well. I come face to face with reality (fictitiously). I become acquainted with the difficulties which I will meet later – fear of unemployment, my fellow workers' arguments, etc. – and if I manage to overcome all these things in Forum Theatre, I will be better qualified to overcome them in reality when the situation arises. Forum Theatre does not produce catharsis: it produces a stimulant for our desire to change the world.

All these forms of Theatre of the Oppressed have developed in response to concrete and particular political situations. When in 1971 the dictatorship in Brazil made it impossible for the people to present popular theatre, we started to work on Newspaper Theatre* techniques, which were forms of theatre easily realisable by the people, so that they would be able to produce their own theatre. In Argentina before the last elections (1973), when the level of repression eased (without completely disappearing), we started doing Invisible Theatre in trains and restaurants, in queues for shops, in markets. When certain conditions arose in Peru, we began to work on various forms of Forum Theatre so that the spect-actors would fully assume their function of protagonist, which is what they were at the time; we thought that the people would have a role to play in the near future. That was in 1973.

In fact, all these forms of theatre emerged when we were barred from traditional and institutional theatre. An experiment I would love to try would be doing Forum Theatre in the theatre, in a conventional theatre building, with an advertised starting time for the show, with sets and costumes, with extant scripts, by single writers or written collectively.†

Wouldn't it be wonderful to see a dance piece where the dancers danced in the first act, and in the second showed the audience how to dance? Wouldn't it be wonderful to see a musical where in the first act the actors sang and in the second we all sang together?

What would also be wonderful would be a theatre show wherewe, the artists, would present our world-view in the first act andwhere in the second act, they, the audience, could create a newworld.

Let them create it first in the theatre, in fiction, to be better prepared to create it outside afterwards, for real.

I think that this is how magicians should be: first they should do their magic to enchant us, then they should teach us their tricks. This is also how artists should be – we should be creators and also teach the public how to be creators, how to make art, so that we may all use that art together.

---

* For Newspaper Theatre, see Augusto Boal, *The Theatre of the Oppressed*, London: Pluto Press, 1979.
† Since writing this in 1978, I have done a number of experiments of this nature in many countries. I have even directed Bertolt Brecht's *The Jewish Wife* and played it in a Forum session in Paris, in 1984. Similarly Sophocles' *Antigone* has been done as a piece of Forum Theatre in Lausanne in Switzerland. *A.B.*

THE GODRANO EXPERIENCE (OR THE ULTIMATE SPECT-ACTOR/PROTAGONIST!)

Godrano is a little village in Sicily, 40 km from Palermo. There are many things Godrano lacks: hotel, hospital, supermarket, cinema, theatre – there isn't even a petrol station or a newsagent's. If you want a newspaper you have to go and buy it at Villa Frati, which is a ten-minute drive away.

Among the few facilities which Godrano does have are a bar, a church, a public telephone, two butchers, two grocers, oh yes, and a *carabinieri* (police station).

Godrano lies in the Busambra valley, in the province of Busambra, overlooked by a mountain of the same name. And right in the middle of the mountain, there is a fissure, a precipice. Into this precipice the local mafia – which holds sway over the whole region – throws the bodies of numerous workers and peasant leaders with whom they disagree.

There have been many mafias. The first mafia, that of Salvatore Giuliano, was a pre-revolutionary form of popular organisation. This was the people armed, the people in revolt, and yet a people without ideology, without a strategy for taking power. So it was defeated. Then the anti-people mafias emerged; the fish mafia (on the coast) used to buy an 11-kilo box of sardines for 1,000 lire and sell the contents in the market at 600 lire a kilo. And anyone who got in the way was warned; his house was burned down. If there was a second offence, the definitive solution was applied; the fisherman was thrown down the Busambra precipice. There were also mafias in the civil construction industry, vegetable mafias and animal fodder mafias.

Because Godrano is essentially a pastoral '*paese*', the community numbers among its inhabitants slightly fewer than 1,000 people and slightly more than 8,000 cows. Why so many cows? Why eight cows for each human being? Because the European Common Market obliges Italy to buy its meat abroad. And the meat one eats in Palermo (all of 40 km away) arrives by plane, when it could just as easily come from Godrano on foot. Foreign cows feed the population of Palermo, and the cows of Godrano live a long life, grow senile and die sclerotic. And these aren't even sacred cows.

Godrano used to have a population of over 2,000, but half had to emigrate. They went to Germany, Switzerland, Sweden, Argentina, Brazil, they went where they had family, friends, or hope. But not one of these emigrants ever stopped thinking of their little *paese*.

That's why building work still goes on in Godrano; there are fewer and fewer people and more and more houses – one day the emigrants will return ...

Such was Godrano in 1977, a peaceful village. A profoundly unhappy village.

Feminism in Godrano

Everyone was unhappy in Godrano, and among the unhappiest were the women and the girls. Everyone was oppressed, but most oppressed were the women who were married or soon to be married. In the afternoons I used to walk around the village's few streets, and in front of almost every house I would see a woman sitting sewing. She would be preparing her trousseau or her daughter's. The trousseau is called the *corredo* and the *corredo* is an Italian national institution. But in Sicily it is even more awful and alienating than elsewhere in the country.

For example, someone told me that it used to be perfectly normal – and is still common today – for the bridegroom's family, before the marriage, to meet the bride's family for what is known as 'the valuation'. Father, mother, uncles and aunts, sisters and brothers, and, sometimes, friends of the family, gather together for this occasion and the bride's family start displaying the contents of the *corredo*.

This cloth cost 20,000 lire.

That's impossible, it's worth far less. I've seen the same stuff in Paoletti's but much better quality and half the price.

Well, that's what it cost –

So the argument goes on till a rough figure can be agreed, then on to the next items, and in this fashion, in front of the assembled company, they parade the bridal nightgown, the handkerchiefs, the sheets, the towels, the carpets and the lampshades.

When everyone is in agreement, the whole lot is written down on a list, with two copies, one for each family. Then, and right up until the marriage, the components of the *corredo* remain on view, for one or two weeks; viewing is open to all friends and family.

The groom is not required to present a *corredo*. Which means, translated into simple arithmetic: 1 bride + 1 trousseau = 1 bridegroom.

There's equality for you.

Another 'detail' – the bride absolutely must be a virgin. Until recently (some say even to this day), in many places in Sicily, it was the custom, the morning after the nuptial night, for the man to hang out the bloodstained sheet so that everyone could see that the bride had been a virgin; no one asked if the groom was a virgin or not.

Now, almost everywhere, customs are developing, but they are still terribly anti-women. For example, at four in the morning the whole family breaks into the newlyweds' bedroom to bring them ... breakfast. And while they're at it they take the opportunity to catch up on the latest news; so, did it all go all right? Did they acquit themselves well?

The police again

Two Palermo newspapers published interviews with me. Immediately, the head of the *carabinieri* at Palermo telephoned the 'brigadier' at Godrano to ask why he had not detected the presence of a 'foreigner'. The *carabinieri* then showed great vigilance in tracking our every movement. And when they became aware that we were planning to do a show in the main square, they decided to ban it. There were lots of comings and goings, one step forward, two steps backward, many discussions. Finally they decided to allow the show if an authorisation came from Palermo – which would entail at least three days' worth of bureaucratic transactions. And there was a further difficulty; the show we were doing had no script on which we could be judged.

The chief of the *carabinieri* repeated his objections: 'When all is said and done, this man is a foreigner; and let's face it, foreigners can cause social unrest. Who knows what sort of ideas they have over there – and who can tell whether or not this foreigner might harm the citizens of Godrano by showing them these ideas?'

My hosts explained in detail the theory of the Theatre of the Oppressed and the policemen listened attentively. It was explained to them that I was not in the least interested in the importation of ideas; all I brought with me was a new way of working. As for ideas, it was the inhabitants of Godrano who would be supplying them, not me.

You mean to say it's the actual people from here who will be expressing themselves through this Forum Theatre? You mean the people are going to say what they think, say what they like, *they're* going to practise doing the actions they think necessary to liberate themselves?

Yes.

The people themselves?

Exactly.

I have to admit that at this point the policeman had a rare moment of lucidity:

Then it's even more subversive and much more dangerous than I thought. It's absolutely impossible.

The only solution was to talk to the *Sindaco* (the leader of the council and the mayor rolled into one). In the name of culture and free expression of thought, the *Sindaco* decided to take full responsibility and we got back to work.

The oppressed and the oppressors

Come the Saturday, we were all in the square. The whole town had got to know about the show; many took part, others were happy just watching, still others watched from a distance, from their window or their doorstep.

It was a wonderful experiment for a number of reasons. Apart from anything else, this was the first time in my experience that Forum Theatre was being done with an audience composed of oppressed and oppressors at one and the same time. In Latin America and in Europe, I had done lots of Forum Theatre, but always with the oppressed. At Godrano the adversaries were face to face.

1 The family

First we did a few exercises and games. Then we started the first scene.

1st action

Giuseppina, a young woman of 20, wants to go out after supper. She asks her Mother's permission. The latter answers that it is up to the Father. Giuseppina says that one of her Brothers will accompany her. The two women prepare supper.

33

2nd action

The Father arrives in a foul mood with everything and everyone – the increase in the cost of living, his wife who isn't bringing his children up right, the children who are all good-for-nothings, the co-operative they were intending to set up and which is making no progress. Enter the sons. Towards Giuseppina each practises a different species of oppression. The first, the violent one, is of the opinion that a woman's place is in the home, and that the stupider and more ignorant she is, the better she is. The second, who is younger, tries to tell on all his sister's smallest misdemeanours: she looked at the neighbour's son, etc. As for the third, he plays the nice guy; he accompanies his sister as long as she behaves as he thinks fit. Giuseppina asks if she can go out that evening, but it so happens they are all busy: one is going to play football, another is going to play cards and the third isn't available.

3rd action

The Father forbids his daughter to go out for a walk. The three Brothers go and do what they want, because they're men. Giuseppina gets back to the washing-up because she is a woman.

The forum

Immediately after the presentation of the play, the model which was to be the starting point of the forum, there were some very masculine reactions. Two husbands ordered their wives to leave their places and go home. The two women refused and stayed to the end. They didn't dare come on stage, but they were brave enough to stay, against their husbands' wishes.

Other men started to say that this was not a serious problem and that we should be discussing serious problems. The women protested, saying that as far as they were concerned, it was very serious.

Then the forum began, with the supper table right in the middle of the stage. Three young women decided to replace Giuseppina and tried to break the oppression. But the oppressors were well coached and on every occasion the women eventually found themselves back at the washing-up. They said just about everything they wanted to say, but in the end they were beaten. Then a fourth young woman came along and showed what was for her the only solution: force. Going against the paternal will, she went out for her walk; and the others accepted this as a solution. The *Sindaco*, who had no daughter of his own, was enchanted with this new form of theatre.

Then the second part of the forum started – the spectators were now encouraged to take the place of other characters as well, to show actors and audience new forms of oppression. Immediately a corpulent man appeared and played out his solution: he ordered his children out of his house and in the end threw his wife out, saying:

Yes, you too, go and find your boyfriend!

Thus he revealed the root of his reactionary thinking: if the girl had committed 'a sin' it was because the Mother was a *putana* (a whore). The women vigorously challenged this.

At the end of the 'forum' of this scene, one of the young women spect-actors commented:

We have dared to say things here, in the main square, in front of everybody, which we sometimes don't dare say at home. But for our parents the opposite has been true; things they say over and over at home, they haven't had the guts to say once here, in front of other people.

The transplanting of the dining-room into the middle of the street had other effects as well. There was another important moment when a young man took the place of the protagonist. We were then able to make the following observation: when a young woman took Giuseppina's place, she immediately excited a feeling of identification, which was experienced by all the other young women present. By contrast, with the young man's performance, there was no identification. The young women watched him, but didn't identify themselves with him.

What are the practical consequences of this non-identification? The male actor (even if he was a spectator at the beginning) was still, as far as the women were concerned, a male actor; the woman spect-actor on the other hand was one of them, a woman on stage, standing there in the name of other women.

It clearly follows that when an *actor* carries out an act of liberation, he or she does it in place of the spectator, and thus is, for the latter, a catharsis. But when a *spect-actor* carries out the same act on stage, he or she does it in the name of all the other spectators, and is thus for them not a *catharsis* but a *dynamisation*.

It is not enough for a theatre to avoid catharsis – what is needed is theatre which produces dynamisation.

In the end, if the men weren't happy, the women, well, they were overjoyed. The next day, when we asked Giuseppina's mother how she liked the show, she answered:

> I thought it was sensational. And all my friends admired my daughter's performance. They told me that it's just the same in their homes. The problems are the same. And one of my friends said that we should look for the solutions together ...

2 *The co-operative: the character assumes his own role and refutes the actor*

In the second show we prepared, something extraordinary happened – an actor was playing the part of a character who was himself present in the audience: the *Sindaco*!

This came about in the following way: at Godrano, the shepherds had wanted to form a co-operative so that they could together find an answer to the problem of the lack of markets for their flocks. They accused the *Sindaco* of not helping them and of positively impeding the co-operative in the pursuit of its goal. They prepared the scene themselves and performed it themselves.

1st action

Three members of the co-operative argue about the role of the *Sindaco*, and decide to broach the subject with him in order to demand certain measures which they deem essential. Everyone agrees.

2nd action

Enter the *Sindaco* in the company of a presiding judge. The former explains that he has chosen this person as a companion on account of his great knowledge of the subject. The three partners protest, declaring that any judge presiding in this case should be an inhabitant of Godrano, someone better acquainted with the problems, not an outsider who knows nothing of them. The *Sindaco* defends his argument and ends up imposing his will.

36

3rd action

The presiding judge reveals his plan, proposing that the base of the co-operative should be located somewhere other than the *paese* where conditions are not ideal. Once again the partners protest, but they are beaten by the cunning arguments fielded by the *Sindaco* and the judge.

4th action

The *Sindaco* insists on getting the signatures of the three partners on a document he needs for his official procedures. The partners refuse, but nevertheless end up giving in.

The forum

At the beginning of the forum, tension was high. The 'accused' was there, in the audience, and while the Actor-*Sindaco* was speaking, the audience could watch the *Sindaco-Sindaco*'s face. The latter smiled and tried to take it all as a joke; but the spect-actors were deadly serious. When anyone shouted 'Stop!', the actor would change and the next spect-actor would give his version of the facts and of the behaviour of the authorities present. Tears in his eyes, one of the spect-actors cried out that if the co-operative had existed, if it had functioned as it might have done, he wouldn't find himself forced to emigrate to Germany. Another inveighed against the benefits the *Sindaco* gained from the non-functioning of the co-operative. Another proposed – still within the theatrical action – that the *Sindaco* be excluded from the co-operative.

And the *Sindaco* was right there, listening to everything, drily swallowing all the accusations and preparing his response.

Then came the inevitable moment. The *Sindaco* himself very nervously shouted 'Stop!' and took the place of the actor playing his part. This happened in Sicily, birthplace of Pirandello – but the motivations on this occasion were very different. There was nothing metaphysical about them, they were as concrete as can be. The motivations here were political; the *polis* was there in the square to discuss the acts of its government, to challenge its government, to attack it.

We experienced a bewildering event; the *Sindaco* entered into the theatrical game, but immediately tried to transform it into a game he knew better, the parliamentary game.

GAMES FOR ACTORS AND NON-ACTORS

Good, now let's talk seriously. Up to now you have been doing theatre, you've been playing around with serious issues. Now we are going to talk seriously.

What did the *Sindaco* want? He simply wanted to play his game. In local politics, it was up to *him* to call on whomever *he* wanted to speak *when he wanted*; he led the action, or interrupted it, or modified it as he wished, and no one dared oppose him. He had been in this position for seventeen years already.

However in the game of Forum, *theatrical democracy* came into play; here any spect-actor could shout 'Stop!' and shut him up. The peasants understood this and one of them said:

No, we are not going to talk seriously, we are going to talk theatre!

In this game, all the characters were equal. And the *Sindaco* did not enjoy this democracy. Because whenever he started to say something which wasn't true, immediately he would hear a shout of 'Stop!' and someone would come on stage, contradict him, unveil opposing evidence and field the counter-argument.

Anyone could do it – this was theatrical democracy. Anyone. A far-from-stupid adolescent girl was one of the most vociferous; she protested the most, she was the most forthright in her condemnation of the *Sindaco*, right there in the middle of the main square, in front of everybody. She talked so much and so often that she provoked the following exchange:

Madam, take your daughter away, ask her to shut up and to stop accusing the *Sindaco*, because if she says one word more, she will never find a husband in Godrano!

The mother answered:

So what? She can just as easily get married in Palermo!

The *Sindaco* continued to try his utmost to have the theatrical game replaced by the local politics game, but at every juncture he would hear the same cry: 'Stop!' Finally he blew his top and screamed:

It's my co-operative, if you want to run it, set up another one.

Clearly this was impossible.

The show had begun at nine in the evening and at two in the morning there were still lots of people on the square deep in discussion. Forum Theatre became forum pure and simple. At great length. Right through till the next day. Even reaching other *paesi* at Villa Frati, at Mizzoiuzzo, because the villagers who had come from there to see the show wanted to take the idea of Forum Theatre back with them, so that the problems of the people would be discussed there too. In the square, in the 'forum'.

Throughout this section, I have tried to stress that in Forum Theatre at no time should an idea be imposed. Forum Theatre does not preach, it is not dogmatic, it does not seek to manipulate people. At best, it liberates the spect-actors. At best, it stimulates them. At best, it transforms them into actors. Actor – he or she who acts.

2

THE STRUCTURE OF THE ACTOR'S WORK

THE PRIMACY OF EMOTION

In 1956 I started working at the Arena Theatre of São Paulo, of which I was the artistic director until I had to leave Brazil in 1971. At this time, the Brazilian theatre was completely dominated by Italian directors, who used to impose pre-established forms on every play performed. To fight against this tendency, in concert with the actors we created an acting laboratory in which we set about a methodical study of the works of Stanislavski. Our first principle at that time was that emotion took precedence over all else and should be given a free rein to shape the final form of the actor's interpretation of a role.

But how can emotions 'freely' manifest themselves throughout an actor's body, if that very instrument (the body) is mechanised, automated in its muscle structures and insensible to 90 per cent of its possibilities? A newly discovered emotion runs the risk of being canalised by the mechanised patterns of the actor's behaviour; the emotion may be blocked by a body already hardened by habit into a certain set of actions and reactions.

How does this mechanisation of the actor's body come about? By repetition. The senses have an enormous capacity for registering, selecting and then hierarchising sensations. The eye, for example, can pick up an infinite variety of colours, whatever the object of its attention: a road, a room, a picture, an animal. There are thousands of greens, shades of green perfectly perceptible to the human eye. The same applies to hearing and sounds, and to the other senses and their sensations. A person driving a car sees an infinity of sensations stream past. Riding a bicycle involves an extremely complicated structure of muscular movements and tactile sensations, but the

senses select the most important stimuli for this activity. Every hu
activity, from the very simplest onwards – walking, for instance
an extremely complicated operation, which is possible only *because*
the senses are capable of selection; even though they pick up all
sensations, they present them to the consciousness according to a
definite hierarchy, and this is repeated over and over again in our
lives.

This becomes even more evident when a person leaves their habitual
environment and visits an unknown town or country; the people dress
differently, speak with another rhythm, the noises and the colours
aren't the same, the faces are differently shaped. Everything seems
wonderful, unexpected, fantastic. But after a few days, the senses once
again learn to select and the routine starts all over. Let us imagine what
happens when a (South American) forest-dwelling Indian comes to
town or when a city-dweller gets lost in the forest. For the Indian the
noises of the forest are perfectly natural, his senses are used to selecting
from them; he can fix his bearings by the noise of the wind in the trees,
by the brightness of the sun through the leaves. By contrast, what is
natural and routine to us city-dwellers can drive the Indian mad,
incapable as he is of selecting from the sensations produced by a big
city. The same thing would happen to us if we got lost in virgin forest.

This process of selection and structuration results in a mechanisation because the senses always select in the same way.

When we began our exercises, we had not yet considered *social*
masks; at that time we were considering mechanisation in its purely
physical form, i.e. by always carrying out the same movements,
each person mechanises their body to execute these movements as
efficiently as possible, thus denying themselves the possibility of
original action every time the opportunity arises.

Wrinkles appear because the repetition of particular muscle con-
structions eventually leaves its mark on the face.

What is a sectarian but a person – of the left or right – who has
mechanised all their thoughts and responses?

Like all human beings, the actor acts and reacts according to mechanisms. For this reason, we must start with the 'de-mechanisation', the
re-tuning (or de-tuning) of the actor, so that he may be able to take on
the mechanisations of the character he is going to play. He must relearn
to perceive emotions and sensations he has lost the habit of recognising.
In the first phase of our work, we did sensory exercises, roughly following Stanislavski's indications.

A few examples follow.

Muscular exercises

The actors relax all the muscles in their bodies and focus their attention on each individual muscle. Then they take a few steps, bend down and pick up an object (anything), doing the whole thing very slowly and trying to feel and remember all the muscular structures which intervene in the accomplishment of these movements.

They then repeat exactly the same action, but this time mentally, without the object, pretending to pick it up from the ground and trying to remember all the contractions and relaxations of muscle which occurred during the previous operation. The object can be varied (a key, a chair, a sock) or the exercise can be complicated – dress and undress, first with, and then without clothes. Or ride a bicycle *sans* bicycle, lying flat on the ground with arms and legs in the air.

The most important thing is that the actors become aware of their muscles, of the enormous variety of movements they *could* make. Other exercises: walk like so-and-so, laugh like such-and-such a person, etc. The goal is not exact imitation, but an understanding, from the inside, of the mechanics of each movement. What causes so-and-so to walk in that particular way?

Sensory exercises

The actors swallow a spoonful of honey, followed by a pinch of salt, and then a taste of sugar. Then they enact the same thing without the original stimulus. They must try to recall the tastes, actually experience them again, and physically manifest all the reactions which accompany the absorption of honey, salt, sugar, etc. This exercise is not about mimicry (smiles for honey, grimaces for the salt), but rather about genuinely experiencing the same sensations 'from memory'. The same can be done with smells.

Another example: we would put on some music and a number of actors would listen carefully to the melody, the rhythm, the tempo. Then, all together, they would try to 'hear' the same music, mentally, with the same rhythm and the same tempo, but without the music. At my signal, they had to sing the bit they were in the middle of 'listening to' mentally – if it coincided, it showed the extent of their original concentration and the precision of their recall.

Memory exercises

We did easy versions of these every day. Before going to sleep, each of us would try to remember minutely and chronologically all that had happened during the day, with the maximum detail – colours, faces, weather – revisualising almost photographically everything we had seen and rehearing all we had heard, etc. Often also, on their arrival at the theatre, actors would be asked what had happened in their lives since the previous day – and they then had to deliver a detailed account to the rest of the group. The exercise became more interesting when several actors had taken part in the same event – a festival, a reunion, a show, a play, a football match. The versions would be compared, and, when there were differences, we would endeavour to arrive at an objective version of the facts or try to understand the reasons for the differences in the accounts. The memory exercises could also deal with a much more distant past; for example, each actor might be asked for a detailed run-down of their marriage day, how it went, who was there, what music was played, what there was to eat, how the house looked, etc. Or the burial of a friend. Or the day Brazil lost the World Cup, in 1950, at Maracana, playing against Uruguay – what radio station did you follow the match on? Were you there? Did people cry? How did you sleep that night? Did you dream? What dreams? And so on. In memory exercises the important thing is to have lots of concrete details. Equally it is vital that this exercise is practised with absolute regularity, as a daily routine, preferably at a particular time of day. The point of this is not only to develop the memory, but also to enhance awareness; everyone knows that they have to remember everything they see, hear and feel, and thus their powers of attention, concentration and analysis develop.

Imagination exercises

We did many of these, of the kind described later ('The dark room' (see p. 203), telling a story, etc.).

Emotion exercises

There is a wall between what the actor feels and the final form which expresses it. This wall is formed by the actor's own mechanisms. The actor feels Hamlet's emotions and yet, involuntarily, he will express Hamlet's emotions in his own way; his own physiognomy, his own tone of voice, etc. But the actor could also be in a position to *choose*, out of a thousand ways of smiling, the one which, in his view, would be Hamlet's; out of a thousand ways of getting angry, the one which, in his view, would be Hamlet's way. To make this choice possible, one has to start by destroying the wall of mechanisms, which is the actor's 'mask'. The bourgeois theatre of São Paulo by contrast used to *reinforce* each actor's mannerisms and automatisms (the actor's 'trademarks') on to which the characters would be glued. The 'stars' would always play themselves – the 'stars'.

We wanted the converse – we wanted the actors to start by nullifying all their personal characteristics, in order to let those of the character flower. These exercises were intended to abolish the so-called 'personality' of the actor – his mould, his pattern – and assist the birth of the 'personality' of the character and its mould or pattern. But how does one arrive at this new mould?

The starting point is to feel the character's emotions, genuinely, so that these emotions may then find, in the relaxed body of the actor, the most adequate and efficient way of 'transmitting' themselves to the audience, so that the spectators may also feel them.

Emotion exercises became routine at the Arena theatre; the actors exercised anywhere and everywhere, on stage, in the office, on the street, in restaurants. Every day, each actor used to do at least two or three such workshop exercises.

What's more, emotion exercises are fascinating to watch and do. At a certain point during our evolution as a theatre company, we gave a quite disproportionate degree of importance to emotion (as yet, the importance of ideas was not so clear to us).

From 1960 onwards, Stanislavski began to be widely used by other Brazilian theatre groups. There were sometimes curious situations and questionable explanations of Stanislavskian instructions on the 'emotion memory'. I remember one occasion, at Bahia, in a university theatre, when a North American director was invited to teach Stanislavski and mount a production using Stanislavskian techniques. He chose Tennessee Williams's *A Streetcar Named Desire*. The rehearsals were already well advanced when the director decided to do some 'laboratory' work on Stella's scene with Blanche DuBois the day after the terrible fight between the two of them and Stanley Kowalski. They couldn't find any way into the scene. They rehearsed and rehearsed, they changed everything, they improvised – impossible, no progress; when it came to running the scene, it was still completely lacking in conviction. Finally the director decided to resort to emotion memory improvisations. And once again, it was fruitless. The director then explained to the actress who had the part of Stella:

> You see, the problem is this: Stella has fought tooth and nail with her husband to protect her sister. But when he starts crying, she is astonished to see him so fragile; he takes her in his arms, carries her into the bedroom, they make love all night long, a wild night of passion, and then she falls asleep. ... Right, so the scene we are dealing with begins the next morning. She wakes up after this marvellous night of sex, obviously she's a little tired, but she is content, she smiles all the time, she is happy. This is a happy woman. And it is precisely that quality that I am unable to detect in your performance. Let's try something – an emotion memory exercise. Try to recall the most beautiful night of your life, a night full of sex, because that is what is missing from the scene.

The poor girl hesitated for a moment before admitting: 'I am a virgin, sir.'

No one knew what to say. It appeared that in a case like this Stanislavski's emotion memory technique was unusable. Then an actor suggested:

> It doesn't matter. She can remember something which made her immensely happy ... and then afterwards she can transfer the emotion. ... It's worth a try.

The director took up the actor's suggestion, the exercise was done, and the scene went incredibly well. There was general joy and excitement; the girl was asked how she had done it, how she had managed to achieve a look at once so sensual, so happy, so alluring. She answered truthfully:

> Well, in the bit where we were talking about sex and how wonderful Stanley was in bed, I was remembering one sunny afternoon when I ate three ice-creams on the trot, under a coconut-tree on Itapoan beach.

These cases of extreme 'transference' are not rare, because no actor has experienced exactly the same incidents as those in the life of the character, only approximate or analogical situations. So it is absolutely inevitable that there should be different degrees of transference.* People remember emotions that they have felt at a particular moment, in particular circumstances which they alone have lived through and which are *similar* to their character's own circumstances. These are absolutely unique circumstances which must be transferred and modified in order to match the character's emotions. I have never killed anyone, but I have felt the desire to do so; I try to remember the desire that I had and I transfer that desire to Hamlet when he kills his uncle. Some degree of transference is inevitable, but I do not believe it should go as far as in the case reported by Robert Lewis: a well-known actor used to make his audience cry out in horror, when, in a scene of great pathos, he used to get out his revolver and point it at his temple, finger on the trigger, ready to shoot, while he pondered aloud the futility of his existence. The actor's performance was absolutely overwhelming, even to the point that he himself was overwhelmed; the spectators cried when they saw him cry, they sobbed when they heard his sobbing.

When Lewis asked him how he had achieved such an impact, such an overflowing of emotion, such a traumatic effect both on the audience and on himself, the actor answered:

Emotion memory, my friend. Haven't you read your Stanislavski? It's all in there.

Uh, right. [said Lewis] So there was this day when you wanted to kill yourself, you use the emotion memory, and then you are there. ... Am I right?

Me, want to kill myself? I love life, my friend. Far from it.

So?

It goes like this: when I point the revolver at myself, I have to think of something sad, threatening, terrible. Fine. That's what I do. You remember how I always raise my eyes to the ceiling when I'm aiming? That's the key. I think back to one winter when I was poor and lived in a house with no heating or electricity, and whenever I took a bath or a shower, the water was ice-cold. When I raise the revolver to my head, I lift my eyes towards the shower-head, I think of the cold water about

---

* The word 'transference' is not used here in its standard psychoanalytical usage, though there is a connection; the essential difference is that here it is intended to describe a deliberate, voluntary process, as opposed to the involuntary nature of transferences recorded in psychoanalytical case histories. *A.J.*

to gush down on my body. . . . Oh my friend, how I suffer, how the tears well up in my eyes!

In spite of such excesses, emotion memory exercises can be effective and useful, especially in the different versions of the 'breaking of oppression' exercises which will be explained later.

RATIONALISING EMOTION

But an intense emotion memory exercise, or for that matter any emotion exercise, can be very dangerous unless one afterwards 'rationalises' what has happened. Actors discover things when they take the risk of experiencing emotions. (There are extreme cases – one well-known actor let herself get so carried away by her emotion in the role of Blanche DuBois, that she ended up being interned in a hospital for the mentally ill.) Which doesn't mean to say that we should dismiss emotion exercises; on the contrary, they must be done, but with the aim of 'understanding' the experience, not simply feeling it. We must know why a person is moved, what is the nature of this emotion, what its causes are – not limit ourselves simply to the how. We want to experience phenomena, but above all we want to know the laws which govern these phenomena. And that is the role of art – not only to show how the world is, but also why it is thus and how it can be transformed. I hope no one can be satisfied with the world as it is; it must be transformed.

The rationalisation of emotion does not take place solely after the emotion has disappeared, it is immanent in the emotion, it also takes place in the course of an emotion. There is a simultaneity of feeling and thinking.

Let me give an example from my own life. I experienced one of the strongest emotions of my life when my father died. During the death vigil, the burial and the seventh day mass, at the same time as being deeply and truly moved, I never stopped seeing and analysing the strange things to be found in such rituals as mass, burial, wakes. I remember that the coffin flowers were changed coldly and dispassionately, 'so the coffin will look prettier' so the man said. I also remember the faces of people offering their condolences to us, each face projecting its owner's greater or lesser affection for us, for the family. I remember the tired expression on the face of the priest, who was perhaps on his fourth or fifth burial of the day. I remember everything, because I analysed everything as it was happening, without for all that being any less upset.

I give this example from my own life, but the same happens or can happen to everyone. Perhaps it is a more frequent occurrence with writers, analysts by trade. Dostoevsky is an extraordinary example. In *The Idiot*, the author describes the protagonist's epileptic fits with an incredible perfection and wealth of detail. Dostoevsky was himself epileptic and managed to retain, during his fits, sufficient lucidity and objectivity to remember his emotions and sensations, and to be capable of describing them.

In this case, the author described his emotions after having felt them. But the case of Proust is even more extraordinary, even more fantastic, and no less real; when he sensed that he was dying, he dictated to his housekeeper notes about the death of a writer – himself! – to amend the description of the death of Bergotte in *La Prisonnière*, the fifth part of his long novel, *A la Recherche du Temps Perdu*. And he retained sufficient detachment to tell her where they should be inserted in subsequent editions. Now that he was actually dying, he corrected the fictional death he had previously depicted. And when he had finished describing the writer's agony, he died.

It matters little whether there is genuine simultaneity here or rapid reason-emotion intermittence. The important thing is to point out the mistake and correct the actor for whom the essential thing is 'to be moved'. When an actor shows himself to be incapable of feeling a true emotion during rehearsals, there is little doubt that he is on the wrong track. But an actor who loses control is also wide of the mark. Very often loss of control is false, is pure exhibitionism. A certain actor became famous for the violence with which he played Othello, it was terribly moving ... and dangerous. When he felt 'possessed' by the character, sometimes he genuinely felt like killing Desdemona. On more than one occasion, the curtain had to be brought down. People were impressed by the wonderful emotive power of this actor. By contrast, my own feeling is that he should have been reported to the actors' union or the police.

Thus we must be absolutely clear that emotion 'in itself', disordered and chaotic, is worth nothing. The important thing about emotion is what it signifies. We cannot talk about emotion without reason or, conversely, about reason without emotion; the former is chaos, the latter pure abstraction.

LA RECHERCHE DU TEMPS PERDU

I have spoken of Proust, and this is a good time to develop another Proustian concept which was very useful in this period of our work and which connects up with Stanislavskian empathic theatre; the concept of '*la recherche du temps perdu*' (literally, 'the pursuit of lost time', usually translated as 'remembrance of things past'). For Proust, the only way we can rediscover time we have lost – in life – is through memory. According to him, while we are living an experience, we are incapable of fully or deeply apprehending it, since each experience is subject to a thousand and one imponderable circumstances. Our own subjectivity is the slave of reality's objectivity. If we love a woman, the love affair is so filled with small incidents that we cannot enjoy it and live it intensely, unless, in the act of remembering, our memory re-creates this love affair for us. In objective reality, love is commingled with such secondary details as a late bus, a painful meeting, lack of money, misunderstandings, etc. But when, via memory, we rediscover the episode lived through, we can purify this love by eliminating all that was not essential. And thus we rediscover the time we have lost by living it again ... in our memory.*

According to Proust, this applies not only to a past love, but to all lived experience. One of his characters, Swann, believes he is utterly, madly, in love; he suffers all the horrors of amorous incomprehension right up till the separation. Years pass, and one day he finds himself back with his ex-love; this gives him a shock. He tries to remember everything that had happened to them, he 'orders' his past experience, he subjectively re-views all its elements and he concludes: 'How was I able to bear her for so many years? It's not even my kind of beauty ...'

Proust allows subjectivity complete freedom to order the past, to organise lived experiences, carefully stripped of what we might call life. In this sense, Proust is very close to Stanislavskian theatre, which, to a certain extent, is also 'memory' – but in the present, here and now! Every time an actor plays a character, he or she plays it for the first and last time. Like we play every minute of our own lives.

There is much Proust in Stanislavski and vice versa. During

---

* In this respect, Proust comes close to Maeterlinck, who considered inactive people remembering their past to be good material for theatre – not an opinion I share with him. *A.B.*

rehearsals, the actor must be allowed time and space to retrieve his 'lost time', with the help of exercises (especially the emotion memory exercises), and subjectively to order his character's experience. However, the actor may then run the risk of moving away from the live experience, i.e. the scene and the conflicts with other characters, which, in theatre, must be staged in the present tense, not as recollections from the past. Theatre is a conflict between or among characters confronting one another, always in the here and now. So memory is important, but only when it is transported to the present – when memory becomes the present, when 'I have felt' becomes 'I am feeling again'. In theatre, to remember is to live again, with the same or even greater intensity, with the same or even broader and deeper knowledge of what has happened, how, and why.

I have worked with an actor who had such a rich imagination that he also imagined how the other characters should be, and, in his stage relationships with them, he treated them as he saw them in his imagination and not as the actors were playing them on the stage. This hypertrophy of subjectivity could be seen in some of the actors who came out of the 'Actors' Studio' in the 1950s and 1960s (though obviously not the Brandos and Deans of this world). They thought so much, they imagined so many things to accompany each phrase, each word they said, that their performances were incredibly slow, stuffed as they were full of secondary actions and activities. No one would answer a question without first stroking their glass, scratching their head, taking a deep breath, clearing their throat, twisting their back, glancing to one side, knitting their brow, before finally saying yes or no. When taken to the extreme, this kind of acting, over-burdened with motivations, even had the effect of changing the style of a piece, moving from realism to expressionism. The real time was the character's subjective time and not the objective time of the characters' interrelations. Their acting tended to expressionism – duration was important, not time.

Thus it is important to understand that the actor's creation must also be, fundamentally, the creation of interrelations with the other actors. In the past at the Arena, we used to construct great lakes of emotion – deep, still, emotional lakes; but empathy, the emotional liaison of character and spectator, is necessarily dynamic. An excess of Proustianism and subjectivity can lead to the breakdown of relations between the characters and the creation of isolated emotional lakes. However, our aim is not to exhibit static emotions, but to create rivers in flux, to create a dynamic. Theatre is conflict, struggle, movement, transformation, not simply the exhibition of states of mind. It is a verb, not an adjective. To act is to produce an action, and every action produces a reaction – conflict.

Thus we began to attribute greater importance to conflict as a source of theatricality, to the dialectical emotion. And we became aware that dialectical emotion is the vehicle for 'transmitting' in what could be called the 'undercurrent'.

Let me explain. Human beings are capable of 'emitting' many more messages than they are aware of sending. They are also capable of receiving many more messages than they think they receive. That is why communication between two human beings can take place at two levels – consciously or unconsciously, i.e. on 'the wave', or in 'the undercurrent', by which I mean all communication established without passing via the conscious mind.

It is frequently the case that an actor will play the same role in the same way in two consecutive shows; in the first, the audience can be in a state of total empathy with the actor, and in the second, not at all. Why? Because in the second case the actor's 'undercurrent' transmitted messages which had nothing to do with the message he was transmitting 'on the wave', i.e. consciously.

The only thing which can bring about an absolute identity of 'wave' and 'undercurrent' messages is the actor's concentration. The actor must never let himself become mechanised, or perform the same actions automatically whether or not his mind is on his role. In the theatrical experience, the actor must give himself utterly and completely over to his task.

THE DIALECTICAL STRUCTURE OF THE ACTOR'S INTERPRETATION OF A ROLE

Now I must explain the meaning of each of the elements of the dialectics of acting which we followed at that time (and still do to this day).

The will

The fundamental concept for the actor is not the 'being' of the character, but the 'will'. One should not ask 'who is this?', but rather 'what does he want?'. The first question can lead to the formation of lakes of emotion, while the second is essentially dynamic, dialectical, conflictual, and consequently theatrical. But the will chosen by the actor cannot be arbitrary – on the contrary, it must be the concretion of an idea, the translation of this idea or thesis into terms of will. The will is not the idea, it is the concretion of the idea. It is not enough to want to be happy in an abstract way, we must want whatever will make us happy. It is not enough to want 'power and glory' in general, we must concretely want to kill King Duncan in very concrete and objectified circumstances. From which we can derive the following formulation: *idea = concrete will* (in particular, specific circumstances).

The will is the essence of the motivation; Hamlet wants to kill his uncle because of his filial duty – how he does it is his characterisation. The will is what he wants, the characterisation is how he will achieve it. 'Character' is a static notion; 'characterisation', combined with will, is dynamic.

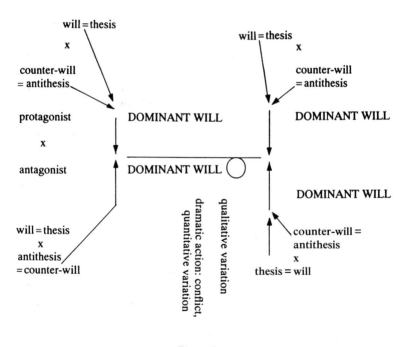

Figure 1

To exercise a will means to desire something which must necessarily be concrete. If the actor comes on stage with abstract desires for happiness, love, power, etc., this will be of no use to him. He needs to have a specific object – to want to sleep with this particular person, in these particular circumstances, in order to be happy and to love. It is the concretion, the objectification of the purpose, which makes the will theatrical. However, this purpose and this will, while having to be concrete, must at the same time have a transcendent significance. It is not enough for Macbeth to want to kill Duncan and inherit his position. The struggle between Macbeth and his adversaries cannot be reduced to a series of psychological battles between a number of people who are desperate for power. In the totality of the play there is a higher idea under consideration, which the characters concretise by their wills; Duncan signifies feudal legality, Macbeth the upstart bourgeoisie. One has a birthright, and the other has the Machiavellian rights of personal merit and power. The central idea of this work is the struggle between the bourgeoisie and feudalism, the wills of the characters concretising this central idea.

From the central idea of the work are derived the central ideas of each character. In the present case, the central idea of the character Lady Macbeth, for example, is the affirmation of individual (bourgeois) *virtu* against rights of lineage. The central idea of the character should correspond to the Stanislavskian 'super-objective'; idea and will are one and the same thing, the former in abstract form, the latter in concrete presence.

Once chosen, the central idea of the work must be respected at all costs, so that all the individual wills may develop in the nurture of a firm structure of ideas. This structure of ideas is the skeleton. Thus one must establish what is to be the central idea of the play – or production – and, from that starting point, deduce the central ideas of each character, so that these central ideas meet head-on in a harmonious and conflictual whole (*central idea = thesis and antithesis*).

If we accept the equation 'idea equals will', as generator of emotion, we must also accept that not all ideas are theatrical. To be more precise, all ideas are theatrical 'in context', but not in their abstract expression. The idea that 2 and 2 make 4, for example, cannot in itself be moving. But if we take this same idea in a context, looking at its impact in a particular set of circumstances – if we translate it into terms of will – then we can arrive at a certain emotion. If the particular situation features a child desperately trying to learn the rudiments of arithmetic, the idea that 2 and 2 make 4 can be moving – just as moving as the incredible moment when Einstein, with all the intensity of his will for knowledge, discovered that

$E = mc^2$ is the formula for the transformation of mass into energy, thus 'concretely' crowning the whole of an 'abstract' scientific research.

To sum up, every idea, however abstract, can be theatrical to the extent that it manifests itself in a concrete form in particular circumstances in terms of will. From which the following relationship can be formulated: *idea = will = emotion = theatrical form*; in other words, the abstract idea when transformed into a concrete will in particular circumstances will give rise in the actor to the emotion which will spontaneously find a theatrical form which is adequate, valid and convincing for the spectator. Problems of style and other questions come afterwards.

Let us be quite clear: the essence of theatricality is the conflict of wills. These wills must be subjective (related to the subject) and objective (related to the object) at the same time. The goals of these wills must also be simultaneously subjective and objective. Let us look at two examples: a boxing match is a conflict of wills, since the two antagonists know exactly what they want, they also know how to get it and they fight for it. However, a boxing match is not necessarily theatrical. A dialogue by Plato also offers characters intensely exercising their wills; their goal is to convince their adversaries of their argument. Here also, there is a conflict of wills. But again, this isn't theatre. Neither the boxing match nor the Platonic dialogue is theatre. Why? Because the conflict in the first case is exclusively objective and in the second case exclusively subjective. Nevertheless, both have the same potential to become theatrical. For example, suppose the boxer wants to win in order to prove something to somebody; in this case what is important is not the actual blows in themselves, but the significance of these blows. What is important is what transcends the fight proper. In the second case, consider the discourse where the disciples try to convince Socrates to flee and not to accept his punishment, death. If the disciples' arguments hit home, Socrates will not die. If Socrates' arguments prevail, he will have to take poison and accept death. In this dialogue, so philosophical, so subjective, there is, however, an important and central objective fact: Socrates' life.

Thus, boxing match and philosophical discussion have equal 'theatrical' potential.

The counter-will

No emotion is pure or constant in quantity or quality. What we observe in reality is quite the reverse: we want and don't want, we love and don't love, we have and we don't have courage. For the actor truly to live on stage, he must find the counter-will to each of his wills. In certain cases this counter-will is obvious – Hamlet wants only one thing, to avenge his father; but on the other hand he doesn't want to kill his uncle. He wants to be and not to be. Will and counter-will are concrete and obvious to the spectator. The same phenomenon applies with Brutus, who wants to kill Julius Caesar, but struggles inwardly with his counter-will, his love for Julius Caesar. Macbeth wants to be king, but he hesitates to assassinate his guest.

In other cases, the counter-will is not so obvious: Lady Macbeth appears to have only one motivation and to be devoid of internal conflicts; likewise Cassius when he is trying to convince Brutus. Whatever the degree of evidence for the counter-will, it must always exist, and must be analysed by the actor in special rehearsals, so that he can genuinely live his character, add depth to it, realise it, and not simply illustrate it. This is valid whatever the character, even in the interpretation of the part of a medieval angel – study the angel's counter-will, hostility to God. The further the actor pushes the counter-will, the more energetically the will appears.

Take Romeo and Juliet, for example: you will not find two characters who love each other more, who desire each other more, who have less by way of counter-will – they are unadulterated love, unadulterated will. Even so, analyse the theatricality of the scenes in depth, and you will see that there is always conflict; conflicts with others, conflicts within themselves, conflicts between the two of them. Take act III, scene v, which opens with her nightingale, his lark. She wants him to stay, so they can make love one more time; he fears for his life, he wants to go, finally she convinces him; and now he wants to stay, and she no longer wants him to.

Let me stress again: if an actor is to play the role of Romeo, he must love Juliet, sure, but he must also look for his counter-wills. Juliet, however beautiful she may be, however adorable and amorous, is none the less a minx at times, an irritating and stubborn little girl. Juliet must have similar reservations about Romeo. And because they also have counter-wills, their wills must be even stronger, and love must explode with even more violence in these two human beings made of flesh and bone, of wills and counter-wills.

The actor who makes use only of wills, ends up looking a complete idiot on stage. He stays the same all the time. He loves, and he loves, and he loves, and he loves. ... People watch him and think: 'Well, looks like he's in love'; five minutes later, the same look; second act, still no change. Who wants to go on watching him? The internal conflict of will and counter-will creates the dynamic, creates the theatricality of the performance and, with this dynamic, the actor will never be the same from one moment to the next, because he or she will always be in a continual state of flux, a constant alternation of coming and going.

Nor is this investigation of the counter-will simply a matter of looking for a will contradictory to the character. It is more than that. For example, it is not a matter of opposing Iago's will to persuade Othello to kill Desdemona against the fear he has of seeing his plan discovered. No, that's not it at all. One must search in Iago for the love he has for Othello, for his hate is also love. We are confronted by a single dialectical emotion, not two opposing emotions. And this doesn't stop other emotions (fear, for instance) existing in addition to the hate-emotion (hate against love). But if fear does also exist, this emotion (fear), this will *not to act*, must also be dialectical; from that point of departure we find courage, the will to do, as counter-will. In graphic, vectorial terms, this would give us something like Figure 2.

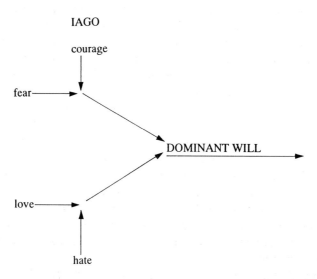

Figure 2

56

Thus the importance, once again, of actors always working on their characters in terms of will and counter-will. This interior conflict will draw from the actor a being always alive and dynamic on stage, internally in perpetual movement; without counter-will, the actor will stay the same, static, untheatrical.

The dominant will

From the interior conflict between will and counter-will there always emerges, on the exterior, a dominant will, which is the manifestation of the will in conflict with the other characters. Search as actors must for all the wills and counter-wills of their characters, they must always refer back to the dominant will which structures the conflict of all these wills. When an actor develops his interior wills to the extreme without objectively exteriorising them, he runs the risk of 'subjectivising' his character to too great an extent and making it unreal. When the actor dwells in the interior life of his character, forgetting objective reality, when the conflict between will and counter-will takes precedence for him over the conflict of character against character (or dominant will against dominant will), he ends up playing the autopsy of a character and not a living, real, present character.

For me it is actually fundamental that the actor must have time to rehearse each of his wills and counter-wills separately, the better to understand and feel them – like a painter choosing his colours first and afterwards mixing them on the canvas. The wills – plus the ideas they underlie, and the emotions they give rise to – are the actor's colours. To use them, he must know them, love them. That is why we do so many exercises on 'separate motivation', 'counter-will', 'artificial pause', 'contrary thought', 'opposite circumstances', etc. The aim of these exercises is to carry out that analysis. Nor must we forget that at every moment there is a dominant will asserting itself, even if we are dealing with a character from Chekhov, painted in the impressionist style, made up of thousands of small wills and counter-wills. If the dominant will is not given due weight, it is impossible to structure the play. Even if they are turned in on themselves, the characters must exteriorise themselves, and in such cases interrelation is fundamental.

In different versions of the same play, each character's dominant will naturally will depend on the central idea imposed on that particular version, but all the other 'possible' ideas can also fit into the character, as complementary wills.

An example to clarify this subject. What is *Hamlet* about?

A familial psychological problem or a *coup d'état*?

What is the central idea?

Ernest Jones has written a book on Hamlet* in which he analyses the latter's incapacity to make his mind up to kill King Claudius. According to him, there is an identity between Hamlet and Oedipus. Hamlet, in his unconscious, wanted to kill his father and marry his mother. But it is someone else who accomplishes precisely these two acts. Hamlet immediately identifies with this man, King Claudius. When he discovers that Claudius is his father's assassin, he wants to be avenged and to kill him. But how? It would be suicide. His filial duty to avenge his father's death is opposed to his fear of killing a man with whom, in his subconscious, he has identified himself. Each time the opportunity arises, Hamlet adjourns the execution. However, near the end of the tragedy, when Hamlet realises that the sword with which Laertes has wounded him is poisoned, that he is fated to die, then he decides to kill Claudius and does it there and then, without the least hesitation, as if he was thinking: 'Since I'm already dead, I'm going to destroy this man, my other self.'

But one can also analyse Hamlet from the national angle rather than the familial angle, taking as the central idea the *coup d'état* instigated by Fortinbras.

These two central ideas – and there is an infinity of others – are completely different. The one which is retained will determine the central ideas of each character, and also their dominant wills, thus leading the other ideas and possible wills to become counter-wills. The love of Hamlet for his mother can perfectly well appear in a '*coup d'état*' version; just as the hatred of the people for their oppressors – among whose ranks Claudius is to be found – can appear in a psychoanalytical version. Starting from the central idea chosen, it is then important to determine what the dominant wills are, relegating all the other possibilities to second place; there is no point in simply making a hotch-potch of ideas, wills and emotions.

* Ernest James, *Hamlet and Oedipus*, New York: Norton: 1949.

Quantitative variation and qualitative variation

This notion concerns the dramatic action itself, with its movement of internal and external conflicts. A conflict is theatrical if it is in movement, which is why the actor must distance himself as much as possible in will and emotion from his eventual destination, i.e. the crisis he is working towards. He must create a counter-preparation to what is going to happen to him, so that the distance to be covered will be as great as possible, and the movement also as large as possible. In order that Iago may eventually have the courage to lie to Othello, it is vital that from the start the dominant will should be fear, for from that fear will be born courage, which will gradually grow stronger. The counter-will – courage – then becomes the dominant will. This change of intensity, the quantitative variation, becomes a qualitative variation.

Oedipus, at the beginning of *Oedipus Rex*, is a victorious hero. He definitely wants to save his city. After Tiresias' revelations, his will increases *quantitatively*, up to the crisis when he discovers that he is the killer of his own father; thus comes the *qualitative* variation – now he wants to punish himself.

That then is a summary of the systems used by our actors at the Arena Theatre, resting on the basic notions (1) that the central idea of the play determines the central idea of the character, translated into terms of dialectical will (the will and counter-will) and (2) that from the conflict of wills is born the action (the quantitative and qualitative variations). For us, this was the nucleus of the character, its 'motor'. Explanation of our exercises, especially those concerned with 'emotional shaping' and rehearsals with or without text, will complete an understanding of the method that we used. As for the joker system, which we used from the *Arena conta Zumbi* ('Arena Tells of Zumbi') production* onwards, and which was characterised by the socialisation of the characters (all the actors performed all the characters, thus abolishing the private proprietorship, the appropriation, of characters by actors) – all that is explained in the exercises under the heading 'Games of mask and ritual' (pp. 139–48) and in the 'Tick-tock' sequence (pp. 221–3). The general rehearsal techniques detailed elsewhere in this book can be used for any method of production, or any style of acting.

---

* For more about this production, given in 1965, see Augusto Boal, *The Theatre of the Oppressed*, London: Pluto Press, 1979.

3

THE ARSENAL OF THE
THEATRE OF THE OPPRESSED

INTRODUCTION: A NEW SYSTEM OF EXERCISES
AND GAMES FROM THE THEATRE OF THE
OPPRESSED

In the poetics of the Theatre of the Oppressed, various words which
can, in other circumstances, carry a number of different meanings
are used in a very precise sense, with a particular connotation. Thus
words such as 'ritual', 'mask', 'oppression', etc., are explained as
and when necessary.

In this book, I use the word 'exercise' to designate all physical,
muscular movement (respiratory, motor, vocal) which helps the doer
to a better knowledge or recognition of his or her body, its muscles,
its nerves, its relationship to other bodies, to gravity, objects, space,
dimensions, volumes, distances, weights, speed, the interrelationship
of these different forces, and so on. The goal of the exercises is a
better awareness of the body and its mechanisms, its atrophies and
hypertrophies, its capacities for recuperation, restructuring, rehar-
monisation. Each exercise is a 'physical reflection' on oneself. A
monologue. An introversion.

The games, on the other hand, deal with the expressivity of the
body as emitter and receiver of messages. The games are a dialogue,
they require an interlocutor. They are extroversion.

In fact, the games and exercises I offer are mostly 'gamesercises' –
there is a fair proportion of exercise in the games and a fair proportion
of game in the exercises. The difference on the whole is one of
didactic intent.

This 'arsenal' has been chosen in pursuit of the general aims of
the Theatre of the Oppressed. Some of the games have been adapted
to our needs (with children's games as the starting point, for example),

some have been invented in the course of our practice, and some are as old as Breughel.

Two unities

We start from the principle that the human being is a unity, an indivisible whole. Scientists have demonstrated that one's physical and psychic apparatuses are completely inseparable. Stanislavski's work on physical actions also tends to the same conclusion, i.e. that ideas, emotions and sensations are all indissolubly interwoven. A bodily movement 'is' a thought and a thought expresses itself in a corporeal form.

This concept is easily grasped in its most obvious manifestations – the idea of eating can induce salivation, the idea of making love can produce erection, love can bring a smile to the face, hate can produce a hardening of the features, etc. The phenomenon is less obvious when it relates to a particular way of walking, sitting, eating, drinking, speaking. And yet all ideas, all mental images, all emotions reveal themselves physically.

That is the first unity, the unity of the physical and psychic apparatuses. The second is that of the five senses – none exists separately, they too are all linked. Bodily activities are activities of the whole body. We breathe with our whole body, with our arms, our legs, our feet, etc., even though our respiratory apparatus takes a leading role in the process. We sing with our whole body, not just our vocal chords. We make love with our whole body, not just our genital organs.

Chess is a highly intellectual, cerebral game. And yet good chess players also do physical training before a match. They know that the whole body thinks – not just the 'brain'.

Five categories of games and exercises

In the following section, I outline a series of exercises and games in five different categories. In the body's battle with the world, the senses suffer. And we start to feel very little of what we touch, to listen to very little of what we hear, and to see very little of what we look at. We feel, listen and see according to our speciality; the body adapts itself to the job it has to do. This adaptation is at one and the same time atrophy and hypertrophy. In order for the body to be able to send out and receive all possible messages, it has to be reharmonised. It is with this end in mind that we have chosen exercises and games which focus on de-specialisation.

No one should undertake or continue any exercise or game if they have some injury or condition which might be exacerbated by taking part – a back problem, for instance. In the Theatre of the Oppressed no one is compelled to do anything they don't wish to do.

In the first category, the aim is to bridge the gap between feeling and touching. In the second, between listening and hearing. In the third, to try to develop several senses at once. In the fourth category, to try to see what we look at. Finally, the senses also have a memory; we try to awaken it.

I   FEELING WHAT WE TOUCH

Death hardens the body, starting with the joints. (In his last years, Chaplin, the greatest dancer, the greatest mime, could no longer bend his knees.) Thus it makes sense to do exercises which dissociate the different parts of the body, so that central cerebral control may be exercised over each and every muscle right down to the smallest portion of the body – tarsus, metatarsus, finger, head, thorax, pelvis, left-hand side of the face, right-hand side, etc.

1st series: general exercises

1 The cross and the circle

We start with the exercise which is theoretically the easiest to do and yet, because of psychological and physical mechanisations, is extremely difficult to achieve in practice. The participants in a work-shop or a forum session can try it sitting down or standing up, on a chair, on a table or on the ground. As there is no need for preparation, non-actors have no fear of throwing themselves into it. As they are warned that it is almost impossible to do well, they aren't ashamed of not succeeding. As there is no compulsion to succeed, they feel free to give it a try.

The participants are asked to describe a circle with their right hand. Large or small, as they please. It's easy, everybody does it. Stop. Ask them to do a cross with their left hand. Even easier. Everyone gets there. Stop. Ask them to do both at the same time ... It's almost impossible. In a group of thirty people, sometimes one person manages it, almost never two. Three is the record!

Variation

Ask the participants to describe a circle with their right foot. They do it for a minute. They forget about the foot, still continuing to make circles. Then ask them to write their first name in the air with their right hand at the same time. . . . Again, this is almost impossible; the foot has a tendency to follow the hand and write the first name as well.

To make the exercise easier, try doing the circle with the left foot and writing with the right hand. This is easier, sometimes people manage it.

Why is this so difficult? Pure psychological mechanisation, since there is absolutely no physical obstacle. So, with practice, it can be done.

2 Columbian hypnosis

One actor holds her hand palm forward, fingers upright, a few centimetres away from the face of another, who is then as if hypnotised and must keep his face constantly the same distance from the hand of the hypnotiser, hairline level with her finger-tips, chin more or less level with the base of her palm. The hypnotiser starts a series of movements with her hand, up and down, right and left, backwards and forwards, her hand vertical in relation to the ground, then horizontal, then diagonal, etc. – the partner must contort his body in every way possible to maintain the same distance between face and hand. If necessary, the hypnotic hand can be swapped; for instance, to force the hypnotised to go between the legs of the hypnotiser. The latter's hand must never do movements too rapid to be followed, nor must it ever come to a complete halt. The hypnotiser must force her partner into all sorts of ridiculous, grotesque, uncomfortable positions. Her partner will thus put in motion a series of muscle structures which are never, or only rarely, activated. He will use certain 'forgotten' muscles in his body.

Variation

Hypnotism with two hands. Same exercise, but this time the actor is guiding two fellow actors, one with each hand, and can do any movement she likes; the 'leader' mustn't stop moving either of her hands – the exercise is for her benefit as well. She can cross her hands over each other and force one actor to pass underneath the

63

other. The two 'led' actors cannot touch; each body must find its own equilibrium without leaning on the other. The 'leader' mustn't do any movements which are too violent; she is an ally, not an enemy, even though she must still try to unbalance her partners. The roles are swapped, so that all three actors have the experience of being the 'leader'.

Variation

Hypnotism with the hands and feet. Like the preceding versions, but with four actors, one for each of the leader's hands and feet. The person leading can do any kind of movement, even dancing, crossing her arms, rolling on the ground, jumping, etc. The actors who are following the feet must follow only the big toe.

Variation

Any part of the body. In this variation, an actor goes into the middle of a circle and begins to move with his whole body, but always in one direction only and staying on the same spot. The rest of the group form a circle around him. A first volunteer comes forward and lets herself be hypnotised by a part of the central actor's body; she must then follow all the movements of that part of the body – ear, nose, back, bottom, foot, whatever it is. Then a second actor comes forward and does the same, choosing any part of either of the two bodies in the middle. A third actor joins, with a choice of three bodies, until all the actors have let themselves be hypnotised by a part of one of the others' bodies. At that point, the first actor can execute one or more full turns with his body – slowly, as these movements will be greatly exaggerated by the others because of their distance from the centre of the circle. Then, if the space is sufficiently large, you can ask everybody to move further away from the part of the body which has hypnotised them. Or to get closer to it.

3 Minimum surface contact

Each actor studies configurations of his body which bring its surface into minimum contact with the floor, varying the options and exploring all the possibilities: feet and hands, one foot and one hand, buttocks only, chest, back . . . . At one time or another during the exercise the surface of every part of the body must have touched the floor. (Make sure you are working on a suitable surface – grass or a soft floor is best.)

The passage from one position to another should be done very slowly, to stimulate all the muscles which intervene in the transition, and to allow the actor to take stock of what is happening.

The actor must feel the force of the weight pulling him towards the ground. In his daily life, he spends his time seated, or lying down, or standing, and thus he is accustomed to dealing with gravity in these positions – but there are a thousand other ways of counteracting this force. Our ordinary, daily movements eventually mechanise our bodies – this exercise is about de-mechanising, de-structuring, dismantling.

After a few minutes, ask the actors to get into pairs. Each actor must touch his partner's body and lean against her, at the same time maintaining the minimum contact with both partner and floor. The actors must counterbalance each other. Their two bodies must move slowly and continuously, at every juncture trying to find a new position, a new arrangement, which must then be changed for another and another.

Afterwards, ask them to get into groups of four, or possibly eight, maybe even everyone in one group.

In this exercise (as with all the other physical exercises of muscular communication), it is absolutely forbidden to talk, make suggestions, or ask questions; communication, in this situation, is solely muscular or visual, never verbal. Talking, even in whispers, spoils the exercise. Nor should the participants try to achieve great feats of strength or to out-perform others. No heroism. No risks. But, within the bounds of the possible, people should try everything, without obliging others to do anything they can't or don't want to do. You make suggestions (muscularly) to others, and either accept their suggestions or don't.

4 Pushing against each other

This is a very important exercise, above all because it shows physi-cally what the actor's *maieutic** action should be during a Forum Theatre session. The exercise is about using all one's strength and still not winning!

The actors arrange themselves in pairs, facing each other, and hold

---

* *Maieutics*: the Socratic process of assisting a person to bring into clear consciousness conceptions previously latent in the mind.

65

each other by the shoulders. There is a line (imaginary or real) on the ground between them. They start pushing with all their strength. When one person feels that her 'adversary' is weaker, she eases off so as not to cross the line, so as not to win. If the other person increases his pushing, the first does the same, so that together both are using all the strength they can muster. This is exactly what the player must do during a forum session: neither give way to the intervening spect-actor, nor overwhelm him, but rather help him to apply all his strength.

Variation

The same thing with two actors back to back.

Variation

The same thing, bottom to bottom.

Variation

Two actors back to back, leaning against each other. Gradually, never breaking the back contact, they walk their way down to the floor, so that they are sitting back to back. Then, without using their hands, they walk their way back up again, to end as they started.

Variation

Back dancing. Two actors set themselves back to back and dance, without music. Each must try to intuit what the other wants to do, and where he wants to go. Back to back contact must never be broken.

Variation

See-saw. In pairs, facing each other, seated on the floor with legs outstretched and apart, the actors take one another by the arms (not just by the hands, which is much more difficult) and brace each other feet to feet. First one partner rises, pulled by the other, and then, as she goes down, the second one begins to rise, in such a way that at a given moment, both will be halfway up – just like two children playing on a real see-saw.

5 Joe Egg (a.k.a. Trust Circle)

Ask the group to form a circle, with everybody standing facing the centre, holding their bodies absolutely upright. Then they must lean towards the centre without bending at the waist, or arching their backs, or lifting their heels off the ground – like the Tower of Pisa. Next, ask them to lean outwards in the same manner (without lifting their toes). Then the whole sequence several times, towards the centre, towards the outside.

Then they do the same thing towards the left and towards the right, still without bending in the middle, without lifting the feet.

Ask them to describe a circle in the air with their bodies, leaning into the centre, to the left, outwards, to the right, into the centre, etc. Then the same thing the other way round: centre, right, outwards, left. Several times.

Ask a volunteer to go into the centre of the circle, close her eyes and do the same thing, but this time she is going to let herself fall. Everybody else must tighten the circle and, when she falls, support her with their hands (giving a little as her body meets their hands so that there is no abrupt impact) and then propel her gently back towards the centre, where she doesn't come to rest, because she starts to fall in another direction, and thus it goes on. It is very important that there are always at least three people taking care of the person in the middle. At the end, if you want, you can roll the person around the circle, instead of immediately standing her up in the middle again.

Variation

Only three people in all, one on each side of a third. The actors on either side face one another. The actor in the middle lets himself fall, either forwards or backwards. In both cases, the actor's feet must not leave the centre.

6 The circle of knots

By way of preparation, make an 'elastic circle': the actors join hands to form a ring and then move apart till only their fingers are touching, while their bodies continue to move as far away as possible. After a time, they do the opposite and gather together in the middle, trying to occupy as little space as possible.

The whole thing can be combined with a voice exercise – when moving apart, the actors vocalise sounds which express their desire to touch one another, and when touching, they make sounds expressing their desire to be apart.

Make a circle again, hand in hand. The actors must not change or loosen their grip, for the duration of the whole exercise. One of them starts to move forward, pulling his neighbours after him (always slowly, without violence, with a lightness of touch) and travels over or under the hands of the people opposite, as if tying a knot; then a second actor does the same, then another, then two or three at a time, over or under, till everyone has made all the 'knots' possible, and no one can move any more. At this point, very slowly and without violence, and above all in silence, without words, everyone tries to get back to their original positions (which is rarely achieved . . .).

Variation

The same thing with eyes closed. This version must be done even more slowly to avoid collisions.

Variation

A line instead of a circle.

Variation

In a tight circle, each person joins a hand with two different people opposite. Then, without loosening their grip, they try to undo the knots.

7 The actor as 'subject': the Greek exercise

One actor in the middle and at least seven or eight others around her. She starts a movement and everyone else must help her complete this movement. For example, if she lifts a foot, someone immediately places themselves under this foot so that the actor is standing on them. The protagonist does whatever she likes, and the others help her raise herself up, roll on to her back, stretch out on her side, climb into the air, etc., by inserting themselves into the relevant space. The protagonist must always move slowly to allow the others (who must move quickly) time to discover her intentions, which should not be spelt out. To make it easier to discern these intentions, the actors must all try to touch any part of the protagonist's body and translate the muscular messages they receive. The most important thing is to avoid manipulating the protagonist actor – it is up to her to decide her movements. If liked, create two or more simultaneous groups, and after a few minutes ask the protagonists to change groups without stopping the exercise – not the group to change protagonists, which would be manipulation. The exercise ends when the protagonist gently returns to the ground. Beware – once, in Italy, I said 'Stop' and the actors dropped the protagonist on the floor. That was a mistake. A serious mistake.

8 *The actor as 'object'*

There are two ways of starting this exercise:
1 the protagonist gets up on a table and lets himself fall backwards on to the hands of eight actors below (two rows of four, facing each other, heads held back, arms extended, hands interwoven with open palms, ready to take the weight – remember to remove bangles, watches, rings, etc.);
2 the actor runs and jumps on to the arms of eight actors, turning on to his back in mid-air. Before jumping, he shouts 'Hup' at the top of his voice. At his cry, the actors stretch out their arms, standing opposite one another, as above.

In both cases, the actor stays stretched out on four pairs of joined hands. At that point, another actor goes and holds his arms and a tenth actor holds his feet. Without speaking to each other, they toss the protagonist up in the air, three times. Then, they lift him right up (all holding their arms stretched up in the air) and turn him over three times. After this, when the protagonist's stomach is facing the ground (it is very dangerous if he is stomach up) the eight throw him higher, kneel down, and catch him below. Then they lay him out on the ground and, on a visual cue, all start giving him an even massage at the same time, with both hands, moving to the right and left, in such a way that the protagonist's whole body is touched with the same intensity – neither caress nor aggression. Then he is rolled over on to his back and the same massage is repeated. The actor at his head touches him around the head, ears, nose, neck, hair.

During this exercise, the actors should make a sound as uniform as their massage, to relax the protagonist, to send him to sleep.

9 Lifting someone out of a chair

One actor sits on a chair. The other actors around her try to press her body into the chair and she tries to stand up again. Everyone uses all their strength. At a certain point, the workshop leader shouts 'Go' and everyone reverses the movement at the same moment, slipping their hands under her and throwing her into the air.

Variation

The person lies flat on the ground and a surrounding group push her into the floor (firmly, but without hurting her). Then, at a given cue, they lift her rapidly into the air, though without actually throwing her. When her body is as high as possible, the actors carrying it try to simulate the waves of the sea.

Variation

Standing, in pairs. One person, with her arms by her sides, her partner holding on to that person's right arm with both hands, stopping it from rising. The first person, keeping her arm straight, tries with all her strength to raise it into the air, but her partner is using all his strength to stop her. After a minute or two, the workshop leader says 'Stop', and both partners cease their efforts – but, magically, the right arm which was being restrained will now rise into the air of its own accord!

10 Equilibrium of the body with an object

Take any object – a pencil, a ball, a chair, a book, a table, a file, a sheet of paper, etc. Try to find as many ways as possible of holding the object, using every possible relationship of body to object – sometimes holding it close to the body, sometimes at a distance, sometimes above, sometimes below – whatever you want to do and can do. A postage stamp, a pen, a postcard, a telephone ... anything will do. The important thing is to study the body-object-gravity relationships.

11 Balloon as extension of the body

The workshop leader throws a number of balloons in the air (one, two, three, as many as necessary) pushing them in the direction of the actors. The actors must keep them in the air, touching them with any part of their bodies, as if their bodies were part of the balloons they're touching; they inflate their whole bodies, as if they were flying through the air along with the balloons.

12 Racing on chairs

A group of five actors in a line, one behind the other, each standing on a chair. There is a sixth, unoccupied chair at the front of the line. Each actor moves along one chair, so that the empty chair becomes the last one; then the last actor passes that chair to the next actor, until this last chair is at the front of the line. Then the actors step one chair forward ... and so on, so that the line of chairs is always advancing.

13 Rhythm with chairs

Five actors, with one chair each. Each actor makes an image with his body and his chair. The workshop leader numbers each image – 1, 2, 3, 4, 5. Then as the actors move around the room, the workshop leader calls out a number, and all the actors must immediately assume the image which corresponds to that number. After a few times, the workshop leader starts saying two numbers at a time, and the actors must try to make both images. Then three at a time, and so on.

Variation

The same exercise without chairs – their bodies are the only material the actors may use.

14 Musical chairs

A well-known children's game. A circle of chairs facing outwards, one fewer than the number of actors playing. The actors sing a song, and from time to time the workshop leader says 'Stop'; all the actors must try to get a seat, but there is one less chair every time. The

71

person who is caught out removes another chair and the game starts again. So on till there is only one person left.

15 Movement with over-premeditation

The actors move their bodies with over-premeditation, in all directions, on several levels, on tables, chairs, the ground, stairs, in an ordered fashion, or in a haphazard, chaotic fashion, standing, lying down, leaning, on all fours.... The important thing is not to stay still and to make transitions gently, trying to think about the body, its muscles, its muscular structures. Thus all movements are pre-planned and mapped out, avoiding all mechanised movement.

16 Difficulties

We are habituated to doing things mechanically – with the smallest alteration of the body, or of the objects we encounter, everything can change. If, for example, the actor has one hand behind his back, how will he lay the table? What if he has the use of only one eye or one leg, or can hardly move forwards or backwards, or his fingers are rigid – how will he get dressed, how will he caress a woman? All physical deficiencies or imperfections of environment produce an immediate increase of sensitivity.

17 Divide up the movement

Break down any continuous movement into its constituent parts – first one leg, pause, then the other leg, etc.

18 Dissociate co-ordinated movements

The co-ordination of movements hardens the muscles and models a physical mask. In this exercise, the actor studies his movements, by dissociating them. He walks with a different rhythm for each leg, his disarticulated hands move out of time. He 'eats' without synchronising the action of his hand with the opening of his mouth, his arms balance his legs out of sync, etc.

2nd series: walks

We mechanise all our daily movements. Our own individual way of walking is perhaps the most mechanised of such movements, and yet it adapts according to place. It is true that we have our own individual gait, particular to each of us, always the same (i.e. mechanised), but it is also true that we adapt our way of walking to suit the place in which we are walking. The Paris Métro, for example, with its long corridors, makes us accelerate our step; certain streets, on the other hand, certain pavements, oblige us to walk slowly. I don't walk the same way in London as I do in Paris, or Rio, or New York, or Ouagadougou.

Changing our way of walking forces us to activate certain little-used muscle structures and makes us more conscious of the possibilities of our bodies. Here are some possible changes, in the form of exercises.

1 Slow motion

The winner is the last person home. Once the race has begun, the actors cannot interrupt their movements, which should be executed as slowly as possible. Each 'runner' should take the largest step forward she can, on every stride. When one foot is being moved in front of the other, it must pass above knee-level. In the process of moving the foot forwards, the actors must stretch their bodies right out, so that in this movement the foot will break the equilibrium, and every centimetre it moves, a new muscular structure will appear instinctively, activating certain 'dormant' muscles. When the foot falls, the sound should be audible. This exercise, which requires considerable equilibrium, stimulates all the muscles of the body. Another rule – both feet can never be on the ground at the same time; the moment the right foot lands, the left must rise and vice versa. Always only one foot on the ground.

2 At a right angle

The actors sit on the floor, arms out in front, parallel to the floor, legs stretched out, back straight. They start *walking* with their buttocks, the right and then the left, as if they were feet. It is important for the actors to be as far apart as possible and not turn it into a race – it's just a walk, which can be slow. When they have covered a certain distance, they must retrace their 'steps' backwards. Legs and arms

73

should always be stretched out in front. The back should not be arched, but should form a right angle with the arms and legs.

3 Crab

On all fours, walking sideways like crabs, to the left and to the right, never straight ahead.

4 Crossed legs

In pairs, standing side by side, the actors hold each other round the waist and intertwine their inside legs, one person's right leg crossed under the other's left leg, lifting the leg on each step. The pairs then start a race, in which each actor must think of her partner's body as her own leg; she must move this body as she would move her leg. Careful – the idea is to walk, not jump. The leg (the actor) doesn't help, it is the other partner who has to do all the work.

5 Monkey

Walking along with hands always touching the ground, head always tracing a line horizontal to the ground. Like monkeys...

6 All fours

Walk on all fours, backwards and forwards.

7 Camel walk

On all fours, right foot moving with right hand, left foot with left hand – so that you move first the whole of the right side forward, then the whole of the left side.

8 Elephant walk

Same as the preceding exercise, except the other way round – right foot moves with left hand, left foot moves with right hand.

9 Kangaroo walk

The actors bend down and take hold of their ankles. They move forward in leaps and bounds like a kangaroo.

10 Leaning-against-each-other walk

Two actors, side by side, touching shoulders (the right shoulder of one against the other's left shoulder) walk along leaning against one another, each trying to keep his feet as far from the other person's feet as possible.

Variation

Same as the above, but with two pairs leaning against each other, one person on either side of the original pair.

Variation

A small circle in which four actors keep their balance by leaning their necks against the opposite person, still trying to keep their feet as far as possible from the centre. It moves around like an eight-legged monster.

11 Strapped feet walk

With feet strapped together, or in a sack, jump first forwards, then backwards, then to the side.

12 Wheelbarrow

Like children: an actor on the floor leans on his hands, another takes him by the legs. The one on the floor walks on his hands, the other as if pushing the barrow.

13 As you like it

Try to modify your normal walk, including its rhythm.

3rd series: massages

The word massage is inadequate as a designation for this series of exercises. A better description would be 'a persuasive *dialogue*' between one partner's fingers and the other partner's body. This dialogue must be carried out without violence, but equally without titillation – neither aggression nor caress. The whole body is combed for tensions; a dialogue takes place, with the participants trying to relax, to release all the muscle tones, all the knots, using repetitive movements, around and across, with the ends of the fingers or with the whole hand.

1 In a circle

The actors sit in a circle, one behind the other, each person placing their hands on the shoulders of the person in front of them, in order to keep roughly an arm's length apart. Then, with their eyes closed, everybody tries to find the hardened points of their partner's body, the neck, around the ears, the head, the shoulders, the backbone. After this has gone on for a few minutes, ask everyone to do a 180 degree turn, still with their eyes closed, turning into the circle (to avoid collisions), so that the whole circle ends up facing the opposite direction. Give the group another few minutes of massage. Then ask everyone to lie back on the person behind them, who must carry on massaging them, this time on the face.

Variation

Face to face. The same exercise, standing, in two lines facing each other. The partners massage each other's faces, as before.

2 The movement comes back

As in the first exercise in the series, except that everyone waits till an actor starts a repetitive action (a rhythmic tap or squeeze or whatever) on the shoulder of the person in front of him, who must then repeat exactly the same thing on the person in front of her, and so on, till the motion returns to the person who started it. At that point, the originator changes the motion or the rhythm (or both).

3 *Sea waves*

Two partners more or less the same height, back to back. One tries to place her buttocks in the small of the other's back and lets herself fall back against him. The latter leans towards the ground, in such a way that his partner is able to 'lie down' on his back. After this has been achieved, he makes gentle movements, up and down, so that his partner feels as if she were floating on the waves of the sea, relaxed, tranquil, without tensions, without fear. After a few minutes, the two partners swap over.

Variation

The same, with two extra people to observe and assist. The preceding exercise is not that easy to do. The most common mistake is for the first partner to put her buttocks at the same height as the second's, rather than finding the small of the back, just above the buttocks. The other problem can be lack of confidence on the part of the first partner. To remedy this, one can do the same exercise, which is in any case very calming, with one or two colleagues on the sides to help the person stretching out on the other's back.

4 *The rolling carpet*

Everyone lies on their back on the floor with their arms stretched out behind them; the first person lies with her legs to the right, the second with his legs to the left, and so on alternately, in such a way that all the shoulders are side by side, but the heads are pointing in opposite directions. Everyone lifts their arms in the air. One person sits on the raised hands and the people lying on the floor make that person's body move along as if she was on a rolling carpet. At the other end, there is one person standing, waiting to receive the arriving person. The latter, once she's got there, lies on the ground to await the arrival of the second traveller on the 'rolling carpet', and so on till everyone has been on the carpet.

Italian variation

Everyone lying on their backs on the ground, heads all facing the same way, bodies all pointing in the same direction. The first person in the row starts rolling on the bodies of his companions till he arrives at the other end. As soon as he has set off, the second person follows, then the third, etc.

Edam variation

Everyone stretched out on their backs, head to toe with their neighbour. This time a little space is left between each body. One person comes to lie across the first three, at a right angle to them. At a given moment, those on the ground begin to roll in the same direction. The person on top of them will also move with them. A second person follows, etc.

5 Back massage

Two actors back to back – each tries to massage the other with his back.

6 The demon

A way to shake out tensions. The actor hops from one foot to the other, doing arm movements similar to those one does to shake water off one's body, or to chase out a demon (in countries where they exist . . .).

4th series: integration games

1 Person to person, Quebec-style

Everybody gets into pairs. The workshop leader calls out the names of parts of the body, which the partners must touch together; for instance, 'Head to head' – the partners must touch their heads together; or 'Foot to elbow' – one partner's foot must touch the other's elbow (and vice versa at the same time, if it is possible). The bodily contacts are cumulative, so that when the partners have put two parts of their bodies together they must keep them together while carrying out the next instruction. The actors can make the contacts in any way they choose, sitting, standing, lying, etc. After four or five instructions which have tangled the pairs together, and taken the game to the limit of physical possibility, the workshop leader shouts 'Person to person' and the pairs separate and everyone finds a different partner – then the process starts again. A number of different people can have turns at calling the instructions.

2 The bear of Poitiers

One participant is designated the bear of Poitiers (a French town where this game is played). She turns her back on the others, who are the woodcutters. The latter are busy at their work. The bear must give vent to an enormous roar; all the woodcutters fall to the ground and must stay there without making the tiniest movement, absolutely motionless. The bear goes up to each one of them, roars whenever she likes, touches them, tickles them, prods them, tries every trick she can think of to make them laugh, to make them move; in short, her goal is to force them to show that they are alive. When she succeeds and this happens, the woodcutter in question becomes a second bear, and the two bears set off to do the same thing to the other woodcutters, who still try not to move. Eventually there are three bears, then four, and so on.

This last exercise is very curious in that it produces an effect exactly opposite to its guiding principle. The principle is: if the woodcutter can send his senses to sleep, if he can feel nothing, see nothing, hear nothing, if he can 'play dead', the bear will not attack because bears don't eat dead people. The instruction 'Feel nothing' provokes exactly the opposite reaction, and all the senses become extraordinarily highly developed – you sense much more, hear much better, etc. Fear hypersensitises us!

3 The chair

An actor sits on a chair, legs held tightly together. He gets hold of the waist of a second actor, who sits on the first actor's knees and then himself hitches up to the waist of a third actor, and so on till everyone is sitting on each others' knees, all with their legs together, with the last person sitting on the chair.

They begin to chant in unison 'left, right' and to move right foot and left foot in time with the chant. The chair is removed and no one falls down, as they are all sitting, hitched up to each other. The head of the line must try to 'insert' himself under the last person – in this way they form a circle of sitting people, still moving. At this point they can let go of the others' waists, because there is no longer any need to hold on to each other, all being comfortably seated.

One can make three lines of people, on three chairs, to facilitate the coupling process. Or four. But the first in the line must still eventually try to join up with the last person in the next line, the closest line.

Or a similar exercise can be done in a standing circle. The circle should be very regular, and quite closely knit. To a count of 'one, two, three', everyone slowly sits down, so that they end up on each others' knees, all sitting, with no chair.

4 Leapfrog

This is the children's game everyone knows. One person bends over with his hands on his knees. His partner jumps with legs akimbo over his back and then bends over with her hands on her knees; her partner then runs and jumps over her, and so on. The game can also be played cumulatively, so that eventually there is a whole succession of backs to jump over.

5 The Breughel game

This game is four centuries old. It features in Breughel's painting *Children's Games*. An actor (called 'the mother') stands with her back to a wall. Five others are facing her, in a line, one behind the other, all bending down with their heads between the legs of the person in front, so that they all make up a sort of ten-legged horse. The person who is closest to the 'mother' rests his head in the latter's arms. The game begins when the other actors, one by one, take a running jump and throw themselves on to the five-person horse, trying to land as close as possible to the mother, but without moving once they have jumped on the horse's back. The first person jumps and either he hangs on, or he falls. The second actor launches herself and she also stays put or falls. When five actors have jumped, the mother starts to rock the horse's body to try to shake off those on top.

There are numerous versions of this game. Usually, in Portugal, each runner warns of his approach with a shout of 'Charge!' One variation specifies that the mother must choose the manner of jumping – shouting, laughing, crying, etc. – and each jumper must do as she says. Equally there can be two teams, and the team which keeps the greater number of jumpers on the horse wins.

6 Grandmother's footsteps

Also a very well-known game. One person stands facing a wall, not looking at the others, who start off some distance back and then move forwards. The person at the wall counts 'One, two, three', and so on, either slowly or very fast, and then swings round to face those approaching. Those she catches moving when she turns to look must go back to the start. The winner is the person who manages to touch her without being caught.

7 Millipede

Everybody sits with their legs apart, one behind another. The work-shop leader gives a countdown: 'One, two, three ... go!' The whole line turns over at the same time, with everybody ending up with their legs on the shoulders of the person in front of them and their hands on the floor supporting them. So the line looks like a millipede. Then, the millipede has to walk. If liked, to make the exercise easier, start with only three participants, then four, and so on, working up to manage a large number – the millipede tends to come out better this way.

8 Apple dance

Two partners dance with an apple clasped between their foreheads (no hands). The apple mustn't be dropped.

9 Sticky paper

One person in the centre. The others touch her or one another, but with a sheet of paper between the touching parts of the bodies. The person in the centre begins to move and the whole group must move with her, but the bits of paper must stay where they are, without dropping. The part of the body which is touching another body can be the head, the shoulder, the neck, the buttocks, anything.

10 The wooden sword of Paris

Two groups facing each other, with a leader in front of each group. They fight a duel as if they had wooden swords in their hands. Each leader can give six different strokes:

1 as if to chop off the head of the opposing leader – in which case all the opposing team must duck;
2 as if to chop off the legs – all the opposing team must jump;
3 striking clearly to the left – the actors must jump to the right;
4 same to the right – the actors jump left;
5 a clear strike at the middle – the actors jump right if they're on the right, left if on the left;
6 the leader thrusts his sword forward – the adversaries must jump back.

The game starts with the workshop leader instructing each leader in turn to give a single strike at a time. The leaders are rotated a few times. The workshop leader suggests two blows at a time; then three, four, five. Then the workshop leader allows the leaders (who should change frequently) to fight however they wish.

11 American football (a.k.a. British bulldog)

Everyone against one wall, except one person who is against the opposite wall. The workshop leader shouts 'Go' and everyone must try to get to the opposite wall, except the lone actor who tries to catch one of the others. Having caught one, these two then try to catch two more; then the four to catch four, etc. Each actor can catch only one actor at a time.

Variation

Same as the above, except that the catcher(s) only have to tag people to catch them, and they can tag more than one each time. This version is less violent.

Variation

Same as the tag version above, except that the catchers have to hold hands.

5th series: gravity

This is a very long series.

It should be done in a very gentle manner, without any violence, without any tension. Each person should endeavour to study the force of gravity, which is an actual, existing force, pulling us towards the ground twenty-four hours a day. We are talking about an enormous force – as great as our own weight! If I stretch out my arm, it requires an enormous effort on my part to keep it stretched out, otherwise it will fall. If I didn't make a huge effort, my head would drop, since it has no particular reason to stay upright on the top of my neck. Without my making a certain effort, my tongue wouldn't stay in my mouth, my knees would bend, my belly button would touch the ground. And so on.

All these feats require an effort. An effort equivalent to our weight. However, this is such a daily effort that we don't even realise it is happening. We make this extreme effort, every day, throughout the day, without even being aware of it.

But, even if we aren't aware of the effort, the body is, the body feels it deeply. And sometimes we say things like: 'I'm tired and yet I haven't done anything.' This isn't true – we have stopped our tongue from falling out, our knees from bending, our head from tumbling to the ground. That's something. A huge something. As huge as the force which we have to counteract all our lives.

In order to combat this force, in order to be able to expend the necessary effort with greater economy, the body mechanises its movements and always finds the most economical way of walking, sitting down, working, etc.

This exercise helps us to become aware of and recognise these mechanisations. In this series, all the body's muscles are continually activated and de-activated, and care should be exercised. Also make sure that you finish the last exercise sequence on the positive, gravity-defeating note specified, otherwise the actors may feel like they can never move again!

1 Horizontality sequence

1 Without moving the rest of the body, which should remain rigid, the actor stretches out his neck and head towards the front.

   A colleague can help him by touching his nose and then immediately pulling her finger away – the nose should try to follow the finger as far as possible, as far in front of the body as it will go. The movement should be executed on a single horizontal line.

2 Again without moving the rest of his body, the actor moves his head and neck backwards on one plane, as far as possible; again,

it is a good idea for a colleague to assist with a finger, to guide the movement to ensure that it is rectilinear and horizontal.

3 The actor bends his neck to the left, placing his head above his left shoulder, still staying in one horizontal plane. A colleague can help by touching his ear with a finger. To make it easier, the actor can cross his hands above his head and try to touch his elbow with his ear. The sideways movement resembles the head and neck movement contained in certain Asian dance forms.

4 Same thing to the right.

5 All the preceding movements must be rectilinear and horizontal; the nose should move in a plane parallel with the ground. Now the actor moves his neck in a circle, trying to touch distant points with his nose, forwards or backwards, to the left or the right. The eyes should be fixed on a particular point, so that all the movement is made by the neck and the head always stays the same distance from the ground, without going any lower or higher.

6–10 The same exercises for the thorax. The whole thoracic cage should be lifted and moved from front to back and from left to right, and should inflate during respiration; the recommended breathing pattern for this is inhalation when the thorax is going backwards and exhalation when it is coming forwards. That is, the reverse of what one does normally.

11–15 The same exercises for the pelvis.

16–19 'Puppet' exercises. An actor takes hold of one of her colleagues by the collar of his shirt, and the latter lets his head hang loosely like a puppet. The head should have no autonomous reaction, and, if touched, should react only to the force of gravity.

Then the same, with head and right arm. The other parts of the body should stay rigid. The right arm and head must be completely supple, responding only to the colleague's handling and to the force of gravity.

The same again, with the left arm as well.

The same colleague holds the actor round the waist and the whole upper part of his body flops over and hangs down.

20 The actor improvises around these base movements, creating any images he wants. For instance, using the image of a typewriter, where his head is the carriage, reacting to the movements of his fingers on imaginary keys: his fingers tap the keys, his head moves over to the left or comes back sharply (carriage

return), reverse key, capital letter key (his head comes up), red print key (his head turns to the right), etc.

2 *Verticality sequence*

1 The actor is seated on the ground, arms and legs spread wide, forming a right angle, thus dividing her body 'vertically' into two parts, each part having one arm, one leg, one shoulder, half the head, half the pelvis, half the chest. She 'advances' in this fashion on her hindquarters, leaning first the right side of her body forwards, then the left side; the two parts of the body should be as dissociated as possible, the movements as isolated as possible.

Having made a few 'steps' forward, still with arms and legs extended, she goes back to where she started from, in reverse.

2 The same thing, on one's back on the floor, arms and legs dead straight parallel to the body; forwards and backwards, left side, right side.

3 Flat on the floor, the actor moves towards the left and towards the right, still 'walking' with one whole side at a time.

3 *Sequence of rectilinear and circular movements*

It is important to be aware of the whole dynamic of this exercise before undertaking it; be aware especially of what is said in the final paragraph of this section (p. 88) about the need to pace the participants, give them breathing space, and then give them all the encouragement they will need to start moving again.

1 The actor moves forward only by means of rectilinear movements of legs, arms and head, like a robot. The movements must be clipped, without a definite rhythm, unexpected, surprising movements. Swinging movements of the arms cannot be used because they are circular. All parts of the body must move.

Very often, in this exercise, actors have a tendency to do abrupt, juddering movements, which should be avoided. While the movements should be straight, they can still be gentle and varied.

As for the rectilinearity of the movements, this is most easily achieved by stating that people's limbs must stay parallel to the walls, the floor, or the ceiling, or whatever diagonals there are in the room.

2 The actor moves forward by means of rounded movements

(circular, oval, spiral, elliptical, etc.). The arms revolve at the same time from front to back, up and down; the head should describe curves in relation to the ground, going up and down, never staying at the same level. The legs and the whole body go up and down. The movement should be continuous, gentle, rhythmic and slow.

Repeat these movements several times while at the same time trying to study (to feel) all the muscles which are active or inactive in the realisation of the movements. Only after having fully studied (felt) a movement should one move on to another, equally round movement. It is important that the whole body is in motion, head, arms, fingers, hands (which should never be clenched into fists), chest, legs, feet. The exercise should be done gently, without violence, with pleasure, almost sensually. It should never hurt. It should warm up the body.

3 Alternate circular movements and rectilinear movements.

4 The right-hand side of the body does circular movements, the left-hand side does rectilinear movements. After a few minutes, swap round.

5 The upper part of the body does rounded movements and the lower part, below the waist, does rectilinear movements. After a few minutes, swap.

6 All the possible variations, with all the parts of the body which the actor has succeeded in controlling and dissociating.

7 Move forwards while dissociating all the parts of the body to as great an extent as possible – stretching out the head, arms and legs to the limit, trying to feel the vertical division of the whole body. Walk on tip-toe with straight movements.

Then progress to very slow circular movements. Then contract the body, drawing in all its parts, until all movement ceases and the body is reduced to a tight little ball. Then do the same thing again, the other way round.

8 Do all the preceding exercises again, moving backwards.

9 Now the participants must keep their knees bent and carry on walking around like this for several minutes, without straightening up.

10 Next, the participants can do any kind of movement they like (circular or rectilinear), towards the sides or backwards, but never the usual way, i.e. forwards.

11 Here the struggle begins. The actors must start making very slightly *less* effort than is required to keep walking, to go from

86

one place to another, to move. Very slightly *less* effort, and immediately afterwards, very slightly *more* effort. They must examine the limits of these two forces, muscular strength and gravitational pull. They try to balance gravity with only the energy absolutely necessary. But each time they use a little less strength than necessary – a hard-won, slow victory for gravity. Always going from a little bit less to a little bit more, but gradually with less and less energy so that on each successive occasion the process of movement is more laborious – but, even so, they try to carry on, walking, kneeling, crawling.

12 Finally, but only after a reasonable length of time, everyone gives up trying to move around and abandons themselves to immobility. But it is absolutely vital that the exercise lasts for some time, and that the actors do not give up immediately, but study the dynamics of force, so that their capitulation is gradual.

13 They stay on the floor, their whole bodies give in. As much of the actor's body as possible should be in contact with the floor. They try to feel the specific weight of each part of their body; the fingers and thumbs – each separate finger should be felt, not 'fingers' in general; head, jaw, etc.

14 After this, when they have had time to feel each part of their body, they start movement again, this time the opposite movement. First a single finger, then each and every part of the body starts to move, tries to rise; the actor still uses the absolute minimum strength necessary, a little more, a tiny bit more, and then a tiny bit less. This time the study is angled towards the little bit more. The hand rises and falls, but it rises again and again, and falls again, but it rises a little bit higher then a little bit higher. And the knees rise and fall, but rise again, and again. And the body starts to move again, but it falls back, but it starts again.

15 The actors move their bodies, shift themselves, with enormous difficulty – this difficulty is genuine, because it is a matter of overcoming the genuine force of gravity, against which we struggle throughout the day. They shift themselves, using only what strength is necessary, sometimes a little less, a little more. They stand up. They fall down, but they are strong and able to right themselves again.

16 They walk. Now it is forbidden to look at the ground, they can only look forwards. Now it is forbidden even to look forwards, they can only look at the ceiling. Now they must walk a little

faster, faster. Then they walk and jump, and each time they jump a little higher, everybody tries to jump even higher, to leave the ground, higher, even higher, they try to touch the ceiling, they try again, they have almost touched the ceiling, now they begin to shout as they jump, they try to take off, to fly, to jump as high as possible, to shout as loud as possible. Running.

This exercise has a very important pivotal moment. In the first stage, the participants are vanquished by gravity. This can give rise to a certain distress, a certain sadness. The more so because they are looking at the ground, because they are becoming aware of a fact of life; the awful power of gravity, against which we must continually struggle. When they reach the moment of inertia, they must be given a chance to rest. They must have all the time they need to start to put themselves back together. They need to be encouraged to stand up, recover themselves, jump, look at the ceiling. They must be told that gravity is a powerful force, but that each one of them possesses a force even more powerful than gravity. The series should end in euphoria (a tired euphoria, yes, but euphoria all the same).

II LISTENING TO WHAT WE HEAR

1st series: rhythm

1 A round of rhythm and movement

The actors form a circle. One of them goes into the middle and executes any kind of movement, as strange or unusual as she likes, accompanied by a noise, to a rhythm she invents. All the others imitate her, trying to reproduce exactly her movements and sounds, in time with her. Then this leader approaches and challenges someone in the circle, who goes into the middle and slowly changes the movement, the rhythm and the sound. Everyone follows this second leader, who then challenges a third person and so on.

The person who goes into the middle can do any rhythm of body and sound she likes, as long as it isn't something she does in her daily life. There must be no fear of the ridiculous, the grotesque, or the strange. If everybody is ridiculous, no one is!

Everyone else must try to reproduce everything they see and hear, as precisely as they can – the same movements, the same voice, the same rhythm . . . . If it is a woman who is in the middle, the men in the circle must try not to produce a 'masculine' version of the movement, but to reproduce exactly what they have perceived; and vice versa.

What is happening here? What mechanism? Simple – in the act of trying to reproduce someone else's way of moving, singing, etc., we begin to undo our own mechanisations. We are relaying to that person our vision of her, but more importantly we are working to restructure our own way of being, in many different fashions (since many actors will go into the middle).

We do not do a caricature, because that would lead us to do different things, but in the same way (our own). We try to understand and make an exact copy of the exterior of the person in the middle, in order to gain a better sense of their interior.

2 Game of rhythm and movement

Two teams are formed. At a given signal, all the members of the first team start making any rhythmic movements that come to mind. They have thirty seconds to unify. If at the end of the thirty seconds the opposing team considers that the members of the first team are all doing the same thing, in a uniform manner, then they start imitating them. If, however, the opposing team thinks that the first team is not acting in unison, they signal as much to the joker-judge. If the judge agrees, those who were doing irregular movements lose and drop out. But if the judge does not agree, the first group has the right to choose an actor to be eliminated from the second group. When the game has been interrupted, it is restarted in the same fashion. If there has been no interruption (no signal to the judge) the second group starts to imitate the first, with this team also having thirty seconds to unify their movements, sounds and rhythms.

3 Rhythms

Using voices, hands and feet, all the actors set up a rhythm together. After a few minutes, they change it slowly, till a new rhythm emerges, and so on, for several minutes.

Variation

Each actor does a different rhythm separately till the joker gives the instruction 'Unify'; everyone unites into a single rhythm. After a few minutes, the joker shouts 'Disperse', the rhythm breaks down into separate parts again, and so on.

Variation

At a given signal, each actor takes a particular rhythm and does a movement in time with it. After a few minutes, each actor tries to get closer to one or more of the others, choosing according to rhythmic affinity. Little by little, those who have the greatest affinity homogenise their rhythm until practically the whole group has the same rhythm and movement. It may not happen – which doesn't matter, as long as the sub-groups which have formed have their own well-defined rhythms and movements.

4 The machine of rhythms

An actor goes into the middle and imagines that he is a moving part in a complicated machine. He starts doing a movement with his body, a mechanical, rhythmic movement, and vocalising a sound to go with it. Everyone else watches and listens, seated on the floor in a circle around the machine. Another person goes up and adds another part (her own body) to this mechanical apparatus, with another movement and another sound. A third, watching the first two, goes in and does the same, so that eventually all the participants are integrated into this one machine, which is a synchronised, multiple machine.

When everyone is part of the machine, the joker asks the first person to accelerate his rhythm – everyone else must follow this modification, since the machine is one entity. When the machine is near to explosion, the joker asks the first person to ease up, gradually to slow down, till in their own time the whole group ends together.

For everything to work well, each participant really does have to try and listen to everything he hears.

Variations

Love and hate. The same exercise, with the following modification: all the participants must imagine a love machine, then a hate machine. But they must continue to be part of a machine, and not human beings.

The same thing, with the regions of a single country from which the participants originate – Germany (Prussian machine, Bavarian machine, Berlin machine), France (Breton machine, Parisian, Marseillaise, etc.), Brazil (Carioca machine, Bahia, Minas Gerais). The political parties – in Britain, the Labour, Conservative, Liberal Democrat, Scottish Nationalist, SWP, etc., machines; in the USA the Republican, Democrat, etc., machines. The different kinds of theatre and cinema – silent films, circus, opera, soap opera, agit-prop, etc.

It is extraordinary how the ideology of a group, its political standpoint, can be revealed in a rhythm of sound and movement. The way people think and the things they find fault with soon become apparent.

5 *The Peruvian ball-game*

This game sounds much more confusing than it is – in essence it is a sort of 'Chinese whispers' with balls. Each participant imagines they are in possession of a ball – a football, a tennis ball, a golf ball, a beach ball, any kind of ball or balloon; they imagine what material their object is made out of, and they play with it, in a repetitive rhythm, in such a way that their whole body is involved in the playing and their voice is reproducing, rhythmically, the sound of their own particular type of ball or balloon. The participants are given a couple of minutes to establish a regular, repetitive, rhythmic action and sound, which they practise while walking around the room.

After a few minutes, the joker says 'Get ready'. At this point each participant finds a partner and the two of them must continue playing with their own balls, facing each other, while at the same time carefully observing the smallest details of their opposite number's ball, its motion and its sound. After a few moments of simultaneous playing and observation, the joker says 'Exchange balls' and each partner must immediately take over the other person's ball, adopting that person's particular movements and sounds as exactly as they can.

After a similar interval, the joker again says 'Get ready', the players find a different partner, and then on 'Exchange balls' they swap again. This process takes place a third time, with yet another partner. Finally the joker says 'Get your original ball back' and from that moment on, all the participants must try to find the balls they started with, while continuing to play with the latest ball they have acquired. As soon as they have located their original ball, they go up to the person who is in possession of it at the time and say 'That's my ball – out you go'. That person then goes and stands on the side and if he himself hasn't yet located his own ball, he searches for it from the sidelines – if he spots it, he goes up to the person who has it and informs her in the same manner. The game goes on until everyone has found their balls ... which rarely happens!

If at the end of the game there are still some people who haven't found their balls, you can attempt to piece together the paths of the various balls by asking them who they first swapped with, and then asking those people who they swapped with, and so on till the eventual destination of the ball is established. This ball 'genealogy' is also usually nearly impossible to establish, but it can provide a useful illustration of the way actions and sounds have been modified, if each player in the history of a particular ball is asked to demonstrate how they played with it; then the various versions of one ball can be lined up side by side, to show the differences.

6 The clapping series

Like the preceding exercise, this is easier done than said. Sitting on the floor, in a circle, all the participants start to beat out a rhythm with their hands on their legs. Everyone must try to listen to the rhythms they hear, and develop a single, simple rhythm.

Once this has been achieved, one person raises her hands and, in rhythm, sends a clap towards the person on her left; then (still following the general rhythm) she does a clap on her legs and, thirdly, a clap towards the person on her right. The latter, when he has seen the first clap to the left, will have been warned and prepares for the third clap of his left-hand neighbour, which he must make coincide with his first clap. His second clap will be on his legs and his third will be to the person on his right, and so on. The claps are always from left, to legs, to right, and the claps on the left and right are always double claps, i.e. claps done by two people at once. Once this group is well in tune (and well practised) you can increase the clapping speed, keeping the same rhythm.

Then, from outside the circle, the joker can say from time to time 'Left' or 'Right' and the claps, instead of following the natural flow, must go back either to the left or the right (according to the instruction).

The next step is for the joker to instruct the first person to send out not one but several claps, at short intervals; several claps will be on the go at the same time.

Finally the joker says 'Go' and the claps must be sent all over the place, anywhere *except* to the left or the right, so that everybody has to watch everybody around the circle, to know where the claps are directed.

7 West-Side Story

So called because of its resemblance to various dance routines in the film of that name.

Two teams are formed, standing in two lines facing each other, with one leader in the middle of each team. The first leader must make a rhythmic movement forward, accompanied by a rhythmic sound, six times in succession. She thus makes six forward movements. After the first or second repetition, her team-mates will have grasped the rhythms of her movement and her sound, and must join in, moving forwards in their line behind her. The opposing gang must retreat the same distance.

At the end of the sixth repetition, the leader leaves the central position and joins on the end of the line. Another leader takes her place, and faces the opposing leader, who goes through the same process – six times, advancing, he repeats his own rhythmic sound and movement, which is copied by his team-mates, who also start advancing, while the first team retreats at the same rate. And so on, alternating advance and retreat, until every member of both teams has been a leader.

8 The Portuguese rhythmic shoes

This is a children's game which is very useful for developing co-ordination in groups. The actors sit in a circle, one shoe in front of each of them. They sing any song or rhyme which everyone knows, and, keeping careful time with the rhythm and the tune, pass the shoe

to their right-hand neighbour, except at certain specified moments.
For example:

The grand	(pass a shoe)
Old duke	(pass a shoe)
Of York	(here you don't pass on the shoe, you beat it in front of your neighbour, keeping hold of it)
He had	(pass a shoe)
Ten thou-	(pass a shoe)
sand men	(same as above)

And so on.

In the past, we used to play this game as a form of competition;
anyone who ended up with more than one shoe in front of him, or
none at all, had to drop out of the game, taking his shoe with him.
The way we use the game now, the important thing is to do it as well
as possible, but with the whole group – so that everyone is looking
after everyone else – thus developing group solidarity instead of
individual competitive spirit.

There is obviously no need to sing or recite that particular rhyme –
every country has popular songs of its own which can be used. Or
you can just use sound on its own:

> Ta ra TAN
> Ta ra TAN
> Ta ra ta ta ta ta TAN

Variation

From time to time, the joker says 'Left' and everyone has to start
sending the shoes to the left. Then she says 'Right', then 'Left', etc.
To make the exercise even more difficult, she can say it in the middle
of the musical phrase instead of at the end.

Blind variation

The same thing, with eyes closed.

Standing variation

This is extremely difficult, don't even try it. But, if you must, do it at your own risk: stand up, pay very close attention and ... the best of luck.

9 The two brooms

Two actors facing each other, with two brooms or sticks which they are both holding; one partner's left hand holds a broom with the other partner's right hand, and vice versa. The two start by putting the two brooms in a horizontal position and then begin a 'tick-tock' movement – one broom rises, the other falls. Tick, tock, one goes up, the other comes down.

The other participants watch from a fair distance away and then approach, one by one, moving in a rhythm which will enable them to go through the two-broom gateway without touching the brooms or changing their rhythm. Each person must arrive when the nearer broom is up, and go into the middle at the right speed to be able to go under the second broom when it is up (and the first is down), without stopping.

It is very important not to stop – the exercise is all about rhythm. A rhythm applied to speed.

10 The four brooms

The same tick-tock rhythm, but now with four brooms – two going up and down, and two others going forwards and backwards, so that at a given moment they all meet in the middle, and at another moment they all open a square hole through which a person can pass.

The process is identical: everyone watches from a distance, then moves forward with a speed and rhythm which will allow them to arrive in front of the four brooms exactly when they start to open to allow the participants' passage through.

11 Horseshoe rhythms

In a horseshoe formation, on the floor, someone starts a rhythm which must travel right round the horseshoe to the other end. Then the person at the other end starts another rhythm and it goes back in the other direction. Each participant will always be in the middle of doing one rhythm till he replaces it with the rhythm which arrives on his left or right.

12 Circular rhythms

The same thing in a circle, standing up, so that the whole body can move, the different rhythms passing right round the circle back to the originator who then starts a different rhythm.

13 The big chief

In a circle, on the floor. One person leaves the room. The group chooses the 'big chief', who is the person who will initiate all the changes in the rhythm and all the rhythmic movements in the circle. The person outside the room is invited back into the room and must try to work out who is the big chief.

14 The orchestra and the conductor

Each actor or group of several actors utters a rhythmic or melodic sound. The conductor listens to them. They must produce the same sound, whenever the conductor asks them with a gesture of hand or baton. They must be quiet when she does not require their sound. In this manner, the conductor can compose her own piece of music. Everyone can have a turn at being the conductor.

15 Rhythm dialogue in teams

Two teams are formed, each with a leader. The game begins: one leader repeats a rhythm four times, directing it towards the opposing leader as if talking to him. The actors of the first leader's group take up the rhythm and repeat it three times. The opposing leader in turn answers with another rhythm; immediately, the members of his team, as if replying to the members of the other team, repeat what he's done three times. The rhythms and the movements should be used as a dialogue, as if the groups were really talking to each other. Each musical phrase can be as long or short, as simple or complex, as people want.

16 Chain rhythm dialogue

One person thinks of something he wishes to express and tries to translate what he has thought into a rhythm of movement and sound (not simply mimicking the sound of the words!). His interlocutor watches him and answers him addressing a third person, who listens to him, and addresses a fourth person, etc. At the end, the participants tell each other what they were thinking, reproducing their rhythm while giving the translation.

17 Brazilian Indians

Lines of five actors. The person at the front of the line is the chief, who must imagine a real or fantastic situation of Latin American Indians in the forest – war, fishing, fighting animals, a religious dance, etc. He then starts travelling around the space, making rhythmical movements and sounds which the other four must repeat exactly. From time to time the joker changes the chiefs, who go to the end of their lines, to be succeeded by the next in line.

18 Lines of five

Similar to the preceding game. The first person in the line makes a gesture and a sound, in rhythm. The line joins in. The first person goes to the back of the line, the next person adds another gesture and sound to what the first person was doing. And so on till the fifth actor has made his contribution.

19 The president's bodyguards

The president in the middle, with one bodyguard facing him in front, and one behind him and one standing each side of him facing the same direction as he. The president makes a rhythmical movement and sound, the guards imitate him (the one facing him as a mirror, the others the same way round as he). The president moves around the room with his escort, making 90 or 180 degree turns whenever he pleases, so that one of the other three becomes the mirror. From time to time the joker elects a new president.

20 Walk, stop, justify

The actors walk around the room in strange and unusual ways. Every now and then the workshop leader says 'Stop'; everyone stops where they are, and each person must justify their strange position or say something which makes sense of it.

21 Carnival in Rio

Several groups of three actors, the individuals in each group numbered one, two and three. The workshop leader says 'Number one' and all the number ones start moving around the room with a rhythm of sound and movement (a different rhythm each). The other two members of each trio must imitate their leader. The workshop leader says 'Number two' and all number twos must initiate a different sound and movement, which the other members of their group must imitate exactly. Then, 'Number three'. When all three have invented their rhythmic sounds and movements, the workshop leader says 'Back to your original movements' and each person returns to their original movement. After a few moments, the workshop leader says 'Unify!'; as soon as one member of each trio decides to copy another, then the third person must follow the majority, so that all three end up doing the same sound and movement.

From time to time, the workshop leader says 'You may change groups'; those who are happy in the group they're in, stay put – those who want to change join on to another group, swelling its size. If one person is left alone (because the other members of his group have both left) he must abandon his rhythm and join one of the remaining groups.

22 Bolivian mimosas

Pairs, made up of one mimosa flower and one person. The person touches some part of the body of the mimosa, who must start moving rhythmically, first the part of the body which has been touched, then enlarging the movement till eventually it takes in the whole body. The person observes to make sure that the mimosa spreads the movement till its whole body is shaking. Three times, starting with different points on the body. Then another three times, with a rhythmic sound added. Then a further three times, but this time the mimosa must make a melodious sound, with a melodious movement. Person and mimosa can swap after each of the three sections, or at the end of the whole sequence.

People with back conditions, beware, the exercise is harder work than it seems at the time.

23 How many 'A's in one 'A'?

A circle. One actor goes into the middle and expresses a feeling, an emotion, or an idea, using only the sound of the letter 'A' in any of its possible inflections and a movement or gesture. All the actors in the circle repeat that sound and action three times. Then another actor goes in and expresses a different idea, emotion, or feeling, and again the circle repeats it three times. And so on. Then the same thing with 'E', 'I', 'O' and 'U'. Then with a single word. Finally with a sentence.

24 Two by three by Bradford

The actors get into pairs facing each other. The exercise has four or more parts. First they simply count up to three out loud a number of times; actor A says 'one', B says 'Two', A says 'Three', B says 'One', A says 'Two', B says 'Three' and so on. They try to get this working as fast as possible.

Then, instead of saying 'One', A does a rhythmical sound and a rhythmical action, which must take the place of the number whenever it would have been said. Thus the sequence now goes: A does sound and action, B says 'Two', A says 'Three', B does the sound and action invented by A, A says 'Two', B says 'Three' and so on. Whatever sound and action A does at the beginning of this second sequence must be repeated as accurately as possible whenever the 'One' would have been spoken.

In the third phase of the game, as well as the sound and action in place of 'One', a different sound and action is substituted whenever 'Two' would have been spoken. Again the partners play for a few minutes, trying to get as fluent as possible.

And of course in the fourth phase, yet another sound and action is substituted for the number three. So now what you see is a kind of sound and action dance, with no words (numbers) being spoken at all.

The game works best if each sound and action is very different from the one which precedes it. This way the players get less con-

fused. Usually people play it better when they discover that each of
the two sequences remains the same: 1–3–2 and 2–3–1. However,
any number of variations are possible – the count can be taken up to
five, or seven, etc.; even numbers do not work, because the players
will then be doing and saying the same things each round, instead of
having to observe and copy each other's actions and sounds.

25 Crossing the room

Two actors cross the room from opposite sides, with a particular
rhythm, movement and sound (one starts and the other copies, or
they reach a happy medium – no pre-planning is allowed). Then
another pair, etc., till everyone has crossed the room.

2nd series: melody

1 Orchestra

A small group of actors improvises an orchestra, preferably with
improvised instruments, while the others invent a corresponding
dance. The rhythm must frequently come to a halt – the actors stop
where they are; the orchestra's rhythm then changes and the dance
must change accordingly.

2 Music and dance

Certain Brazilian rhythms of African origin, like the samba, the
batucada and the capoeira (all involving circular movements and
almost all involving moving backwards), are excellent at stimulating
all the muscles in the body. One can also run a tape at a higher speed
than it was recorded at. In all these conditioning exercises, the
important thing is to begin slowly. Only little by little can these
exercises be done with greater intensity. I repeat that the exercises
must be fun to do, the experience should induce pleasure, not pain.

3rd series: sound

1 Sound and movement

A group of actors vocalise a particular sound (the sound of an animal,
of leaves, a road, a factory) while another group does movements

which correspond to the noises, in some way 'visualising' the sounds. If the noise is 'miaou', the representation need not necessarily be a cat, but whatever visualisation the actor associates with that particular noise.

2 Ritual sound

Same thing, except that the group which makes the noises must restrict itself to the noises of a particular ritual – waking up in the morning, going home, getting to work, a classroom, the factory, etc.

4th series: the rhythm of respiration

We have voluntary muscles which we can command at will. I tell my hands to type what I want to type and my hands obey me. I tell my body to stand up and, without hesitation, up it stands. If I want to talk, I order my vocal chords, my mouth and my tongue, to do what is necessary to produce the sounds I intend to utter.

These are voluntary muscles, consciously controllable. But there are muscle reactions which are not controllable – when I am afraid of something, or if I see the woman I love, I can't stop my heart beating faster than usual. There is no point in my saying to it 'Be quiet'. It will beat as it wants to beat, in a manner which is beyond my control. I exercise absolutely no power over it.

But there are also muscles which are controllable, which are voluntary, but have fallen into neglect, so that one isn't even aware of them – they have become mechanised. This category includes, among others, the muscles involved in respiration.

Because of their mechanisation, we breathe badly. Inside our lungs there are huge expanses of impure air which is not renewed. We use only a tiny part of our lungs' capacity.

The exercises which follow are intended to help us become aware that we can also de-mechanise respiration, we can control our breathing.

1 Lying on your back, completely relaxed

1 Place your hands on your abdomen, expel all the air in your lungs, then breathe in slowly, filling the thorax as full as it will go. Breathe out. Repeat slowly several times.
2 Start again, placing the hands at the base of the thoracic cage;

inflate the chest, making a particular effort to fill the lower part of the lungs. Do the exercises several times.

3 Same thing again, hands on the shoulders or up in the air, trying to fill the upper part of the lungs.

4 Connect up the three types of breathing in the order shown.

2 Leaning against a nearby wall

Supporting yourself on your hands, do the same respiratory movements; then start again, this time leaning on your elbows.

3 Standing up straight

Do the same respiratory movements. All the muscles should be tightened on the in-breaths. Respiration should be a whole-body activity. Every muscle should react to the entry of air into the body and to its expulsion, as if one could feel the oxygen circulating around the whole body through the arteries, and the carbon dioxide being carried through the veins to be expelled by the lungs.

4 Breathe in slowly

Slowly and deeply breathe in through the right nostril and out through the left nostril; then the other way round.

5 Explosion

Having breathed in as much air as possible, expel it violently, all in one go, through the mouth. The air produces a sound similar to a cry of aggression. Having breathed in to capacity, do the same thing, this time energetically discharging the air through the nose.

6 Breathe in slowly while lifting the arms

Lift the arms as high as possible, standing on tip-toe as you breathe in slowly; expel all the air slowly, first returning to a normal position, then gathering in the body till it occupies as little space as possible.

7 The pressure-cooker

Hold your nose, pinching together the nostrils and closing the mouth, making the maximum effort to expel the air. When you can go on no longer, open mouth and nostrils and release the air.

8 As quickly as possible, breathe in

Breathe in as much air as possible as fast as possible and immediately expel it as quickly as possible. The whole group can do this exercise, with the joker marking the time of the in-breath and out-breath, as if they were runners in a race trying to 'shift' as much air as possible in one go.

9 As slowly as possible, breathe in

Breathe in very slowly, then breathe out vocalising a sound, trying to make the sound audible for the maximum length of time.

10 Breathe in deeply through the mouth

Do this with gritted teeth, then breathe out through the nose.

11 With clear definition and lots of energy, breathe in

Breathe in and out as described, following a particular rhythm – the rhythm of the heart, or of a piece of music (with a well-defined beat), or a tune hummed by one of the actors.

12 Two groups

The first group sings a melody which the second group accompanies with its breath, marking the rhythm with the in-breaths and out-breaths. To start with, to make things easier, the tunes should be relatively slow. They can get faster later on; extremely difficult rhythms can even be used to accompany the breathing. But I repeat, always start with a slow piece of music, 'The Blue Danube', for instance.

13 Standing in a circle

The whole group breathes out making an 'Ah' sound, then the actors let themselves drop as if they were deflating, ending up on the ground, completely relaxed.

14 One actor pretends to pull the stopper out of another's body

The actor does this as if the fellow actor was an inflatable doll full of air. The part of the body 'unstoppered' can be the finger, the knee, the ear, etc. The unstoppered actor acts as if he was in the process of 'emptying'; at the same rate as he breathes out, he deflates, until he falls to the floor like an empty rubber doll. Then the first actor approaches the doll-actor's empty body and does the movements and sounds of someone filling a balloon up with an air pump. The 'balloon' must fill up with the same amount of air as the actor is pumping, sometimes a lot, sometimes a little. After the relevant time, without any motor movement (as if he was a real doll, a real balloon) he reinflates as much as he can, and his colleague helps him into an upright position (a doll wouldn't be able to do it alone).

This game-exercise should be done with several people. Once the body has been blown up again, everyone plays like a child with their 'balloon-doll', which should bounce on the ground or off the wall (but never walk). After a few minutes, the joker should ask all the children to swap balloons, two or three times. Finally, the balloons begin to deflate very slowly, and bounce less and less, till eventually they fall to the ground, completely empty.

15 A, E, I, O, U

All the actors cluster in a group, and one person comes and stands in front of them. The group must make sounds, using the letters A, E, I, O, U, changing the volume according to how near to or how far away from them the single actor is. When the 'volume-control' actor is far away, the group gets louder, and when he is close, they get quieter. The actor can move anywhere he likes around the room. The individual actors who make up the group should be trying to communicate a thought or emotion to the actor, not just making noise.

Variation

In pairs, each actor directs a vocal sound at his partner actor who is around 50 cm away; this second actor moves back 1 m, then 2 m, 3 m, 10 m. The first actor tries to adjust his voice to the distance. This exercise can also be done with singing. Thus, in the same way as the eye 'aims' naturally at the object it wants to see, the voice also 'aims' naturally at the person it wishes to address.

16 All the actors, standing facing the wall

Standing side by side, the actors 'make holes' in the wall with their voices, all at the same time and in unison.

17 Two groups of actors, facing each other

Each group gives vent to a different sound, and tries to force the other group into submission.

18 With their bodies in maximum possible contact with the floor

So placed, the actors exercise their voices.

19 Lying on their backs on tables

Lying as described, heads hanging off the end, the actors vocalise a continual sound till they feel an itch in their throats and can go on no longer.

5th series: internal rhythms

Each of us has one or more personal rhythms; our heartbeat, our breath, our walk, our laugh, a rhythm of speech, a rhythm of attention, an eating rhythm, a love-making rhythm, etc.

1 Rhythmic images

In this exercise-cum-game, an actor goes into the middle and the rest try to express with their bodies, each in turn, a rhythmic image of that person, of how they perceive him. After every actor has had a turn individually, they all repeat their rhythms together. Then the actor can try to integrate himself into this 'orchestra'.

105

Variation

A single actor does someone's rhythm; when that person recognises herself, she does someone else's rhythm, and so on.

In this exercise-game it is vital that the actors try to see as deeply as possible into the person being observed – caricature must be avoided at all costs.

III DYNAMISING SEVERAL SENSES

Of all the senses, sight is the great monopolist. Because we see, we don't bother to perceive the world outside through the other senses, which remain dormant or become atrophied.

The first part of this section is entitled 'The blind series'. In these exercises, we voluntarily deny ourselves the sense of sight in order to enhance the other senses and their capacity for perception of the outside world – just as people who really are blind can accomplish feats of perception which astonish those of us who are sighted. In this series we do the same, with the advantage of being able to open our eyes when the exercise is over . . .

The blind series

In all the games which feature a 'blind' person and a guide, it is best if one can do the game a second time, swapping the blind/guide roles.

1 The point, the embrace and the handshake

The participants are asked to fix their gaze on a static point in the room, which can be anything they like – a window, a mark on the wall, a radiator, etc.; they each choose their own point of focus. They must then close their eyes and try to make their way slowly towards their own particular point. When they collide with another person, if they think they have been diverted from the straight line they have mentally traced, they must try to correct their movement. After a few moments, the joker asks everyone to open their eyes again and take their bearings. Are they close to their chosen target? Are they miles away? A second attempt is made; this time, all those who found their mark choose a more distant point, and all those who had difficulty choose a closer point. The process is tried a third time.

Next, they must get into pairs and hug their partners. In mid-embrace, they must close their eyes, release one another, and walk backwards, either till they meet an obstacle (probably the wall) or for a pre-ordained number of steps; then they retrace their footsteps to reconstitute their embrace with the same person ... not someone else. The same exercise is done at least three times, changing partners each time.

Finally, the most difficult version. In pairs, the actors shake hands, close their eyes, break the handshakes (while keeping their hands extended in handshake position), go back till they meet an obstacle, return and try to reshake the same hand ... not just any old hand!

2 Noises

The group divides up into pairs; one partner will be blind, the other will be her guide. The latter makes a noise like an animal, a cat, a dog, a bird, anything and her partner listens. Then the blind people close their eyes and all the guides, at the same moment, start making their noises, which their blind partners must follow. When the guide stops making the noise, the blind person should also stop. The guide is responsible for the safety of his blind partner; he must stop her (i.e. by stopping his noise) if she is in danger of colliding with another blind person or bumping into an object. He should change his position frequently. If his blind charge is 'good', if she is managing to follow him, the guide should move as far away as possible. The blind person must concentrate on her own noise, even when there are lots of other noises right beside her. The exercise deals with the selective functioning of the ear.

3 The imaginary journey

This is done in pairs. The blind person must be led across a series of real or imaginary obstacles found or invented by the guide, as if the two of them were in the middle of a forest (or any real or fantastic environment the guide has in mind). As in all the exercises of this kind, speaking is forbidden; all information must be given by physical contact. Whenever possible, the guide should make the same movements as the blind person, imagining his own story.

The guides should sow obstacles throughout the room – chairs, tables, whatever's available – so that the obstacles are sometimes real, sometimes imaginary. The blind person must try to imagine where she is. On a river, for instance? Are there crocodiles? Lions? Rocks? And so on. The guide can use physical contact or breath or sound, as a means of guidance, but the blind people are not allowed to do any movement which they haven't been 'instructed' to do.

After a few minutes, the exercise stops and the blind person must very quietly tell her guide where she is in the room, who is next to her, etc. – in short, she must give all the real information she has been able to gather by means of all her senses, bar sight. Then the guide tells his story, and they compare notes.

Variation

At the end, the blind person describes both her imaginary journey and where she thought she was in the room.

4 The glass cobra

Everyone stands in a circle (or in two or more lines if the group is very large), with their hands on the shoulders of the person in front of them. With their eyes closed, they use their hands to investigate the back of the head, the neck and the shoulders of the person in front. This is the glass cobra in one piece.

Then, on an instruction from the joker, the cobra is broken into pieces and each person sets off around the room, still with their eyes closed. In Brazilian legend, this type of cobra, 'the glass cobra', shatters into a thousand pieces; but one day the pieces find each other again, these small fragments which are harmless on their own, but become dangerous the moment they get back together, because when they do they turn into the dangerous steel cobra.

The cobra in the legend is the people, obviously! In the game it is simply the participants who, after having moved around the space for a few minutes, on a signal from the joker must find their way back to the person who was in front of them before the cobra broke up. They must reconstitute the cobra(s). As in the legend, this can take time ...

Variation

The same thing except that the whole exercise is done with the participants lying on the ground and dragging themselves around like snakes.

5 One blind line, one sighted line

Two lines of actors, facing each other. In one, the actors have their eyes closed; with their hands, they try to feel the face and hands of the actor facing them. Then the sighted actors separate and shuffle themselves, and each 'blind person' has to find the person who was facing them, by touching hands and faces.

Variation

An Image Theatre exercise. The line of people with their eyes open form themselves into individual statues. The blind partners have to discover the shape of their opposite number's statue, in a few minutes, and then return to their line and form themselves into that image. Then they open their eyes and compare their image with the original it was based on.

6 The magnet – positive and negative

All the participants wander round the room for a few minutes, eyes closed, trying not to collide with one another. It is best to have crossed arms, with the hands covering the elbows, so that small people do not get elbowed in the eye; as long as people move slowly, no one gets hurt. In the first part of the game, whenever anyone touches anyone else, they must both immediately back off – the magnet is negative. They must find their bearings in the room, while avoiding touching others; this exercise develops all the other senses.

After a few minutes, the joker announces to the participants that the magnet has become positive. From that moment on, when anyone touches anyone else, they stay stuck together for a few moments. This is very difficult because the participants must not stop moving around, their feet must keep walking, which sometimes means that in order to stay stuck together, they have to walk sideways, backwards, etc. Touch with the hands should be avoided – other parts of the body are preferable. If it feels okay, a person can remain stuck to someone else; otherwise they have the right to go off looking again. A person who has been turned down (as a sticking partner) has the right to insist, but only once; the point of the game is not to hunt down particular people. One can stay stuck to one, two or several people.

Eventually, the joker gives the signal to stop. Everyone stops where they are, and each person tries to find a face, just one, with their hands. This is where the most beautiful part of the game starts – each person must try to 'translate' the tactile sensations into an image. In other words, by touching the other person's face, they must try to imagine what that face is like, looking for general features as much as small details. This process of translation is very delicate and also very pleasant. People are allowed to touch the face and head, that's all. After a few minutes the joker tells everyone to open their eyes and compare the image they constructed with the image in front of them.

7 Swedish multiple sculpture

Half the group is made up of blind people, the other half of guides. The guides each pronounce the name of a blind person who must walk towards them. The guides change position frequently, till at a certain point they come to a halt and continue calling their blind people, always calling very quietly. When the blind people are close to the guides, the latter take them by the hand and model their bodies into a complex sculpture in which they are all touching – that is, a single sculpture made out of a number of bodies.

Then the guides move away and reproduce the same sculpture with their own bodies; the reproduction must be exactly the same as the original it is modelled on, each guide taking up exactly the same position as the blind person they modelled (or else it may be the mirror image – but it must be made clear at the outset which version of the exercise is being used).

When the second sculpture is in place, the joker calls the blind people, who must come towards her, slowly, on all fours. She then conducts them to the sculpture made out of the guides' bodies. When they get there, each of the blind people must try to identify their own guide. When they think they recognise their guide, they say their own name. If they are right, the guide says 'Yes' and the blind person drops out of the game and can open his eyes. But the guide must stay put, so that the sculpture isn't altered. And so on till the last blind person finds their guide.

8 The vampire of Strasbourg

The title of this exercise is slightly alarming – and so is the exercise itself. It goes like this: everyone walks around the room with their eyes closed, their hands covering their elbows in the manner described on p. 109, without touching each other or colliding. The joker applies a little squeeze to the neck of one of the participants, who then becomes the first 'vampire of Strasbourg' – his arms extend in front of him, he gives a scream of terror, and from this point on he must seek out a neck in order to vampirise someone else. The vampire's scream gives the others a clue as to his whereabouts so that they can try to escape him.

The first vampire finds another neck and gives it a little squeeze, like the joker. The second victim screams with terror in the same fashion, her arms rise in front of her and now there are two vampires, then three, and four, etc.

Sometimes one vampire will vampirise another vampire; when this happens, the latter lets out a cry of orgasmic pleasure, which indicates that someone has been re-humanised, but also that there is still a vampire beside him. The participants must flee the most vampire-infested areas.

It is curious (though understandable) how the participants experience a certain feeling of relief on being vampirised, when instead of fleeing other people they must now persecute them. Without doubt the same mechanism operates in all situations where the oppressed becomes the oppressor. It is even richer than that. On the one hand, the oppressed (participant) becomes the oppressor (vampire); he escapes from his oppression, his fear, his anguish. He ceases to be a victim and becomes a tormentor. On the other hand, he develops in himself the mechanism of struggle – he understands that all oppressive situations can be broken, smashed. The two aspects go hand in hand.

9 The blind car

One person stands behind another, who is the car. From behind, the driver guides the movements of the 'blind car' by pressing a finger in the middle of the back (go straight on), on the left shoulder (turn left – the nearer the shoulder, the sharper the corner), the right shoulder (similarly), or with a hand on the neck (reverse). As there will be a number of blind cars driving round at the same time, it is important to avoid crashes. The cars stop when the drivers stop touching them (like bumper cars). The speed is regulated by harder or softer pressure with the finger.

10 What is the object?

With eyes blindfolded and hands behind his back, the actor has to 'guess' with the rest of his body, the nature of the object he is touching – chair, pen, glass, sheet of paper, flower, etc. This exercise greatly stimulates the sensitivity of all the parts of the body which enter into contact with the object.

To make the exercise more complex, give the blind person several objects at the same time. For instance, everything on the top of a desk, the entire contents of a wardrobe, everything there is in the kitchen, etc.

11 The smell of hands

Like the 'line of blind people', with the difference that this time a line of people go up to a blind person (someone with her eyes closed), and each person tells her his name and gives her his hand to smell. After they have all been past her once (say, five people), they return, but this time in a different order, and the blind person has to say the name of the person, by trying to remember the smell of their hand.

12 The figure-of-eight chicane

Two actors are positioned a couple of metres away from each other. Then, in a line, with eyes closed, the participants try to do a figure of eight around these two people.

Variation

'Slalom à la Flaine' (as in skiing), with two lines of four or five actors, around whom the others have to slalom, blind, at walking pace.

13 Goalkeeper

A trust game. Six actors standing side by side, not too far apart, form the safety net. Another actor, a few steps in front of them, is the goalkeeper. Facing this group, say 6 m away, are the other actors. One by one, the other actors look at the goalkeeper, close their eyes and start to run towards him, as fast as they dare. The goalkeeper must catch the runner round the waist. When an actor strays off course, one of the six members of the safety net can catch him.

The most important thing is to try not to slow down when approaching the goalkeeper – this is a test of trust. The idea is not to slow down or stop or end up far from the goalkeeper.

14 In pairs, one partner kneels with eyes open

One partner kneels with her eyes open, on one knee, the other sits on her knee, with his eyes closed. The sitter then stands, takes seven paces forwards, goes back again and sits down slowly on the same knee. The person who is kneeling can stop the blind person falling if he starts to sit down in the wrong place.

15 Draw your own body

Normally we would do this exercise at the beginning of a session. All the participants lie on the floor and think about their body as a totality, and also about each of its constituent parts: fingers, head, mouth, tongue, legs, sex, eyes, hair, belly button, neck, elbows, shoulders, vertebrae, etc. They try to move the part of the body they are thinking about.

After a few minutes of concentration, the joker gives each person a sheet of paper (the sheets of paper must all be the same size) and a pencil or felt pen (all of the same colour if possible, or else don't let the participants see what colour it is). The joker asks each actor to draw their own body on the paper, with eyes firmly closed. Once this is done, the joker asks the participants to write their names on the back of their drawings, still with their eyes closed. She then collects up the drawings, arranges them on the floor in any order, and tells everyone to open their eyes and come and look at this impromptu exhibition. She asks them what strikes them most about the drawings – are the bodies naked or clothed, lying down or standing up, resting or working, in a relationship with objects or on their own, do they have important details like the eyes and the sex or only general outlines?

Finally, the joker invites them to identify their own drawing.

This exercise greatly sensitises the group: first, when everyone is thinking about their own body, about each individual part of their body; then, when everyone is trying to reproduce by hand what they felt; lastly, after the exercise, when they pay much greater attention to themselves, to their movements, their way of sitting, their way of approaching other people, etc. The exercise makes the participants extremely conscious that we are each of us, first and foremost, a body. We may be capable of constructing the most profound abstract ideas and devising the most extraordinary inventions, but it is only because we have, before all else, a body – before we have a name, we inhabit a body! And we rarely think of our body as the fundamental source of all pleasures and all pains, of all knowledge and all research, of everything!

Usually we do this exercise before the game of the 'Masks of the actors themselves' (p. 143).

16 Modelling clay

This is basically the same exercise, except that in this version modelling clay is used instead of paper. This makes a difference, because the hands can return to details already constructed. On paper, if you have already done the head, for example, you have to remember this but you cannot come back to it. With modelling clay, you can always come back to what you have already done.

17 Touch the colour

The joker gives the (blind) actor five pieces of clothing of the same kind (all socks or all shirts or whatever), but made of different material and different colours. The actor must feel each of the pieces of clothing and try to recognise the colours.

18 The blind person and the bomb

A blindfolded actor, surrounded by the other actors. The 'blind person' must imagine that a bomb will explode if she touches someone for longer than a second. At each contact, she moves as far away as possible. This exercise produces an incredible development of the senses.

19 Find the hand

Starting in pairs, each actor touches their partner's hand; then they split up and walk around. After a few moments, they must try to find the original hand again, by touching all the hands they come across.

20 The siren's song

Very difficult, very delicate. Each actor must think of an oppression she actually experiences. Then everyone closes their eyes and assembles in the middle of the room. Whoever wants to start utters a sound (a cry, groan, shout, lamentation, etc.) which must be the translation into sound of the oppression she has in mind. The joker takes her by the hand and leads her on a trip around the room, eventually stopping in a corner. Same with the second person. Three or four others do the same, each in their own way, with their own specific cry. It is important for the joker to choose quite different sounds to inhabit the four corners of the room. Then the four let loose their cries together. Those remaining in the middle listen to the four and each choose the sound which best suits their own oppression; four groups form. After this everybody opens their eyes, and they make four circles, and, in their separate circles, each person recounts to the others the oppression she was thinking of, the episode which was in her mind. It is no magic that within each circle, the story is almost always about the same type of oppression, on the same theme.

21 Find a convenient back

Sit on the floor, move around, find a convenient back. Then, still with closed eyes, do the 'Pushing against each other' exercise (p. 65), back to back.

22 Who said 'Ah'?

Everyone closes their eyes and wanders around the space. The joker designates (by a touch) one person to 'Ah' in any way they like. The rest of the group must work out who it was.

23 The melodic hand

Seated in a circle with eyes closed, each actor touches hands with his neighbours; his left hand resting *on top* of the hand on his left, his right hand *under* the hand on his right. Thus he controls the movement of the left hand of his right-hand neighbour, and his own left hand's movement is controlled by the person on his left. The actors move their right hands in a rhythmical, melodious fashion, allowing their left hands to be similarly moved by their neighbour.

115

Then the joker says 'Heads' and the actors bring their heads into the movement; then 'Chests'; then 'Stand up' and the whole body dances, and then 'Sing' and the whole group (still with closed eyes) is standing, swaying and singing together. Then they open their eyes.

Variation

The same exercise, except that the controlling hand is placed *over* the hand it controls, rather than under.

The space series

This series also engages all the senses.

1 Without leaving empty a single space in the room

All the actors must *walk around very quickly* (not running) trying to ensure that their own bodies are always more or less equidistant from everyone else's, and that they are all spread out over the whole floorspace of the room. From time to time the joker says 'Stop!' At that moment, everyone must immediately come to a halt – it should not be possible to see an empty space in the room.

The main thing is not to come to a halt before the 'Stop'. Whenever anyone sees an empty space, they go and fill it with their body, but they can't stay there, so a moment later it is empty again, except that someone comes to fill it, but he can't stop there either . . .

2 Instead of simply saying 'Stop', the joker says a number

Everyone must get into groups of that number as quickly as possible – groups of three, five, eight, etc. As quickly as possible, the groups must site themselves so that they are all an equal distance apart, to ensure that there are no empty spaces on the floorspace of the room.

3 The joker says a number and a geometric figure

The participants have to arrange themselves in that number of figures of the shape specified by the joker – four circles, three diamonds, five triangles, etc.

4 The joker says a number and a part of the body

If the joker says, for example, 'Three noses, seven feet', then seven feet and three noses must be touching. Again the floorspace of the room must always be occupied by equidistant groups.

5 The joker calls out a colour and an item of clothing

The joker calls out as described – a part of the body (hair, eyes) may be used instead of clothing. The participants must form into groups accordingly, still trying to ensure that they are equally distributed throughout the room.

6 The participants run slowly

(Running slowly is not the same as walking quickly.) From time to time the joker says 'Stick' and immediately the actors stick together in groups of three, five, or more, but without stopping. Everyone must keep running, which is extremely difficult. Then the joker says 'Separate' and everyone must separate. And then it starts over again, with the participants still trying not to leave empty spaces on the floor of the room.

7 The participants touch each other

The actors touch with hands and feet, while moving around the room, no one ever remaining completely separate from the rest. The joker says 'Stop' and at that point everyone stops on the spot, but each person should be able to touch other people with both hands and at least one leg, without anyone being left isolated in a corner of the room. The result is like a spider's web.

The integration games series

1 Stick in the mud

Two actors run after the rest and try to tag them. When they have been tagged, the actors stay on the spot, standing with their legs apart. They are only released by another actor going between their legs. The game ends either by dint of exhaustion, or when all the actors have been immobilised.

117

2 The hat game

Two teams of six in two rows facing each other, 2 or 3 m apart. They are numbered in reverse order, so that 1 is opposite 6, 2 opposite 5, and so on. One person stands in the middle, holding a hat (or any object) and calls out a number. If, for example, he says 'Four', the fourth member of each line must come into the middle as quickly as possible and, without going beyond the centre line, must carry off the hat. Having taken the hat, she must not allow her adversary to touch her, otherwise she loses.

The person in the middle can shout out two or three numbers and four or six adversaries will come and play for the hat.

Variation

A British version called 'Dog and bone' – same as the above, except that the caller stands out of the way at the end of the lines, and the hat lies on the floor between the two teams. If a player carrying off the hat is touched by an opposing player before he gets back to his own line, he has to drop the hat on the spot; and both players then try to carry off the hat again, without being touched.

3 Three Irish duels

1 In pairs facing each other, each actor tries to step on one of the feet of the opposing player (gently) without being stepped on himself;
2 in pairs facing each other with hands on knees, swapping from knee to knee – each actor tries to touch the other's knee with his hand, without being touched himself;
3 with an open left hand held behind his back, palm facing out, and the index finger of the right hand held in front like a sword, each actor tries to 'stab' the flat hand of his adversary.

4 Little packets

A version of a very well-known children's game, excellent for developing the participants' attention and concentration. Three or four (or more) groups of three people in a line one behind the other, all the lines facing in the direction of the same central point, all equidistant. Two people not in the lines are the hunter and the quarry. The quarry must flee the hunter; whenever the former is in danger of capture he can take the place of the person either at the front or the back of any line. If he stands at the front of a line, the last person in that line becomes the quarry and must escape; if he goes to the back of a line, the front person must escape. If the hunter catches the quarry, they swap roles immediately and play on.

To complicate the game, you can decide that all the people in the front position in the lines have to count from one to twenty and, at the end of the count, must also escape. Thus there can be more than one quarry at a time. The lines must never have more than three people.

5 Good morning

Each actor has to say 'Good morning' (or whatever salutation suits the time of day) to all the other actors, at the same time shaking hands with them. But she must always have one hand shaking hands with someone – so only when both hands are occupied in handshaking can she disengage one to find someone else.

6 Cat and mouse

A variation of a well-known game, similar to the 'Little packets' game above. Everyone has a partner, with whom they hold hands and move around the space – except two people who are on their own, one being the cat, one being the mouse. The cat chases the mouse, as usual. But if the mouse wishes to avoid getting caught, it can join up at one end of a pair and hold hands, which means that the person at the other end of that pair becomes the mouse and has to run away; there can only ever be two people holding hands together. As with the other version, you can decide that if the cat catches the mouse, they exchange roles.

Variation: homage to Tex Avery

The person released when the mouse takes her partner's hand becomes not a mouse but a dog, which chases the cat; the cat being chased can then join hands with one partner of another pair, releasing a player who becomes a bigger dog, which terrifies the first one; and so on with progressively larger animals.

7 Consequences (a.k.a. Cadavre éxquis)

This game takes its French title, 'Exquisite corpse', from the Surrealist poets. It can be done as a verbal game or a drawing game. In the drawing version, one actor draws something, usually a body starting from the head, and folds over the paper, leaving only a small part visible; a second actor draws on the next bit, folds it over, and so on. At the end the paper is unfolded to see what has been created.

In the speaking version, one actor starts telling a story, which is continued by a second actor, and so on till the whole group has contributed a part of it. This can be done in the same way as the drawn version, with one actor coming into the room at a time, saying a line, and only repeating the last few words when the next actor comes in; or with a tape recorder, the whole thing can be recorded to be played back at the end.

IV SEEING WHAT WE LOOK AT

There are three main series of exercises which help us see what we are looking at – the mirrors sequence, the sculpture or modelling sequence, and the puppet sequence. These first three sections in particular form part of the arsenal of Image Theatre and are also useful as part of the process of developing models for Forum Theatre.

The exercises develop the capacity for observation by means of 'visual dialogues' between two or more participants; obviously the simultaneous use of spoken language is excluded. In Image Theatre the use of words would interfere with the language of images or superimpose itself on top of that language. Symbolic gestures, such as those used to signify 'OK' or 'yes' or 'no', should be avoided, as should any sign corresponding exactly to the word(s) it replaces.

Sometimes people find the silence required for these exercises a hindrance – it can at first seem irritating and even tiring. However, the more the participants concentrate, the more they discover the fascination of this work, and the richer the dialogues become.

The exercises can be done in isolation, each having its own specific function and application. Nevertheless, when they are done in sequence and without interruption, the participants are stimulated not only by each exercise in itself, but also by the transition from one exercise to another; this transition sometimes bears more interesting fruit than the exercises it links together. This is particularly the case in the three 'exchanges' of exercise 8 in the mirrors sequence (p. 124).

The mirrors sequence

Each element of this sequence can last one, two, three minutes, even longer – it all depends on the degree of participation by the group, their interest, their unity, and what the objectives of the work are. The important thing about the work is that it be as meticulous, detailed, exact, and rich in discoveries, as possible.

1 The plain mirror

Two lines of participants, each person looking directly into the eyes of the person facing them. Those in line A are the 'subjects', the people, those in line B are the 'images'. The exercise begins. Each subject undertakes a series of movements and changes of expression, which his 'image' must copy, right down to the smallest detail.

The 'subject' should not be the enemy of his 'image' – the exercise is not a competition, nor is the idea to make sharp movements which are impossible to follow; on the contrary, the idea is to seek a perfect synchronisation of movement, so that the 'image' may reproduce the 'subject's' gestures as exactly as possible. The degree of accuracy and synchronisation should be such that an outside observer would not be able to tell who is leading and who is following. All movements should be slow (so the 'image' may be able to reproduce and even anticipate them) and each movement should follow on naturally from the last. It is equally important that the participants be attentive to the smallest detail, whether of body or facial expression.

2 Subject and image swap roles

After a few minutes, the joker announces that the two lines are going to swap roles. He gives the signal, and at that precise moment the 'subjects' become the 'images' and vice versa. This change-over should be carried out without affecting the continuity or the precision. Ideally the movement which was happening at the moment of change-over should be continued and completed, without any sense of break-down or hiccup. Here again, the outside observer should not be able to perceive the change of roles, and this invisibility of change-over can be achieved if the synchronisation and imitation of actions are perfect.

3 Subject-image, image-subject

A few minutes later, the joker announces that when he gives the signal, the participants in both lines are to be simultaneously 'image' and 'subject'. From that point on, each partner has the right to do any movement he wants, together with the duty to reproduce movements made by his partner. And this must be done *without either partner tyrannising the other*. It is absolutely vital that each feels completely *free* in his movements, but at the same time *in sympathy** with his partner, so that the partner's movements are followed as faithfully as possible. *Freedom and sympathy* are essential. In the whole of this sequence, the aim is not to make movements which are difficult or impossible to imitate; going fast does no good, quite the reverse. The key to the exercise lies in *synchronisation* and *fidelity* of reproduction.

Up to this point, communication remains exclusively visual, and everyone's attention should be *concentrated* on their partner – first on the eyes, then taking in the whole body, in concentric circles. It is not advisable to watch hands or feet; in the act of looking into someone's eyes and following the movements of their body, hands and feet will enter naturally into the field of vision.

4 Everyone joins hands

Once again the joker gives first a warning, and then the signal for everyone to join hands with their left- and right-hand neighbours. The two lines are still facing each other, each person fixing their gaze on their partner. But in this stage a new element comes into play; if, thus far, communication has been exclusively *visual*, now it becomes *physical* as well. Each partner receives visual stimuli from their facing partner and physical stimuli from colleagues on their left and right. Suppose one of the participants does a movement which is accepted by his own neighbours to the left and right, but which cannot be followed by his opposite number because *his* neighbours are physically stopping him from echoing the movement; in that case, the originator of the movement must go back a step as quickly as possible, so as not to break the synchronisation and the perfection of the imitation. If movements are slow and continuous, the process of visual and physical 'consultation' which enables the two lines to

* The French word *'solidaire'* combines the senses of solidarity and sympathetic action. A.J.

be identical will not be interrupted. One person will always be the image of the other, and within this image, each actor will retain his own freedom of movement together with his responsibility to imitate the opposite number's movements (within the limits of his physical capability).

5 *The two lines form a curve*

The joker takes the person at the head of one of the lines round the space, in such a way as to make the line into a U-shape. The other line will form a matching curve opposite.

There is still *a single, long mirror* between the two lines. When the participants move away from the imaginary mirror, in the process of making the curve, those facing them must also move away. And when they are approaching the mirror, the same mechanism applies. The worst thing that can happen is for an actor to bump into the actor opposite on the way in to the mirror – the conceptual space must be respected. (It's a mirror, people don't usually walk into mirrors!) The participants must keep up their eye-to-eye scrutiny.

The fact of forming a curve adds a new and essential element to this progression for the participants. Having passed through the stages of direct, individual, visual communication, followed by visual and physical communication (with opposite number and neighbours respectively), now the actors become aware that each line forms a group; in other words, the actors bring into play the whole space of the exercise, though their scope for invention is still limited and defined by physical contact.

6 *Symmetrical groups*

The joker gives the signal for the players to release each other's hands, without letting this break the continuity of the exercise. Now free of physical contact but aware of the whole space, and all the while having regard for the imaginary mirror bisecting the room, the participants try to form a collective, symmetrical image with the other people in their group. Sometimes all the members of one group develop a single image reproduced by the facing group. (Remember, the two groups are simultaneously *subject* and *image*; just as no tyranny was exercised on an individual level by one person over another, so a group must act with the same freedom and sympathy towards the group opposite.) Sometimes each group divides into

123

subgroups; it is important that they do not then further fragment into separate individuals – at least two or three, if not all of the members of the group, must be involved in the mutual reproduction, still with great attention to detail and careful synchronisation.

7 *The mirror breaks*

When the mirror breaks, we are again left with pairs of facing partners watching each other. They exactly reproduce each other's suggested movements, without either person tyrannising the other. But now each couple has their own little piece of the mirror. The large central mirror, which was dividing the room in two, has shattered into small pieces all over the room. Consequently, each couple can evolve as it pleases, moving closer to their bit of mirror, or backing away from it, or turning round, but always staying in the same relationship to each other. At this point a redoubling of attention and concentration is required – an awareness both of one's partner and of the whole space, a space which is continually being modified by the evolution of each pair and their piece of mirror; a space no longer limited by the huge, long mirror, now for ever broken. The space becomes more dynamic. It requires a higher level of care and concentration. It is important that each pair moves and evolves using the whole of the room.

8 *Changing partners*

Three times the joker gives the signal to change partners. On the signal, as quickly as possible, each person abandons his partner and tries to find someone else with whom he can establish the same mimetic relationship. Sometimes this person is quickly found, but sometimes it can take time. Whatever happens, the actor must continue moving at the same slow pace, without interrupting his rhythm, without interrupting the movements he was doing with his previous partner, till he finds another. At the first signal, each person must choose one of his neighbours. At the second change-over, a more distant partner must be sought, and at the third, someone who is as far away as possible. It is important that the continuity is not broken, that an actor doesn't (for instance) suddenly cross his arms while looking for someone else who is partner-less. His own movement is the force attracting his future partner.

During this part of the sequence, it often happens that two partners choose the same person and believe for some minutes that they have established contact with that person. However, if they had both kept their eyes on the chosen colleague, if all their attention had been channelled into that eye contact (even though the whole room might have been within their field of vision), they would have been able to tell straight away whether or not their contact was being reciprocated.

Each time a new partnership forms, a fertile dialogue must be established between the two players, each 'observing' the other's gestures, sensing the difference between this person's movements and the previous person's. The idea is not to move rapidly from one thing to another, but to conduct a dialogue on a visual and a physical level, to get to 'know' the other person.

9 The distorting mirror

The joker should always warn the group before giving any signal to move the sequence on to its next stage. In this case when the signal is given, the relationship between the two partners changes completely. Up till now all movements, facial expressions and gestures have reproduced in an identical, 'mimetic' fashion; now there is 'commentary', 'response'. Each person is allowed to do whatever feels right, and at each new stimulus, their partner 'answers', 'comments', 'enlarges', 'reduces', 'caricatures', 'ridicules', 'destroys', 'relativises' – in sum, produces an image responding to the received image, but in a contrapuntal relationship to it.

There should be no sense of adjustment between the 'image' (gesture, movement, expression) and its 'response'; on the contrary, they should be simultaneous, or virtually so, and continuous. The idea is not to do something and wait for the other person to repeat it, and then respond to that while he waits; there should be a continual dispatch and reception of visual messages answering each other, distorting each other. Of course, absolute simultaneity is impossible, but any period of waiting (and loss of concentration) should be avoided.

10 The narcissistic mirror

After distortion, criticism, corrosive commentary, the attempt to destroy the partner's mask, caricature, now the mirror becomes narcissistic. And this is perhaps one of the most beautiful moments in the whole sequence. Here, each participant looks at himself in the mirror and sees himself beautiful. However, the image he sees is his partner. Each person must try to display, as precisely as possible, all the signs of pleasure we give out, all the joy we experience, when we feel happy deep down, when we are glad to be what we are. I feel happy, I make a gesture of happiness, and I look at myself in the mirror; but what I see is my own image in the body of another. At the same time, this other looks at himself in me; in me, he sees himself happy, he sees himself contented. And it is I, with my gestures and my movements, who must offer him this happiness, this satisfaction.

A Portuguese poet, Fernando Pessoa, wrote these wonderful lines:

> One never loves another,
> One loves what there is of oneself in them
> Or what one thinks there is.

That is partly the idea of these exercises; we seek ourselves in others, who seek themselves in us.

11 The rhythmic mirror

Gently, in this loving search for oneself in the other, the dialogue becomes one, changes into monologue – both seek movements which have rhythmic affinities. Both must find rhythms and movements of the body which both find pleasing, movements which can now be slow or fast, gentle or vigorous, simple or complex, staccato or glissando. The most important things are (1) that both partners feel good, at ease, and happy in the execution of the movements; (2) that these movements are rhythmical and identical; and (3) that the whole body is involved in them.

12 Unification

Finally, the joker gives the signal to attempt unification – 'attempt' meaning that there should be no obligation. Sometimes at the end of this sequence the whole room is totally synchronised, totally united in one rhythm, one movement. But equally it may be the case that the room is united in complementary rhythms and movements, which are different but harmonious. A third situation can also occur, in which the different groups do not become unified, and end up as several small groups and subgroups, continually returning to and re-creating their own particular rhythms and movements.

It is vital that this last stage be properly understood, without ambiguity – this is not a competition, it is not about imposing one's own rhythm and movement on others; more than anything, it is about seduction. The aim is to undertake a rhythmic study of the participants, and to try to unify the group at least on a minimal basis. But this can prove impossible. This phase of the exercise brings out the violence, the volatility and aggression of each member of the group; it also reveals the degree of compatibility, of dialogue, the capacity for collaboration, within the group. The joker must be careful not to force anyone, not to manipulate the group to bring it to unification at any cost. It is a matter of *analysing, studying* and *not imposing*. It is up to each individual to express themselves freely so that the results of this study may be real.

A great variety of forms of visual communication appear in this long sequence, though all have a common base – *mimesis* (with the exception of the 'distorting mirror' where mimesis is present but not dominant). Throughout the sequence people study their partners, in order to imitate them down to the smallest detail and as simultaneously as possible. In the sequence which follows, the modelling sequence, the dialogue takes a completely different form.

The modelling sequence

If in the 'mirror' the dialogue was mimetic, here it must be translated. The actor 'sees' what her colleague does, and translates the action or gesture she has seen, by changing her own position. She does not reproduce the gesture with her body, she extends it, she shows what results from the gesture. This becomes clearer as the sequence unfolds.

1 The sculptor touches the model

The participants arrange themselves in two lines facing each other. One of the lines is made up of sculptors, and the other of statues. At the beginning of the exercise, each sculptor starts using her hands to model the statue she has in mind. To this end, she touches the 'statue's' body, taking care to achieve the effects she is striving for, down to the smallest detail. The sculptors cannot use 'mirror' language, they cannot use their own bodies to show the image or expression they want to see reproduced; here neither mimesis nor reproduction comes into the equation, this is no longer a dialogue, this is modelling. Consequently, it is necessary to touch, to mould;

127

each action on the part of the sculptor provokes a corresponding reaction, each *cause* produces a different *effect*. In the mirror dialogue both partners are always synchronised, carrying out the *same action*. In the 'modelling' dialogue, though synchronised, the partners' actions are complementary.

The joker lets this first exercise last as long as is necessary – two or three minutes, or even longer, it all depends on the participants, on what sort of atmosphere has been created, etc. – for the sculptor and the statue to understand each other, so that the sculptor's gestures, *seen and felt*, may be easily translated by the statue.

2 The sculptor doesn't touch the model

In this second stage, the joker tells the sculptors to move away from their statues, but all the while continuing to do the same gestures as they were doing before, when they were touching them. The statues, who previously 'saw' and 'felt' these gestures, still 'see' them, but no longer 'feel' them; but they must continue to respond as if they were feeling them, as if the sculptors were still touching them.

The sculptors must always make *realistic* gestures – the actual motions which would be necessary to cause the statue to do the desired movements, form the particular facial expressions, or make the required gestures.

During this exercise, the sculptors frequently fall into the three basic traps: the first mistake is to allow oneself to be drawn almost irresistibly closer to the statues; the second is to fall into the temptation of making symbolic signs of the 'Come this way a bit', or 'That's not it' variety; and the third temptation, the worst of all, is speaking. This last must be resisted at all costs, for by introducing the violence of verbal language, one abruptly breaks the visual communication. If by chance the statue doesn't manage to grasp what the sculptor is after (and only as a last resort), the sculptor can touch her to make her understand what is wanted; and then, without fail, the statue must revert to the position she was in before the 'explanation', the sculptor makes her gesture again and this time the statue gives the desired reaction, now that she has understood.

The statues are also frequently tempted into an error, which is to execute movements which haven't been asked for. For example, if the sculptor makes a gesture of grabbing the statue round the waist or pulling it by the arm, it must fall over, and not take a step forward to regain its balance. The step forward has been neither asked for nor caused by the sculptor's actions. Clearly the statue should have no faculty of autonomous movement. If the sculptor wants the statue to move forward without falling over, it is up to her to take care of its balance, to make it first move one foot forward, then the other, making sure that the centre of gravity never moves too far from the feet, so that it won't fall over. All movements made by the statue must be generated, directed by the sculptor.

3 The sculptors spread out around the room

If in the previous exercise sculptors and statues were lined up facing each other, without obstruction, now the sculptors must spread out around the room, taking care that their faces don't move out of the statues' field of vision (since the statues cannot move themselves). The sculptors make movements and gestures to make their statues move backwards or forwards, to one side or the other, up or down.

4 The sculptors fashion a single sculpture together

With as great a distance as possible between sculptor and statue, the sculptors try to bring their statues together, so that they form a single, multi-person sculpture, which the sculptors must give meaning to.

5 Sculpture with four or five people

Thus far, the sequence has been without interruption, each exercise following on from the last, with the transition being as important as the exercise proper. Here, continuity is broken. The participants divide into four or five groups. One sculptor and a number of statues. Each sculptor fashions the bodies of her colleagues into one significant image – as if she were saying, 'This is what I am thinking.' When she has finished visualising her thought, reifying it, she takes the place of one of her companions in the sculpture, who in turn becomes a sculptor. This new sculptor starts work, as if she was thinking: 'That is what you were thinking, but have a little look at my response,' and she alters the work of the previous sculptor, moulding the bodies of her colleagues into a multiple statue rep-resenting what *she* wants. All this is done without the sculptor touching her statues; the movements are done at a distance, are 'seen' but not 'felt', are translated by the sensibility of each statue, which acts as if it really had been touched. And so on, till everyone has given their 'visual' opinion.

The puppet sequence

Finally, there is a third form of 'visual' dialogue, the 'puppet'. The premiss is that between subject (puppeteer) and object (puppet) there is a string which conducts the movement. This is the shortest of the three sequences, it contains only two movements.

1 String puppet

The puppeteer and puppet are some distance apart. The former pretends to pull a string and the latter answers with the corresponding movement. Both must imagine that the string goes directly from the puppeteer's hand to a part of the puppet's body, which the puppeteer designates with a look: arm, hand, knees, head, foot, neck, etc.

2 String puppet with rod

We imagine a rod 3 m high over which is slung the string, one end of which leads to the puppeteer's hand, the other being attached to the puppet's body – all movement is reversed. With the string puppet in the previous exercise, the puppeteer lifted his hand to lift the corresponding part of the puppet's body; here, whenever the puppeteer makes an upward movement, the puppet does a downward movement.

Image games

1 Complete the image

A pair of actors shake hands. Freeze the image. Ask the watching group what possible meanings the image might carry: is it a business meeting, lovers parting for ever, a drug deal, etc.? Various possibilities are explored.

Everyone gets into pairs and starts with a frozen image of a handshake. One partner removes himself from the image, leaving the other with his hand extended. Now what is the story? Instead of *saying* what he thinks this new image means, the partner who has gone out returns to the image and completes the image, thus *showing* what he sees as a possible meaning for it; he puts himself in a different position, with a different relationship to the partner with the outstretched hand, changing the meaning of the image.

Then the first partner comes out of this new frozen image, looks at it, and completes it, changing its meaning again. And so on, each partner alternating. The players should look quickly at the half-image they are completing, arranging themselves in a complementary position as fast as they can; like the modelling exercises, the actors should think with their bodies. It does not matter if there is no literal meaning to the way an actor chooses to complete the image – the important thing is to keep the game moving and the ideas flowing.

Then the joker can add a chair to the game, two chairs, an object – how does this affect things, how does it change the dynamic?

2 Ball-games

Football, basketball, volleyball, etc. Two teams play a match without using a ball, but acting as if there was one. A referee must check to see if the imaginary movements of the ball correspond closely to the real movements of the actors, and should correct them if necessary. Any kind of collective sport can be played for this kind of exercise – ping-pong, tennis, etc.

3 Boxing match

Two people standing several metres apart must react immediately to blows doled out by their partner. This works best if one person beats up the other, then the roles are reversed – it is difficult to react to imaginary blows and dole them out at the same time. We would usually close this exercise with gestures of tenderness, or by moving on to the 'lovers' variation which follows.

The lovers variation

The same as above, except that one person is caressing rather than attacking the other. The partner must react to every tender gesture offered.

Variations

Make a bed without bedding and synchronise the movements. Or two teams have a tug-of-war with a non-existent rope. Or else draw a net full of fish out of the sea. Or move a piano. There is an infinity of possible variations.

131

The dancing variation

The actors dance in couples, then they draw apart and continue dancing as if they were still in each other's arms.

Variation

This kind of exercise can also be done in another way, making the cause precede the effect – for instance, I feel the pain of falling before I fall, then I fall and compare.

4 One person we fear, one person is our protector

All the participants must be scattered around the room. Without saying anything, each person must think of one person in the room who frightens him (for the purposes of the game only). Everyone moves around the room, trying to keep as far away from the person who frightens them as possible, but also not letting that person be aware of the fact. After a short time, the joker asks everyone to think of another person who is their protector (who should also not be aware of having been chosen as such). Now everyone moves around again, trying to keep their protector between them and the person they fear. Eventually, the joker gives a countdown and everyone must freeze where they are – then the players find out who has succeeded in evading the one they fear.

5 Furnish the empty space

Two actors face to face. One moves and the other fills 'the empty space'; if one draws back her hand, the other pulls hers in, if one shrinks, the other grows taller, etc.

6 Atmosphere of snow

An actor imagines that the atmosphere is malleable, as if the air was snow; she makes a sculpture out of it. The others observe and must discover the nature of the sculpted object. The game is not about mimicry – the actor must really feel the atmosphere and the relationships between the muscles of her body and the outside world; if she is striking blows with a hammer, the muscles of her body should work as if she really had a hammer. This exercise can be simplified or complicated at will. You can start with elementary movements, using real objects (carry a chair from one place to another, for instance), and observe which muscles are stimulated, the nature of the stimulus. Then you try to stimulate the same muscles repeating the action without the object. The exercise can be enriched if it is done collectively – an actor makes an object with the atmosphere, she passes it to another actor, he changes it and passes it to a third actor, etc.

For example, several actors can be put on the same car production line – one actor puts on the wheels, another puts on the wings, and so on, from the important parts to the tiniest parts, until the whole vehicle emerges. The accent should always be on the physical relationship to the outside world and not on mimicry or signs.

7 Building character relations

This exercise can be either silent or with sound. One actor starts an action. A second approaches and, by means of visible physical gestures, establishes a relationship with him, in keeping with the nature of the role he has chosen – brother, father, son, uncle, etc. The first actor must work out what this role is and respond accordingly. Immediately after, a third person starts up a relationship with the first two, then in comes a fourth, and so on. The first part of this exercise must be silent, so that the relationships with the outside world develop via the senses and not through words.

8 Characters in movement

One or more actors come on stage and do various actions to show where they come from, what they do, and where they are going. The others must try to understand them by these few actions; they have come in from the street, they are in a waiting room, they're about to have a tooth pulled out; they've come from a bar, they are in the lobby of a hotel and they are about to go up to their room; they've come out of their house in the morning, they are in the lift, and they're about to start work at the office, etc.

9 Observation

An actor fixes his gaze on his colleagues for a few minutes, then with his back turned or wearing a blindfold, he tries to describe them with as much detail as possible – colours, clothes, features, particular characteristic behaviours, etc.

133

10 Complementary activities

An actor starts any movement, and the others try to discover what she is doing so that they can then engage in complementary activities. For example, the movements of a referee during a match are completed by the defending and attacking players; a priest saying mass is completed with the addition of an altar-boy and the priest's congregation, etc.

11 What has changed

Two lines, the actors facing each other and observing. They turn their backs and alter some detail of their appearance; then they turn back to look and each must work out what the person opposite has changed.

12 Tell your own story

An actor recounts an experience, of any kind, as long as it is something that really happened to him; his colleagues then illustrate his story. The actor/story-teller must not intervene or make corrections during the exercise. At the end they discuss the differences. The story-teller can thus compare his reactions with those of his colleagues.

13 The French telephone

A circle of people watching each other. Number 1 is watched by 4 who is watched by 7 who is watched by 10 and so on; 2 is watched by 5 who is watched by 8 who is watched by 11 and so on; 3 is watched by 6 who is watched by 9 who is watched by 12 and so on.

   The aim is to do nothing. You watch carefully without doing a thing. But whenever our model moves the tiniest bit, we also move, a tiny bit more. As someone is watching us, he will move a tiny bit more than we did and a tiny bit more than our model. The whole thing escalates. With the instruction 'Do nothing' as the starting point, we end up with all extremes of behaviour.

14 Concentration

A concentration circle is set up; the actors look around them for, say, two minutes, in which they must find as many colours, shades, shapes and details, as they can. These can be a table, the end of a floorboard, a corner of the wall, a colleague's face, a detail of a hand, a white leaf, etc. Then they close their eyes and say everything they saw.

Like all human beings, actors are used to 'synthesising' reality in order to be able to operate within it; we would go mad if our consciousnesses perceived and registered the infinite variety of colours and shapes our eye can perceive. Which is why the actor must endeavour to 'analyse' reality and discover its smallest details. This exercise can be done with two actors face to face; each informs the other of everything he has managed to discover in his face. The same thing can be done with sounds.

15 Animals

To make best use of this game, it should be pushed as far as possible. Each actor is given, at random, a piece of paper bearing the name of an animal, male or female; though they do not know it, there are two of each animal. The joker gives the signal and all the actors start playing their animals at the same time; i.e. they begin to create an image of their animal which can be realistic, surrealistic, symbolic, poetic, etc. The joker stresses that the actors should not limit them-selves to a single informing detail, and that, as the image develops, they should try to find as many details as possible – tail, wings, head movements, fast or slow ways of walking, sitting, hanging, etc. After a few minutes, the joker suggests a number of activities:

1 The animals are hungry. The actors must show how their animals eat. Greedily? Slowly? Secretly? In a stationary position? In motion? Timorously? Aggressively?
2 The animals are thirsty. How do they drink? In great gulps or little sips? With their mind on other things or with total concentration?
3 The animals fight among themselves. The actors must show how each animal manifests its rage, its aggression, its violence, its hatred.
4 The animals are tired and go to sleep. How? Upright, sitting, lying down? On a branch?

5 The animals wake up and, little by little, take a fancy to one another. Each must thus go in search of its partner, male or female. The joker reminds the actors never to stop playing their animal, since that is the only way they will be recognised by their partners. If an actor stops playing in order to observe the others, then clearly it will be impossible to recognise him. When two 'animals' think they have found each other, they perform the 'love scene' of their encounter, always staying faithful to their animal's way of behaving. The bull and the cow, for example, are hastier and more violent than the stallion and the mare, who exhibit great tenderness, kissing and nuzzling each other. The cock and the hen don't act in the same way as the rhinoceros and his mate.

Finally the two 'animals' leave the playing space and reveal their identities to each other. But the game doesn't end there! For that reason it is important not to talk and above all not to reveal to the rest of the group who you are. The joker invites the couples to come back into the middle of the room if they like, to replay the scene of their lovers' meeting. When the other participants are sure that they know what kind of animals they are watching, they give the appropriate animal call – the lion's roar, the cock's crow, or whatever. If they are right, the couple goes out of the game.

Equally the joker can offer watching actors the chance to come into the ring and show other elements, other 'visual' characteristics which the 'couple' in question has not been able to find, so as to enrich the performance, especially as far as the image, the representation, is concerned.

The animals chosen must be very different from each other: felines, reptiles, fish, big birds, little insects, etc. It is also not a bad idea to slip a 'man' and a 'woman' in among the couples. Very often spectators have some trouble identifying them.

16 Professions

This works on the same principle as the previous game, but animals are replaced by professions; the professions chosen should by preference be ones the group has strong feelings about (love or hate). The people playing the various professions also go through a variety of activities – they eat, amuse themselves, drink, etc. For instance, they might get dressed, travel, go to an exhibition, have an accident in the street and pick themselves up, chase women (or men), and, finally, they do their jobs.

Again the game works best if words are not used, though sounds are allowable (as long as they aren't 'signposts', like the repeated note of a police-car). As before, no one should reveal his identity to anyone else till the end of the game.

This exercise can be done having pairs of actors in the same profession who have to recognise one another, or form partnerships with others. On one occasion when we played this game, six actors were completely unable to recognise each other. They were respectively pairs of policemen, of concierges and of foremen.... One can guess why they had difficulty identifying each other. The same thing happened with cabaret artistes, athletes and prostitutes ... they were all too busy showing themselves off to identify their partners.

17 The balancing circle

There must be an even number of participants in this game. The actors arrange themselves in a symmetrical circle around a cup or other object. The cup represents a pivot on which the whole circle is balanced, like a saucer balanced on a stick. The joker starts at one point in the circle and numbers the actors – 1, 2, 3, 4, 5, etc. – till he has got halfway round the circle. Then he starts from 1 again, numbering the second half of the circle. Thus both number 1s should be standing opposite each other, with a straight line between them crossing through the central pivot; and everyone should be equidistant from this pivot.

The first actors to be numbered are the leaders, the second actors with the same numbers are their followers. The joker calls out a number, and the first actor designated with this number starts moving about the space slowly, in or out of the circle; his opposite number must move in such a way as to keep the circle/saucer balanced. So if the leader moves in towards the pivot, the follower must move in to the same distance; if the leader moves towards his right, his follower must move towards his own right – if they both moved in the same direction (i.e. the leader's right and the follower's left) the saucer would overbalance.

Gradually, the joker calls out other numbers, till all the pairs are playing at the same time. Once the moving pairs have developed a working relationship, the leaders can start to vary their movements, going fast and slow, back and forth, crawling, jumping, etc. At any given moment, there should be a straight line between leader, pivot and follower.

At a certain point, the joker can shout 'Change leaders' and, without any break in continuity, the leaders become the followers, and vice versa. The joker can also eventually shout 'No leader' and the pairs have to keep moving and working together without either leading.

At the end of the game the joker can bring the pairs out one by one, shouting a number at a time, till all are out.

18 Charades

This is a very well-known game in which the group divides into two teams. The first team sets the members of the second team the title of a film, the name of a politician, or a phrase used recently by any public figure or popular politician. One member of the second group must mime the phrase, name, or title he has been given to his colleagues, and they must work out what it is. Each actor has two minutes in which to do their charade. With more experienced actors, this game can be played starting from the subject-matter or central idea of a scene. The actor must not make any explicit exhibition or use explicit identifying traits or hints; he may only embody the central idea, according to its possibilities and his imagination.

19 The Indian in the city, the city-dweller in the forest

The senses function as selectors when they send messages to the brain. The selection of conscious stimuli depends on the rituals of each society. People say that a mother who doesn't hear the alarm clock go off is up immediately if her child starts crying.... In a forest a bird can hear the song of its mate even if a lion is roaring by its side. The huge choice of visual and auditory stimuli in a big city is easily filtered and selected from by a child crossing a road, whereas a forest-dwelling Indian would go mad in the same circumstances. This exercise consists of precisely that, an actor trying to be the forest Indian in the city, the city-dweller in the forest. A person not cognisant with the forms of our civilisation has to 'codify' and 'order' its elements. That is why everything he sees he 'finds strange', even the most elementary things, and it is also why he is unaware of genuine dangers he is courting.

The same exercise can be done the other way round: a 'civilised' person in the middle of the rituals of a society which is called 'primitive' – or any other kind of change of circumstances overtaking a person 'educated' according to certain rituals, who suddenly has to assimilate new ones and adapt himself to another society. This kind of thing happens to all of us when we travel and find ourselves in another town; so long as we are not used to it, we can wonder at everything; but after a few days, we no longer see or feel half of these marvels.

Of all the physical conditioning exercises in this book, not one is 'acrobatic' because then we would be in danger of creating the mask of 'the athlete'. We use only exercises which help to relax or stimulate muscles which are little-used in our daily routines, or exercises which focus on altering these habits which mechanise and 'ritualise' our bodies, our movements, our sensitivities, and even our ideas, creating rigid, hardened 'structures' of ideas, muscles, movements, etc. With the help of exercises, the actor must destroy these structures, and try not to replace them with others (like 'athlete').

Games of mask and ritual

1 Follow the master

An actor starts talking and moving around normally, while the others try to capture and reproduce his mask. It is important not to caricature, but to reproduce the inner force which drives the actor to be as he is. The actors imitate the 'master', but imitation in the sense of the word as defined by Aristotle: trying not merely to copy appearances, but to reproduce the inner creative forces which produce these appearances. For instance, one actor's visible characteristics included extreme volubility; in reality he was a timid person, unsure of himself, a person who sought self-assurance by talking non-stop, as he was afraid others might attack him.The actor must create the fear impelling this excess verbosity. Moreover he must discover in the other person the social rituals which have prompted him to be victim to this fear. The foundation of the mask is always a social necessity determined by rituals.

2 Follow two masters who metamorphose into each other

Two actors start talking or arguing. Each has their own team of 'followers' who begin to imitate or create the masks of their respective master. After a few minutes, the two masters initiate their meta-

139

morphosis into each other; each master imitates the other, in such a way that the followers of one end up imitating the masks of the other.

3 Rotation of masks

Five actors talk, move around and observe each other. After a few minutes have passed, the joker calls out one of their names, and the others start to imitate that person's mask; a few minutes later the joker names another actor and everyone changes into that person's mask, and so on.

4 Unification of masks

A group of actors, in the middle of a conversation, decide to imitate the mask of one of their number, spontaneously, without verbal communication, till that person becomes aware of it. This can start with a number of different masks being played, till a unity occurs.

5 Collective creation of a mask

A group of actors talk and move around. In the course of the conversation, an actor introduces some characteristic or other of her way of walking, or talking, or thinking, or one of her personal obsessions. All the others try to discover this characteristic and reproduce it. Once unification has been achieved on this first characteristic, a second actor adds a second characteristic which must also be assumed by the rest and added to the first. Then a third ... and so on until in the end all the actors are performing the same collectively created mask.

6 Addition of masks

Without dropping any of the characteristics or elements of his own mask, an actor is asked to add other characteristics or elements corresponding to the mask of one of his colleagues. How would so-and-so be if, on top of everything he is, he possessed the violence of such-and-such a person? Or what if this strong, aggressive actor had that actor's timidity, without, however, losing his own strength and aggression? There is an infinity of possible combinations, depending on whether elements are added to the masks or swapped between actors. One can also make the mask which is the 'sum' of all the members of the group, taking the most representative parts of each person.

7 Pushing the mask to its extremity and annulling it

Once conscious of her mask, the actor affirms each element of it, pushes it to the extreme, and wears the mask in its most exaggerated form. Then, slowly, she annuls it, and in place of each element she creates the opposite characteristic.

8 Following the master in his own mask

Sometimes an actor encounters difficulties in pushing his own mask to the extreme or in annulling some of its elements. So four actors join him, he starts talking and the others follow the 'master'. When the five masks are unified, the four actors move to the opposite stance, and the 'master' must try to transform himself instantaneously into the 'follower' of the four other new 'masters'.

It was by the former process that an extremely timid male actor in our company ended up shouting and vociferating violently. There was also a female actor who was unable to externalise her cruelty. We formed two groups; the first, made up of three people, started to attack (not physically) and humiliate the second, which was also made up of three people, one of whom was this actor. After violent humiliations and provocations, on a cue from the director, the situation was reversed, and those being humiliated started humiliating. The actor, helped by her two colleagues, unleashed all the cruelty she had inside her, hidden by her mask. The situation was so violent that, on coming out of it, the actor experienced a feeling of guilt. So we ended the exercise with a children's game which all six actors played to the full with great delight.

There is always the danger in exercises like this which violate the actor's intimacy, of wounding people. The workshop exercises should not have a therapeutic intention nor should they risk prejudicing the actor's health. Ending with an exercise of emotional violence within a charged 'psychological climate' can be dangerous; such a session should end in an atmosphere of physical play. In Cuba, the intellectuals take part in the harvest of the sugar cane; this is important so that these people do not become alienated from the processes of production or from reality. It is also important to place 'psychological' problems back in a more general context of external, physical and social reality.

9 Changing masks

One actor talks and moves around naturally. The others show her how they see her mask, and how they would like to change it. They point out each of the elements of the mask and the actor cancels or modifies them, according to the criteria of her colleagues – transforming gentleness into violence, indecisive movements into decisive movements, her deep voice into a high-pitched voice, etc.

10 Mask exchange

We play out a typical ritual; for instance, the ritual of the man taking a young girl to his flat for the first time, with intentions which are obvious. In the first rehearsal, the scene is played true to type: in perfect Don Juan style, he puts on the *macho*, the powerful conquering man, and she acts the 'pretty little thing' waiting to be conquered. Typical actions in this ritual are listening to a record, showing her round the flat, having something to drink, etc.

In all the above, the young girl plays with the mask of the 'object of desire'. Then, without changing parts or changing the essential characteristics of the ritual, the two actors change masks. He, while still remaining the man, behaves as the 'object of desire'; she, without losing her womanhood, dons the role of the aggressive conqueror, that is, with the mask usually worn by the *macho* Don Juan character.

Another example is a worker asking his boss for a raise in a particularly exploitative society, with the actions and gestures which correspond to that ritual: taking his hat off, describing his family problems, explaining that the cost of living has gone up, etc. Then, staying in the boss role, the actor takes on the mask of the worker, and the latter, without ceasing to be the worker, takes on the mask of the boss.

An infinity of relationships can be uncovered and brought to light with the help of this exercise – father/son, teacher/pupil, torturer/victim, officer/squaddie, landowner/peasant, etc.

142

11   The masks of the actors themselves

This game is usually done after the 'Draw Your Own Body' exercise (see p. 113). If the game is being done separately, all the actors write their names on slips of paper which are folded over and then randomly distributed; if it is done with the aforementioned exercise, then the actors will already have written their names on the back of the drawings they have made of their bodies. The more participants the better the game – it requires at least 16 to be effective; 30 is a good number.

The group divides into two halves. One half of the group go on stage and act out their own daily lives – the 'Image of the Hour' technique can be used to facilitate this, so that various times of day are specified by the joker and the actors on stage do what they do at that time of day. While the actors are on stage, the other half of the group is watching, each person closely observing the actor whose name they were given.

After five minutes or so, the two groups swap places. The actors who were in the audience now try to show on stage the mask of the actor they were observing; as always in the mask exercises, they are not necessarily trying to replicate exactly what their assigned actor did, but rather trying to show what they saw as important or central to that actor's mask. If the 'Draw Your Own Body' exercise has preceded this exercise, then they may also use whatever evidence they deduce from the actors' blind self-portraits.

The actors now in the audience have to try to work out which actor is playing their mask; as soon as they have located their masks, they say so. Thus, eventually all the actors are paired off; as the numbers diminish, it becomes easier to work out who is playing your mask.

Once every mask has been identified, the joker may then ask each actor/mask pair in turn to play side by side on stage, so that the observing group can note the similarities and differences between the actors and their masks. Other actors may also join in at this point, coming on stage and adding elements which they think are missing from the mask. It is worth asking the actors how they identified the masks of themselves, or why they failed to identify themselves till the very end.

12 Substitution of mask

This exercise points up the economic character of certain relationships. In some parts of Latin America, the clergy is extremely progressive, but in other areas it is terribly reactionary. In this exercise, we first create the masks determined by the rituals of dependency between peasant and landowner. Straight afterwards, we enact the rituals of the confessional, between the pious and the priest. Then we enact the ritual of the economic dispute, with the actors using the masks of priest (great landowner) and pious (peasant).

13 Separation of mask, ritual and motivation

The actors rehearse these elements separately, then put them together. In one enactment of this exercise, an actor told of a day spent with her family after the death of her father. Everyone had assembled to celebrate the mother's birthday and during the celebration, they had argued about problems connected with the inheritance, each relative anxious to get more than the next.

First we rehearsed the ritual of the birthday with all its details – the arrival of the children, the presents for the mother, sitting down at table, champagne, birthday greetings, singing 'Happy Birthday', taking pictures, and the loving departures. The actors rehearsed this ritual several times so that they would afterwards be able to reproduce the whole sequence of actions down to the last detail; how people raised their glasses, how they drank, how each person walked, the time given to taking a photograph, etc.

Then, seated, with their eyes closed, the actors argue violently, their arguments informed solely by their own 'motivations'; in this case casting back and forth the blame for the economic failure of the business, demanding financial compensation from each other, dredging up old accusations, frenetically washing their dirty linen.

The third phase of the exercise is to choose the mask of one of the participants, in this case the actor telling the story, and have all the actors imitate it. Here, the actor in question was pregnant, so everybody acted like pregnant women (even the men).

At the end, having been released separately, all three elements are brought together – the economic motivations, the deadly hatred some characters feel towards others, and the exclusive use of the repressed mask of the actor. Then the actors carry out the happy, smiling, mother's birthday ritual again. Every so often, the motivation runs slap bang into the mask, and both collide with the rigidity of the ritual, the three elements revealing their autonomy.

In the same exercise, one can choose a particular mask for each person, instead of a single mask for everyone; the mask of 'fascist general' ('General gorilla' was our term) for the elder brother who refuses to explain his conduct in running the business; that of 'middle-class matron' for the mother with all her appearance of power and actual incapacity; the 'peasant' aspect of the exploited younger sister, etc.

14 Changing a whole set of masks into a different social class

When she was little, an actor who lived with her mother in Buenos Aires was called to Rio by her father who had been living there for the past year. The father had said in a letter that mother and daughter should move to Rio, and that the little girl must go there first to see the city, the flat, etc. On her arrival in Rio, her father told her the truth – he was living with another woman and he wanted his daughter to tell the mother. Although it gave her no great pleasure, the little girl accepted the mission and returned to Buenos Aires. The three characters were rich and could afford the luxury of staying in good hotels when travelling. The mother had no financial difficulties.

First we performed the scene as she had told it to us, within the same social context. Then we put the masks in place; the father is working-class, living with a woman in a dismal house in a suburb of Buenos Aires; the mother and daughter live in Cordoba; the girl abandons her job to go to see her father in Buenos Aires.

In this particular instance, the working-class father was unable to resist his daughter's persuasion that he should bring the mother to Buenos Aires as well and set her up in another house until she finds a new job. The 'sacrifice' in the first case was quite simply the fruit of economic power – there is no real sacrifice, mother and daughter could afford themselves the luxury of forgiving the father. In the second case, that option of benevolent understanding and forgiveness is quite simply not available.

Another example – a middle-class man learns that his daughter is pregnant and that the guilty party has disappeared. The father shows himself in a very good light, very understanding, and helps his daughter as much as possible. If, in place of him, we substitute the mask of the proletarian, the situation becomes different. The rigidity of this morality is determined by an economic reality – where will he find the money to feed an extra mouth if the man who made the girl pregnant has gone? This is a case of economic morality – the bourgeois can be good because he has money. The girls of Copacabana beach can afford to be free in their choices of sexual liaison, they don't have any sexual prejudices. But those living in the slums of Copacabana do. The girls who populate the beaches have money, those who inhabit the *barrios* are household servants.

15 Making the mask all-encompassing

The mask superimposes itself on the human being, but under the mask life goes on. This exercise consists of making the mask invade the whole of the human being, to the point of eliminating all other signs of life. The 'human' component of the worker is not adequate for the mechanical work he has to achieve; thus the less human the worker, the more efficient he is and the more he turns into an automaton. The actor makes his body do the movements which the worker normally does, the mask gradually gains the upper hand, till the worker 'dies'. For example, the seamstress who ends up sewing up her own body; the priest for whom the righteousness prescribed by the rituals of the cloth ends up transforming him into an angel of the Middle Ages, of the pre-Renaissance period, without a sex, without individuality, without any personal physiognomy; the prostitute who is just a moving body, etc.

16 Changing actors mid-ritual

Two actors start any scene and construct the masks appropriate to the ritual they want to represent. After a few minutes, one of the two takes the other's place, maintaining her mask and continuing the ritual. A second actor replaces the first, a third replaces the second, and so on. There must be an absolute continuity of motivations, masks and rituals.

17 A round of masks in different circumstances

One actor places himself in the middle of the circle. One of his colleagues goes in and shows what she imagines to be his mask in other circumstances – furious, happy, nervous. The actor in the middle must follow her, playing each mask he is shown, one by one.

146

18 Natural and ridiculous

A round of rhythms and movements. An actor goes into the middle and does all the movements and rhythms which seem to her 'natural' and 'relaxed'. Another actor goes in and gets her to do movements which seem to him unnatural and contorted; the actor in the middle and those in the circle follow him. The actor in the middle, once her colleague has gone, returns to relaxed movements; a second actor enters and makes her change again.

The natural is often a defence against the ridiculous.

19 Several actors on stage

Those not on stage make up a story and the people on stage mime it. The off-stage people argue, talk, those on stage do the actions.

20 The game of complementary roles

A variation of the professions game (see p. 136), with the difference that on the bits of paper are complementary professions or social roles: teacher/pupil, husband/wife, priest/worshipper, doctor/invalid, policeman/thief, worker/bourgeois, etc.

21 The politicians game

Another variation of the professions game – the pieces of paper contain the names of well-known politicians.

22 Exchange of masks

The actors invent a character in the following manner. The actors start going round in a circle, in their own persona. They concentrate on the changing positions of each part of their bodies. The hand, its swinging movement. The head – does it accompany the movements of the feet or not? The vertebral column – is it curved or upright? The knees – locked straight or bent double? Etc.

After close self-observation, they start to change. What if I was different? What if I had a different gait? What if my head moved differently? Each person experiments as much as they want and then constructs a 'mask', a 'physical character' different from themselves. Next, sound is added in the guise of language; no words are spoken, only the melody and the rhythm which suit this type of character.

The next section is played just like the rhythmic 'Peruvian ball-game' (see p. 91). The joker warns, 'Get ready.' Each person chooses a partner, they 'talk' to each other, they shake hands when they are ready to exchange masks, then they do the exchange. Three times. The point of the game is then to find your original mask again.

23 Exchange of roles

In order for the whole group to be able to contribute to the creation of all the characters (even if the 'joker system' is not being used and each actor is playing the same part throughout the piece), the actors rehearse parts they are not playing (each person doing someone else's character). In this way each person can give their version of the other characters and study the versions of their own character put forward by others.

The image of the object

In this section we use 'joker-objects', transforming their size, multiplying them or dividing them, placing them in unconventional relationships to each other and other things, always using objects which are symbols, 'charged' objects, which can be manipulated ideologically.

1 The found object

The members of the group are asked to bring in five objects each, objects which have been used. They all then place their objects around the space. Once all the objects have been positioned, the group analyses the relationships between the objects, why they have been placed where, what the connections between the different groups of objects are, whether there are 'families' of objects, what meanings we project on to the objects.

2 The object transformed

This game is to be used in combination with a number of the character-creation games, for instance 'The embassy ball' (see p. 157) or 'Cops and robbers' (p. 156). Taking the objects that people have brought in, the participants change their meaning by using them differently or in different contexts (see also 'Homage to Magritte', p. 149).

3 The object created out of simple things

Again, this can be used in combination with any of the character-creation games (pp. 150–61). Using simple materials like newspaper, string, leaves, tissue, etc., the participants make objects and use them in different contexts.

4 Homage to Magritte – 'this bottle is not a bottle'

This game takes as one of its two starting points Bertolt Brecht's words:

> there are many objects within a single object, if the final goal is the revolution; but there would be no objects within any object, if that goal were to disappear.

The other starting point is the work of René Magritte, some of whose pictures bear titles or slogans which disrupt the identification of the objects they depict. 'This bottle is not a bottle', what could it be? This chair is not a chair, this table is not a table, etc. The game consists of giving the group an object, which each actor in succession must discover a use for, by the addition of his body to the image; what could this object have been? A piece of wood can be a gun, a baton, a stake, a horse, an umbrella, a crutch, a lift, a bridge, a ladle, a flagpole, a fishing rod, an oar, a whistle, an arrow, a spear, a violin, a needle, many other things, even a piece of wood . . .

The invention of space and the spatial structures of power

1 Space and territory

Space is infinite; my body is finite. But around my body is my territory, which is subjective.

A woman is sitting on a crowded subway. All the seats are taken, except for one seat beside her, which is empty. A man boards the carriage and sits beside her – her territory has not been invaded.

The same woman is sitting in the same seat, and the whole carriage is empty. The same man comes and sits by her: her territory is invaded. In this forum game, spect-actors replace the woman and show different ways of regaining their territory.

Other examples: a man is at a public telephone – if the people standing in line keep a certain distance, they do not invade the man's territory; but if they come closer, within hearing distance, they do.

or the same thing in a bank, queuing behind someone at the cashier's window. Or a couple kissing on a public bench in a public garden – someone sits down in front of them and looks at them.

In none of these cases were the protagonists' bodies touched but in every case their subjective territories were unquestionably invaded. What should they do?

2 Inventing the space in a room

Using their bodies and any of the objects from the previous sequence, the participants create an environment in the room – a boat, a church, a bank, a ballroom, a desert, the high seas, etc.

3 The great game of power

A table, six chairs and a bottle. First of all, participants are asked to come up one at a time and arrange the objects so as to make one chair become the most powerful object, in relation to the other chairs, the table and the bottle. Any of the objects can be moved or placed on top of each other, or on their sides, or whatever, but none of the objects can be removed altogether from the space. The group will run through a great number of variations in the arrangement.

Then, when a suitable arrangement has been arrived at, an arrangement which the group feels is the most powerful, a participant is asked to enter the space and take up the most powerful position, without moving anything. Once someone is in place, the other members of the group can enter the space and try to place themselves in an even more powerful position, and take away the power the first person established.

Games involving the creation of characters

These are particularly recommended when starting a new group with non-actors – for instance, workers and students. Some are parlour games – and not workshop games – which help people accept the possibility of trying to 'play' as we play in the theatre; they help people lose some of their inhibitions.

150

The great game of power - as played by members of Augusto Boal's Theatre of the Oppressed Centre in Paris. (Photos: Fabian Silbert)

1 Murder at the Hotel Agato

This game was taken from a 'suspense' story. In the lounge of a hotel, when all means of communication with the outside world have been cut, someone finds a piece of paper on which is written: 'I am a murderer and I'm going to kill you all.' As quickly as possible, all the participants must discover the identity of the killer – who will preferably have been appointed secretly by the joker. The killer has an agreed signal (for instance, two taps on the shoulder or a wink) by which he can kill everyone, but he can only start killing after the others have had ten minutes to study and get to know each other. The actors can, by a majority vote, 'kill' suspects.

This parlour game can also be done as a workshop exercise, with the actors actually creating characters and developing their emotions. In the latter situation, the 'dead' people do not leave the stage, they die 'for real'. However the game is being played, the death of a person who has been murdered must be slow; the actor must wait a few minutes before dying, so as not to give away the identity of the assassin.

This kind of game is excellent for stimulating the actor's powers of perception. Generally our senses select what we are to become conscious of; this game greatly enlarges this field of consciousness, and each actor analyses their colleagues in much greater detail, seeing as they are all, potentially, 'murderers'. The joker can choose one killer, or several, or none, thus keeping up the 'suspense', generating an atmosphere of tension and a much greater alertness on the players' part.

2 Cops and robbers

This is a variation of the preceding game. The group is divided into two halves, one made up of guerrillas, the other of policemen. Without knowing each other's allegiances, they are all travelling in the same bus, which breaks down on the road. They all know that the bus contains only guerrillas and policemen, but they do not know which is which. The exercise consists of trying to work out who is a friend and who is an enemy, and agreeing a signal for 'killing' members of the other side. The exercise ends when one side has been completely wiped out. In this exercise, imagination plays as important a part as observation; each actor, whichever group she is in, has to come up with a convincing story to show her friends her true identity and to make her enemies think she's one of them. The formation of small groups is allowed, so everybody doesn't start speaking at the same time, but there should also be separate interrogations, isolated 'deaths'. This exercise can take on a high degree of emotional and ideological violence, as it does not involve the creation of 'general' characters, but rather of combatant characters on one side and repressive characters on the other, with each side trying to justify their antagonistic stance.

3 The embassy ball

Each person chooses an establishment character to play, a judge, a politician, a business-person, etc. A ball is being held at the embassy, or the office, or wherever – any ritualised gathering – and all these characters attend, on their best behaviour, dressed in their smartest clothes. They are announced at the door, they meet, they mingle.

Unbeknown to the guests, the waiter is a member of a revolutionary movement; he hands round drinks, and slices of a cake which has been spiked with a hallucinogenic drug. A first round of cake is distributed, loosening the inhibitions of the guests who start to behave slightly oddly. A second round of cake contains more of the drug, and the guests reveal more of themselves, behaving as they would really like to; their desires come to the surface and override their masks of respectability. The third round of cake drives them to wild extremes of behaviour. Finally they get a last slice of cake, which contains an antidote which brings them down and returns them to their socially acceptable selves. Each round is initiated by the joker at suitable intervals.

4 The child's dream – what I wanted to be when I grew up

Half the group write their names on pieces of paper together with the name or description of the person, hero, or mythical figure they dreamt of being when they were children; the other half of the group watch.

First, the participants move around the playing space using only their bodies to show the main characteristics of the characters they are playing. They must reveal what fascinated them about this dream when they were children, using only gesture, facial expression and movement, all at the same time, but without at this stage relating to one another.

After a few minutes, the joker tells them to look for a partner. Then they start dialogues with their partners, but without saying anything which will obviously reveal who their characters are.

After another few minutes of this, the joker tells them to change partners, and the new couples engage in a dialogue, each person maintaining and developing his own character. Then after the same period of time, a third partner is chosen.

When this is over, the joker reads out the names of the participants one at a time, and those in the group who were watching the game, as well as those who were playing it, must describe the characteristics they saw in that person. They should not try to guess the actual name of the childhood aspiration (Superman, Mother Teresa, Pele, Grace Kelly, etc.), but rather try to describe how the person they were watching behaved, because this will reveal what he really wanted to be or what capacity she wanted to develop in herself, using the name or image of someone real or fantastic as the vehicle for that aspiration.

Two examples. In Zurich, a man wrote 'Tarzan'. The comments of the participants showed that he wanted to be superior, a leader, a commander, a chief, high above all others – i.e. the animals. In New York, two young women both wrote down the same name – Cinderella. One of them showed narcissism, beauty, cruelty; the other, a Puerto Rican as it happened, chose to show the moment when her Cinderella had to go back to the kitchen – all the woman wanted was a few hours of happiness.

This game is effective because somehow it reveals characteristics and aspirations which the participants still cherish.

After the first half of the group has acted out their childhood dreams, the second half do the same.

5 The child's fear

The same rules as the previous game, with two differences: (1) the participants must play the character or thing which frightened them, not themselves being afraid; (2) when they engage in dialogue with their partners they must try to frighten them, just as they were frightened of the characters they are playing when they were children.

The chosen character must be concrete, a person, an animal, a 'tangible' ghost, etc.; for instance, instead of 'fear of darkness', they must play the person or thing they are afraid of, hidden in the darkness. Even if the fear is something like 'fear of being struck by lightning' they should try to play the person (perhaps even God Himself) who wanted to strike them.

By playing the subject that I was afraid of, I gain a better understanding of my childish fear (which may still live on inside me).

6 *What grown-ups wanted me to be*

The same as the preceding games. This allows each person to compare what they actually are with what their elders expected from them.

7 *The opposite of myself*

Still the same rules. The participants write their names on pieces of paper, along with a characteristic they would like to try to possess, which must be completely different from their actual behaviour.

During the playing, after a while the joker must give the instruction 'Back to your normal behaviour' and then 'Back to your opposite self'.

8 *The two revelations of Saint Teresa*

The title of this exercise relates to the place in Rio de Janeiro where it was invented – there is no religious connotation to it. The group decides what kind of interpersonal relations it wishes to investigate – husband/wife, parent/child, teacher/student, doctor/patient, etc. Only close, charged relationships should be selected. Then the group forms into couples, in which the partners decide only: (1) who plays what; (2) where they usually meet; (3) their age.

The improvisation begins when the couple meet. They must say to each other the things they think those characters would usually say, and do what they believe they would usually do, including all the usual clichés.

After a few minutes the joker says, 'One of you make the first revelation.' Then one of the partners must reveal to the other something of great importance which has the potential to change their relationship, for better or worse. The other partner must show what they think would be the most probable reaction.

A few more minutes of this, and then the joker tells the second one to make an important revelation as well, and the first person

reacts accordingly. Another interval, then the joker says one of them must leave: they improvise the separation – a 'see you tomorrow' or a 'good night' or a 'goodbye for ever'.

This game is especially useful for showing the stratifications of a particular culture. First, where do husbands and wives, for instance, usually meet and talk – in the kitchen or in bed? What revelations do young girls make to their mothers – are they pregnant by a married man and want an abortion, do they want to leave home, do they want to leave the country?

Comparisons of the different couples, where they meet, what they reveal, is very effective as a means of exposing the mechanisations of a given society. Usually I do this game on the same day as the 'Image of the hour' game (in which everyone has to show what they usually do at 7 o'clock, at 8, 9, 10, 12, etc.) and the 'Ritual gesture' game (see p. 182) (in which you show in image form the critical movement in a series of mechanised movements you make every day).

9 The fighting cocks

A game to develop facility of improvisation. In pairs, one person accuses the other of having done something wrong. The other person has to defend himself and justify his action, in the process creating a character.

10 Catchphrases

Think of two or more phrases, popular sayings, formulas or recent declarations by leaders or demagogues. Each actor gets one word of one of these phrases. In the course of the game, she must answer the questions the others put to her while always trying to insert her key word into the answer. She can have one conversation or several. The game is finished when the actors manage to identify those of their number who have the words of their catchphrase. It is important that each actor, when answering, does so with phrases compatible with the ideology which is behind the catchphrase or slogan from which the key word has been lifted. For instance: with the slogan 'Only the people can save the people', one actor will have the word 'only', another 'the', a third 'people'. Nobody knows who belongs to their group, it is up to each person to work it out by answering using the word they've been given.

11 What am I? What do I want?

Very simple, terribly difficult. Each person writes down on a piece of paper three definitions of themselves; they should not add their names. What am I? A man, a teacher, a father, a husband, a friend, a Brazilian, a writer, a director, a playwright, a traveller, a politician? Which comes first? What does each person choose?

What do I want? To be happy, to travel, to be rich, to win elections, to swim, to make people happy, to play, what?

The joker collects all the pieces of paper and analyses, systematises and reveals their contents to the group without identifying anyone.

V THE MEMORY OF THE SENSES

If I bang my hand, I feel the impact. If I remember banging my hand yesterday, I can awaken in myself an analogous sensation. This series helps us to reconnect memory, emotion and imagination, when rehearsing a scene or preparing a future action.

Reconnecting memory, emotion and imagination

1 Memory: remembering yesterday

The actors must be sitting quietly on chairs, completely relaxed. They must slowly move each part of their body in succession, concentrating solely on that part, in isolation. Eyes closed.

Then the joker starts encouraging them to recall everything that happened the previous evening, before they went to bed. Each detail must be accompanied by bodily sensations – taste, smell, tactile sensations, shapes, colours, outlines, depth, sounds, tone, tunes, noise, etc. The actor must make a special effort to remember his bodily sensations and try to re-experience them. To make the operation easier, he should repeat the movement of the relevant part of his body; if he is thinking about something he's eaten, he moves his mouth, lips, tongue. If he is thinking about a shower he's taken, he moves his body, the skin which was in contact with the water; if he is thinking about a walk he took, he moves the muscles of his legs, his feet.

After this, the joker continues the probing, now pushing the actors to recall what happened to them that morning. How did they wake up? With an alarm clock? Did someone wake them? The sound of the alarm, the person's voice – what were these things like? They are asked to give the most minutely detailed description of the face of the first person they saw. All the details of the room they slept in, of the room they breakfasted in: outlines, colours, sounds, tones, tunes, noises, smells, tastes, etc.

Then, the means of transport they used. Their travelling companions? Underground, bus, car? The sound of the door closing, etc. Always searching for the details, the most minute details of the bodily impressions, and always with the small movements of the relevant part of the body, which must accompany the memory.

Finally, their arrival in the room they are in. Who did they see first? Which voice did they hear first? A sensory description of the room, with as much detail as possible. Now – where are they? Next to whom? How is everyone else dressed? What objects are there in the room?

Open your eyes. Compare.

2 Memory and emotion: remembering a day in the past

This is the same exercise, but perhaps nothing important happened the day before or that morning. So each person must have by their side a *co-pilot* to whom they recount a day in their past (last week or twenty years ago) when something really important happened, something which made a profound impression on them, the memory of which provokes emotion, even today.

Each participant must have a co-pilot because people's experiences are not the same. The co-pilot should help the person to link the memory to the sensations, by asking lots of questions related to sensory details. The co-pilot is not a voyeur; he should use the exercise to try to create the same event in his own imagination, with the same details, the same emotion, the same sensations.

3 Memory and emotion and imagination

The same system – with the help of the co-pilot you try to remember something which really happened. You try to reawaken the emotions and sensations you felt at the time, but this time the co-pilot (who must be a genuine co-pilot, co-feeling the same sensations and sharing the same images) now has the right to introduce various elements which were not in the original version: extra characters, additional events. And the actor-protagonist must introduce these new elements into his imaginary world.

Thus both protagonist and co-pilot are participants in the creation of a story, part reality, part fiction, but moving in its totality, evocative of powerful images and sensations.

With practice, the fictional elements introduced by the co-pilot can become further and further removed from the reality, even to the point of surrealism. But people should set out from the probable and the possible to arrive at the improbable and impossible, which can still generate emotions and awaken sensations.

4 Remembering an actual oppression

Same exercise. This time the co-pilot may only suggest possible actions which might eventually lead to the breaking of the oppression being related. It is up to the protagonist herself, in her imagination, to break the oppression, even if she is following the co-pilot's suggestions.

5 Rehearsal on the stage of the imagination

Everything you have done in imagination must immediately be played on stage. The other actors help, the protagonist and the co-pilot play director, and you try to play physically everything that has been played in the imagination. You use the same objects, you try to repeat the same phrases, etc.

6 Extrapolation

The theatre, the fiction, stops with the previous exercise, but the real goal, the final objective, is to extrapolate into real life solutions which have been found in the imagination and rehearsed on the stage. We have already done this a number of times. With no regrets.

These are five categories of exercise, game and 'gamesercise' which we use to prepare the actor and non-actor. Their goal is the development of the individual and the group.

These five categories are preliminaries to the introduction of Image Theatre, Invisible Theatre and Forum Theatre techniques.

IMAGE THEATRE

To make it easier to understand the systematisation of these Image Theatre techniques and how each one works, I shall endeavour to describe the most effective methods of 'dynamisation' for each type of model. Of course, any of the various types of 'dynamisation' can be applied to any of the various models; the choice of method depends on the nature of the group, the occasion and the objectives of the work. Thus I have tried to start with the most simple techniques and end with the most difficult.

I stress again that use of the Image Theatre exercises and games which precede these techniques is by no means *obligatory*. Indeed nothing in the Theatre of the Oppressed is obligatory, because each exercise, game and technique, while having specific objectives of its own, in itself contains the totality of the process. There is a built-in and continuous interplay between the exercises, games and techniques of all the forms of the Theatre of the Oppressed: Newspaper Theatre, Image Theatre, Forum Theatre, Invisible Theatre, etc. That said, a teacher could well suggest that his pupils use image techniques in the course of their work, even if he has not previously taken them through the preceding exercises. Equally, during the preparation of a Forum Theatre production, it is not necessary for the joker to take the participants through all, or even any, of the suggested image exercises, simply so that they can then use the image techniques.

Image techniques: models and dynamisations

1 Illustrating a subject with your body

The model

The model can be developed in one of two ways.

1st method   The joker asks five or more volunteers to express the chosen theme(s) in a visual form. Each works without seeing what the others are doing, so as not to be influenced by them. One after another they come into the middle of the playing space and use only their bodies to express the theme they have been given. When all the volunteers have been, the joker asks if anyone in the audience can suggest an image different to those shown. The response is almost always in the affirmative. One by one, anyone who wants to comes into the middle and shows their own image of the subject being treated – whatever image occurs to them. When they have all been in the middle, the joker goes on to the dynamisation of these images.

2nd method   When dealing with small groups (and, in my view, only in such cases) the joker can suggest that the participants form a circle and, at a given signal, *all* simultaneously depict with their bodies their version of the subject. Then as a second stage, still holding their poses, they look round at what everyone else is doing.

The images made by each participant must be static images, even if they *presuppose* movement; the actor can show a static image of something *captured in mid-movement*. Similarly every image must be isolated, though it may presuppose the presence of other people or objects or whatever.

The dynamisation

Once the model has been constructed, the joker suggests 'dynamising' it. This should be done in three stages.

1st dynamisation   At a signal from the joker, all the participants who have already been into the middle go back there, and present exactly the same images as before, but this time all together, and not in succession. What happens? Previously, each actor was showing their own image, in a subjective, personal way, as they saw the subject. Presenting all these individual visions together gives us a multiple vision of the subject, in other words, an overview, an 'objective' vision. In this first part of the dynamisation, the object is no longer to know what each individual thinks, but to see what everybody thinks. The individual presentation of images gave us a 'psychological' representation, now we are given a 'social' vision; that is, we are shown how this particular theme influences or affects this particular community.

A few examples will clarify this. In a workshop in Florence, one of the participants suggested religion as the theme. First, several people dwelt on pious, religious images in their illustration of the subject: Christ crucified, bleeding Virgin Marys, saints, penitents, priests, worshippers . . . and so on; then other actors came on stage and showed lovers in churches, beggars receiving alms, strict, sententious curates ... and finally tourists casually wielding their cameras and flash-guns.

In a town in the South of France, a teacher asked his pupils to make representations of famous people, real or fictitious: Joan of Arc, Berenice, Napoleon, etc. In these images he discovered many things! Everything he himself had taught in class about these characters appeared, but *not as he had taught it*, but as each child or adolescent had *been able to understand it* from within his or her own frame of reference and experience. It was not unusual, for instance, for Phaedra to appear in these images hunched over her supermarket bill, or Napoleon dealing with his bank statements ... children's ideas, but ideas all the same! Ideas revealed in their image presentations.

Another example: in Brazil, someone suggested treating the theme of violence. Rio de Janeiro, where the workshop was taking place, is one of the most violent cities in the world, with the highest rate of theft, the highest incidence of murder, taking a lead from the government dictatorship.... Thus it came as no surprise to me when one of the group (on a course I organised in December 1979) proposed violence as a theme. But what transpired did strike me as extra-ordinary – everyone, without exception, played the roles of *victims* of violence ... and not without good reason! Violence on all levels: physical (military and police aggression), economic (payment of rent), religious (penitence), educational (domineering teachers), sexual (rape).... In spite of everything, it was always the victims who appeared in these images; because the course in question was made up of twenty-four victims! In the dynamisation, as we will see later, the causes came across loud and clear.

2nd dynamisation   At a signal from the joker, the participants try to interrelate with the other participants on stage. In other words it is no longer enough simply to present your vision, you must try to link it to other people's. Each person can choose one or more themes, can move further in or out, whatever they like, as long as their pose relates in some way to other people's poses, and to the objects others have placed or imagined. If each image was previously valid in itself, now the important thing is the interrelation, the collection of images, the macrocosm. Now what we see is not merely the social vision, but an organised, organic, social vision. The image no longer shows multiple points of view, but rather a single, global, all-embracing vision.

For example, on one course someone suggested the French theatre as a theme. The participants, who were mostly professional or amateur actors, were not very taken with this idea. So, in the construction of the model, each person in turn proffered an unflattering image: one person gazed in wonderment at his navel, another tried to kiss her own bottom, another seemed to be looking for someone (probably a member of the audience) through binoculars, a fourth was counting his pennies, a fifth was yawning, a sixth was asleep, etc. Basically, they were not happy! In the first dynamisation, nothing particularly startling happened – they all faced the audience, in one multiple image of their expressions of discouragement and boredom. By contrast, during the second dynamisation a surprising development took place: all the images which in one way or another 'symbolised' the 'artists' entered into relationships with each other, but not one of them made any approach to the images which represented the 'audience' – who, for their part, stayed in their corner yawning and snoozing.... The actor who was contemplating his navel went up to the one who was counting his pennies, the one who was admiring her bottom acknowledged the presence of a woman who was showing off her breasts ... and so on; but no one, I repeat, no one, made the slightest effort to form a relationship with the disheartened 'audience' ... and, equally, the latter made no progress towards the 'artist' group.

We should be wary of generalisations – this happened on one occasion, on one course, with one particular group. But the whole of a group. It has to mean something!

3rd dynamisation It often happens, as it did in Rio, that the participants show only the 'effects' and not the 'cause'; the *result* of the violence, but not its *origin*. In this particular case (Rio), all the participants were victims of the same repressive system. Thus, when in the second dynamisation they wanted to compose a 'whole', the social macrocosm, the images which emerged were first the absence of solidarity, of unity among the victims, and then the absence of 'agents of violence'. Everyone had found it preferable to play *their own role* rather than that of their enemy. In such cases, it is a good idea to use the third method of dynamising the model. The joker tells the group that on his signal all the images of 'victims' (objects) should transform themselves into oppressors (subjects). The young woman who has been raped must show her rapist; the man paying

167

the rent plays the recipient of his cash; the beggar shows the person who gives him alms; the citizen plays the policeman, etc.

So in the first round each actor must show one of the two poles of conflict, and in the second round the opposite pole. Which is where another interesting aspect of the work comes into play, which can be of considerable assistance to us in terms of 'reading' the thoughts, the emotions, the ideology of the group. If when showing their own oppression the participants generally use *real images*, when they are showing their 'enemy' they have a tendency to portray *subjective images* (one might almost use the term 'expressionist'), distorted images. Distorted, yes, but not simply on a whim – because the makers of these images have experienced this aggression. The images cease to be realistic, they become larger, they become misshapen – monsters! Everybody reveals themselves *as they are* (or how they think they are) and their enemies, *as they see them*.

Now this is, in my view, one of the most important problems for theatre. Is there such a thing as *objective realism*? Is it really possible to show *life as it is*? Does such a vision exist? I believe it could not exist unless the artist were capable of expressing a cosmic point of view. But as artists are themselves part of a society, I do not think it can be possible for them to see the world other than from their own particular angle. The realist style is as subjective as any other, but it is dangerous because it pretends to be the opposite.

I like the vision that victims have of their tormentors: *if they see them in this way, it is because that is how they are*. For us, that is how they are. And when I say 'us' I mean that in the aesthetic process we must identify ourselves with someone – us or them, there is no alternative.

In this work, the more victimised the victims, i.e. the greater the oppression they are suffering, the more they will distort their images. But the term 'distortion' should be taken here in the opposite sense to its normal usage. The sense should be of restoring the actual, true image; for instance, a torturer has a normal 'appearance', he comports himself in a 'normal' way. His 'realistic' image will be no different from other men. His 'real' image is the image which the tortured person will give of him. In actuality he is as the tortured sees him, even if, in the 'realistic' style of theatre, he's just like everyone else. I have never had much confidence in realism and I have become even less happy with it since I have been working with images – the more I 'see' what I am 'looking at', the further away from the realist style I find myself moving.

But it is also important to underline that the aim is not to create a neo-expressionism, to construct a strange, subjective, individualist style. In this process of image construction, what is important is not to see how *one oppressed person* sees *one oppressor,* but to find out how *the oppressed* see *the oppressors.* If we were compelled to give a name to this approach, we would be forced to call it, contrarily, social expressionism, objective expressionism, etc.

But let us return to the dynamisation – in order to be able to delve as deeply as possible into the vision of the image, and not simply accept it as a statement of evidence, one has to lead the actor to complete the image he showed at the start. This complementarity often bears fruit, it can throw light on and add depth to the first image shown.

2 *Illustrating a subject using other people's bodies*

The resources of the first technique are limited to the extent that the actors can use only their own bodies. In this second technique, they can use the bodies of others, and even objects as well.

The model

The joker asks a first volunteer to illustrate the theme proposed by the group, using the bodies of other members of the group. When the model is finished, the joker consults the group, who may well disagree with the image shown (in which case the model is taken to pieces), or may agree with it (the model is retained as it is), or partially agree with it. In this last case, the joker consults the group and removes from the image those elements the group considers to have no function or convey no meaning. At every point the group should be consulted, as it is ultimately the 'constructor' of a collective image on the proposed subject.

It is important that the person who is 'sculpting' the image works fast, so that she will not be tempted to think in words (verbal language) and then translate into images (visual language). If the work is not done in this way, the images are generally poor, like a translation which is an impoverishment of its original.

It will sometimes be the case that the group cannot arrive at a collective image which everyone finds acceptable. I remember, for example, in Turin when a group I was working with was trying to present an image of 'the family', but the images suggested were so numerous and various that even a modicum of agreement proved impossible. At first I found this disconcerting, but I rapidly worked it out – Turin has a population of around two million people, of whom only a quarter are genuine Turinese, the rest being people drawn to the city by the chance of work (especially in the Fiat factories). They come from all over Italy, especially the south. They are all Italians, but hail from completely different cultures – Calabria, Milan, Naples, Sicily, etc. – each of the sculptors was thinking of his own family, his own culture!

The subject of 'the family' is, however, a constant in the trajectory of the Theatre of the Oppressed, being probably the most discussed of all topics. In all societies the family exists – but which particular version of 'family'? On each occasion the subject arises, a different family emerges, according to the culture, class, country, regime, age of 'sculptor', etc. I have cited some examples earlier in this book; a few more follow.

A Swedish family   In 1977 during a workshop I was leading in Stockholm as part of the Skeppsholm festival, the participants made an image of the family; two years later at the municipal theatre of Norrköping, another group reproduced exactly the same image: a table in the middle, with two or three people around it, but all with their backs to each other. At the back of the image, by the door, a woman with her back to everyone. A group of people gathered together around a table, not seeing each other, not looking at each other, not speaking to each other.

A family in Godrano (Sicily)   The table again, with men, only men, playing cards; further off, on a chair, a woman caressing (and stifling) a young girl of 20, hugging her to her breast as if she was a newly born child. Still further off, another woman sitting sewing a trousseau. No need for further explanation for us to understand the patriarchal relations of this society.

A North American family   This image was presented to me in New York, in Berkeley, in Milwaukee, in Illinois – from north to south, east to west, everywhere, every time, to the extent that it became almost a cliché: a man seated on a chair (the table is also there, but pushed against the wall) and around the male character, a woman and several children, heads leaning together, mouths chewing gum.... I am only saying what I saw.

A German family   First seen in Hamburg in 1979: a seated man, apparently at the wheel of a magnificent car, concentrating completely on the task in hand – driving. By his side, a woman, also very proud of the car, but taken up with the three small children in the back, who are fighting, biting each other, hitting out at each other, vying for supremacy. Faced with this image, I at first thought that they were exaggerating – the man seemed so proud of his car that he wasn't even glancing at his family. I made a comment to this effect, and someone answered, with laughs of approbation from the rest of the group: 'That's the way it is! Here in Germany, the male preoccupations are, in descending order: the car, then the wife, then the dog, and finally the children.' Everyone broke into laughter and applause, but I was still not convinced – till a few months later, working in Berlin with a completely different group, I saw exactly the same image . . .

A Florentine family   A family procession walking to church: the grandmothers led by the grandfathers, the husbands by their wives, the children by their mothers . . . . A long line of oppressed/oppressors travelling to holy mass, with little piety visible on their faces. All the participants accepted the image, except that one vital element was lacking – a man pissing against a wall . . . freedom!

A Mexican family   In the middle, a statue of the Virgin Mary, arms outstretched, with two women on each side, on their knees, praying. On one side, a male character, obviously drunk, hitting a woman who was deftly fending off the blows. Behind, a drunk man was hitting three young men making vague gestures of aggression – in fact they were at the start of their apprenticeship; by the side of the woman defending herself, there were three young women who were also learning to defend themselves. The whole scene took place under the complacent, beneficent gaze of the Holy Virgin . . . Mexico is a very religious country.

A lesbian family   It should be stressed that these images are not necessarily universal on every occasion. Thus, in Sweden, I was shown two women holding hands with each other and with a child. Some people protested: 'That isn't a family.' The actor replied: 'It's *my* family . . .' and she continued calmly sculpting the image, working on the characters' faces, giving them all gentle, kind expressions. It

171

was her family and she was happy with it. It wasn't 'the Swedish family' but that did not matter to her.

An Egyptian family A splendid portrait: a seated woman with her arms uplifted as if she was bearing a dish; a man standing behind her, on a chair, eating from the dish she was holding up and at the same time keeping out of the reach of a compact line of young people (their legs spread, sitting one behind another) whose arms were stretched out towards this forbidden dish.

An Argentinian family Moving, sad, shocking. Several people seated, others, the majority, standing; one empty chair and everyone's gaze directed towards this empty chair, towards its absent occupant.

I lived in Argentina for five years. I knew tens, maybe hundreds of Argentinian families. I did not know one, not a single one, which did not have an empty chair, a chair belonging to someone killed under the torture of the military dictatorship, to one of the 'disappeared' (of whom, according to the incomplete statistics of Amnesty International, there were more than 15,000), or to one of those driven to flight or exile. This image of the empty chair was made by an Argentinian, but could just as easily have been offered by a Uruguayan or a Chilean, a Paraguayan or a Bolivian, by any of the inhabitants of any of the countries in a bloodstained continent, Latin America!

The dynamisation

1st dynamisation Make a rhythmic movement which is contained within the image. Take, for example, a static image of a man eating; it offers us a certain amount of information, allows us to understand a certain amount – it is an image which *speaks* to us. But there are a thousand ways, a thousand different rhythms, of eating. In this phase of the dynamisation, 'the image' must eat in a rhythm which will provide us with more information, supplementing what was contained within the static image – does he eat fast or slowly, does he wolf his food down or savour each mouthful?

2nd dynamisation The image, as well as making its rhythmic movement, utters a phrase which, in the actor's view, fits with the character on show. Let us be absolutely clear about this – the speaker is the character, not the person playing him. Thus if a nice actor is playing a nasty person, it is the nasty person who has the line, and not the kind-hearted actor.

3rd dynamisation   The image repeats its rhythmic gesture, saying its phrase, and then starts doing something, some movement or action of which the static image contained a hint; in other words, if the subject is eating, what will he do afterwards? If he is walking, where will he go afterwards? If he is being aggressive towards someone, what will the consequences of his aggression be?

3 Image of transition

This third technique consists of working on a model, generating an argument, by visual means alone. More than ever, it is vital that words are absent here; but not discussion, which should be as rich and full as possible.

The model

You proceed along the same lines as in the previous technique, to arrive at a model which the whole group (or most of it) is willing to accept. The subject-matter of this model must be an *oppression*, of whatever kind, which the group has suggested. Consequently this will be a real model of oppression. Then you ask the group to construct an *ideal model*, in which the oppression will have been eliminated and everyone in the model will have come to a plausible equilibrium, a state of affairs which is not oppressive for any of the characters. After this, you return again to the *real image*, the image of the oppression, and go on to dynamise it.

The dynamisation

The joker makes it clear that every participant is entitled to give their own opinion on all the ways of moving from the 'real' (oppressive) image to the 'ideal' (non-oppressive) image. Each participant acts as sculptor and changes whatever he feels necessary to transform the reality and eliminate the oppressions. Each person has a turn. The other participants must simply give their opinion, say whether they consider each solution to be realisable or magic, but without using words, since the actual discussion should develop only by means of modifications of the images.

173

After everyone who wants to has shown the two images of transition (in the process revealing their thoughts, ideology, expectations, hopes) you then proceed to a *practical verification* of what has been discussed. Thus, at a signal from the joker, all the characters in the image start moving. Every time the joker claps his hands, each character (each actor in the image) has the right to make one movement, and one alone, to free himself (if he is playing one of the oppressed) or to increase the oppression (if he is playing an oppressor). The movements made must be *appropriate to the characters and not to the people playing them.* Having clapped his hands several times – thus after several movements – the joker suggests that all the characters continue their movements in slow motion, and at each clap (the claps now coming at a much slower rhythm), they take a look round so that they can consider their positions in relation to others. Movement ceases when all the liberation possibilities have been studied visually; when the image has come to an almost complete halt, when all the conflicts have been resolved one way or the other, with happy or unhappy endings...

4 Multiple image of oppression

The previous technique allows the group to concentrate very directly on a single problem, a single form of oppression, a single concrete case. Society is represented *en bloc*, in one image. Macrocosm is presented in microcosmic form.

And this can be a very effective way of achieving a more thorough and sometimes more detailed analysis of that microcosm. However, it is often the case that the possible solutions to that problem, and even a proper understanding of it, can be found only in the social macrocosm, and not the microcosm – in multiplicity rather than unicity. This is the function of the fourth image technique.

The model

The required model here is no longer the unique, it is the multiple. Whatever the subject, the aim is no longer to show *one*, but *several* images which represent it, either at several different moments in time, or from several different perspectives. Thus, instead of one image, the group can prepare five, seven, ten images. Preferably the images should not be too repetitive, unless the oppression being studied has only one essential characteristic. With the exception of the latter case, the more varied the images, the better.

The dynamisation

Once the multiple model has been established, the dynamisation is done in three stages.

First, the makers of the images of the oppression under consideration must enter into the image themselves, to give us their perspective on this oppression. They must replace one of the people participating in the image they have made so that both the overall image and *the sculptor's point of view* may be better understood. Then, in the first phase of the dynamisation, the sculptor is allowed to move around all the people in the image, however she likes, to show an *ideal image*. Thus in the model we see the oppression as it is experienced by the sculptor, and in this modification we see her desires, her vision of how things would be if they were the opposite of how they are now.

Second, the image returns to its real model state, and, on a signal from the joker, all the participants in the image must, in slow motion, effect the *real-ideal* transition the sculptor desires. Thus, by means of autonomous movement (no one is guided by the sculptor, each person acts on their own initiative, following her instructions), one can get an idea of the *magical* or *realistic* nature of the sculptor's proposal. If the ideal image, or even the transition to that ideal, is in the realms of magic, the ridiculousness of the situation immediately makes this clear.

Third, the image returns to the original model. Once again, at a signal from the joker, the figures move, but this time *not necessarily towards the ideal*: each figure must act in accordance with the character they represent. Now it becomes possible to determine how realisable the sculptor's proposal actually was.

This multiple image of oppression always throws a good deal of light on the thinking of the group. It is one of the most revealing techniques.

At this point I must stress one thing: the rules of the game must be clearly and simply stated at the very beginning. If something is not described as 'forbidden' in this opening declaration of the rules, then no such interdiction exists. If the participants, or some of the participants, 'believe' that such-and-such a thing is forbidden, then that is their concern, and not the game's.

For instance, in Hamburg we used this technique. The chosen theme was the family. The images which made up the model were almost all absolutely terrifying – violence, physical and psychological aggression. At the moment of dynamisation, I realised that the participants were all looking for the 'solution' to their problems *within* each image; they went on beating each other up, hurting each other, arguing among themselves, in each of the grouplets which made up the whole image. No one tried to leave the *microcosm* of their family, to look for solutions in the social *macrocosm*, in the multiplicity of other families, other groups, other people. When all movement came to an end (with lots of dead and wounded) I asked why the participants had stayed so obstinately within their particular groups, when if freedom was to be found it was certainly beyond these immediate confines. Almost everyone gave the same answer – we thought that it was forbidden to leave our groups (their families)! Who forbade it? On the contrary, the multiple image technique is open to everything, to the outside world, people are free to join other images – its function is not to close us into our own little worlds.

Such self-inflicted oppression is very common. We are so oppressed that we oppress ourselves, even when external oppression is absent, does not exist. We all carry within us our own 'cops in the head' (see pp. 191–201 in 'New Image Theatre techniques'). At Montélimar, the reverse of the Hamburg experience happened, all the people playing images of 'children' escaped through the window...

This technique brings forth revealing, sometimes totally unexpected things. I remember at Bari, on the Adriatic coast of Italy, someone suggested treating the subject of sexual violence against women (in 1979, an ordinary year, there were more than 26,000 cases of rape in Italy, not counting the thousands of cases not reported by women out of fear or shame). Several images evoked this kind of aggression. I especially remember Angelina's. In the image she created, three men were brutally attacking her. In the dynamisation, we thought that she would beat back her aggressors violently. But to our amazement, Angelina contented herself with modifying their expressions and their postures, filling them with tenderness in place of hate. The essentials of the scene she hardly changed at all. When her colleagues questioned her, Angelina answered: 'For me the horrific element of rape is the physical violence of the act, not the sex...'

In cases when this technique is being used and the subject-matter divides the participants, as, for example, when dealing with men's oppression of women and vice versa, it greatly enhances the effect if the scenes are played in succession; first the women show how much they are oppressed, then the men show their multiple images of oppression – which are also numerous....

There is also a fourth kind of dynamisation, applicable in such cases: the men show the images of what *they believe* is an oppression against women, and the women show images of what *they consider* to be the oppressions of women against men. Parents *vis-à-vis* children and vice versa; teachers and their pupils, etc. Whenever the situation allows it, this kind of dynamisation of the model offers new possibilities of knowledge of the subject and the participants.

5 Multiple image of happiness

This technique, though quite specific, is very close to the preceding one. It reveals, better than any other, the oppressed/oppressor side of the participants.

The model

The model is constructed in the same way, with different volunteers sculpting their images of happiness. The images are distributed throughout the room in such a way that each can be seen both as part of the whole and as a separate image. The joker must not seek to influence the images, but should by contrast make it clear to each participant that she is free to illustrate the image she desires. What is happiness? Without doubt, it is the absence of oppression. Consequently the images of happiness shown will be devoid of oppression – i.e. the sculptor will not show her oppressions, but her happiness, real or ideal, true or imaginary. This image can be located in work, in love, in peace, wherever the participant wants. The joker must encourage people with different ideas of happiness to create their own images in order to avoid the repeated production of the same type of image, the same type of happiness (unless it is a particular characteristic of the group).

The dynamisation

Ideally there should be the same number of images around the room as people out of play, not involved in any of them; if there are six images, six people should be outside them. The dynamisation takes the form of a game. The joker takes the 'outsiders' around the room to look closely at all those who are 'in' the images, and at their positions in relation to each other. Each of the outsiders must come to a decision in their own minds as to who is *happiest*.

The game (the dynamisation) begins when the joker gives the first signal. All those who were outside have to run into the images and take the place of the person who, to their mind, is the happiest. The people who have been replaced come out. If by chance two people have chosen the same character, the first one to get there replaces her, and the second has to go and find another character, 'the second happiest', and replace him. Thus the same number of people go in as come out.

At the second signal, all those who have been replaced have the right to go back in, free to choose the 'happiest' person, which can be the character they were showing or another. But this time, instead of replacing the person, each must combine their own body with the other person's, in the same position; and so if two or more people have chosen the same figure, they all take up the same position. All the participants stay on stage.

At the third signal, all the participants start to move with the aim of placing their bodies in a happier relationship than the position they started in. This includes the people who sculpted the images, those chosen as statues at the start, everyone – all at the same time, they can move around trying to form relationships of maximum happiness to each person.

Beware: in this third stage, all the characters move at the same time, *simultaneously*. Everyone is a subject, no one is an object – though the latter status may emerge and usually does in the earlier stages.

However, if everyone is a subject, inevitably at any given moment the whole multiple image in the room (the multiple images of happiness) is in a permanent state of flux and modification. Thus one person 'sees' a group of figures or a single figure which she wishes to enter into a relationship with, as she thinks she will be happier there. She heads towards this group or figure, but her target can itself be dynamically in the process of heading for other figures which it wants to relate to; thus when the first person arrives she may well no longer find the characters she hoped to meet. At every moment each person has to reconsider the overall structure of the multiple image in all its aspects and adjust accordingly.

In order that this analysis may get to the very heart of things, the joker should suggest that the movements follow a particular pattern: one action each time the joker claps her hands, then a gradual slowing down, and finally the cessation of all movement (still marked with a clap); that is, no body movement – facial movement is still allowed, so that people can see what is happening in the room.

This technique is very enlightening. Certain constants recur wherever the exercise is done. For example, rare are the images of happiness which show the person happy at their work. In general, happiness is associated with relaxation, sex, sport, music – but not work, especially not manual work. In some countries (for example, the Nordic countries) it is very common to see a solitary image: a man or woman reading, or sunbathing, alone...

Inevitably there is always someone who objects: 'I cannot give my image of happiness, because for me happiness is not an isolated entity, it is the sum of many moments, of many activities...' And that's true; but it is also true that when someone is invited to show, to sculpt, their image of happiness, they show the image they feel most strongly at the time, in that particular place and those particular conditions. And the following is also true: normally the game is complete when all the characters have found an ideal relationship (within the limits of circumstance) with the other people – however, sometimes a person finds happiness in the *search* and is at their happiest in the continual movement from one image to another.

On occasion it can also happen that the *sculptor* seeks to express *his own* happiness, forgetting to create a general image of happiness, shared by the other actors in the image. I remember once someone made the following image: he was lying on his back, surrounded by seven women who were taking care of him, caressing him, singing and dancing for him.... Fine. When the dynamisation started, several men ran like lunatics to play this image of happiness. They all wanted to put themselves in the same position, they all wanted seven women to pander to their needs – but they never asked themselves whether the women wanted the same thing. So, when the third part of the dynamisation started, when each element of each image was free to act autonomously, the first thing the seven women did was to beat up the 'pasha'.... This man had shown his

179

happiness, and this happiness resided in the unhappiness of others. In order to achieve happiness, the man became an oppressor. Thus the third part of the dynamisation also provides an opportunity to bring to light the oppression dwelling in some people's visions of happiness.

6 Image of the group

This technique can be used any time in the work process. But it is particularly effective when the group itself presents a problem. With the help of this technique, the problem emerges more clearly and the solution can be sought with a greater likelihood of success.

But even in the ostensible absence of problems, it is always good to 'see' how each participant of a group 'sees' the group as a whole.

The model

If there are tensions at the heart of a group, it is highly probable that the group will not actually manage to construct a single model which is acceptable to all its members. It may even be that the mere presentation of different models gives rise to a visual discussion of the differences which exist in the group. The simple search for one model can already be in itself a reflection of what problems there are, and a pointer to the possible solutions.

If the construction of a single model is achievable, it is usually done in stages. Thus the joker, in continual consultation with the group, adds or takes away elements of the image which the group considers to be essential or superfluous respectively.

The dynamisation

Once the model has been agreed on, and assuming that it contains some or other kind of oppression, the dynamisation goes through the following stages.

The joker reminds everyone that *the whole group is by necessity part of the image.*Those who are outside the image which has been constructed are still part of the general image of the group; even if they are 'happy watching', they are part of the overall image and are taking on the roles of people who are 'happy watching'. Within the room a single, general image has formed, structuring and organising itself, in which everyone is a participant. But this overall image has a nucleus: the image that the group agreed on. So the joker asks those who are happy and have no problem with being in the nucleus, to stay where they are, in that position; and those who are there against their will, those who are unhappy, dissatisfied with their positions, are asked to leave the nucleus and join the 'spectators'. The joker also suggests that those in the watching group who feel uncomfortable or unhappy in their spectator positions enter into the nucleus if they want. Or they can also leave the room.

After these movements, the joker asks the participants once more to come out of the image and go back in, but this time positioning themselves as they wish and not in the manner which was imposed on them. At this level, objectively, everyone should assume the pose, play the role, make the image which *corresponds exactly to the image each of them desires and is capable of realising*, in an ensemble of people as *subjects*, where each person has their own personality, and their own desires. The final image obtained in this way will reveal the existence or non-existence of the possibility of harmonious functioning of the actual participants of a group.

At Dijon I was invited by two groups which were in conflict. My position proved very delicate – how could I pursue my work without exacerbating the crisis or hardening the divisions? The task was not to form a permanent group, but to do a five-day course, to live and work together for a certain period of time, in pursuit of common objectives.

We made the image of the group, which, as a whole, was agreed on. At the centre, one character was trying to catalyse, to dynamise, to stimulate the rest; some people were paying full attention to him, others less so, still others were not concentrating at all. Some people were turning towards others with threatening looks. All in all, the central figure, in spite of all his efforts, was failing to magically expunge all these latent conflicts, the exact causes of which he did not know.

Once the image had been composed, I attacked the dynamisation. In the first stage many people abandoned the central image and stayed outside (even though there was no 'outside'), watching. In the second stage, they had to choose: either leave the room altogether, that is, go and abandon the course midway through, or else stay. If they stayed, it was obvious that they could no longer maintain the marginal position they had adopted. They understood that no one could stay *outside*; that those who had not been used in the central image were just as implicated as those who had taken part in it. Slowly, those who had retired came back. They took up different positions from the ones they had been placed in, while gradually getting a little closer to the central image. After a few minutes, they had all established links with the central figure. Nobody left the room. I waited a bit, then asked the young man who was representing the catalysing person to rejoin the others. Then *I* put myself in his place and announced: 'The seventh technique – the ritual gesture.'

Which brings us to the next technique.

7 Ritual gesture

When two soldiers meet, they look at each other and salute. *Looking at* each other, mechanically and without thought, they make *the ritual gesture* of the military salute. We, who are not soldiers, *look at* and *see* one another. At the same repeated stimulus, the soldiers answer mechanically. They do not hesitate, they have no doubts, they do not try to imagine new ways of saluting; the one gesture invites another such gesture by way of response.

When tourists enter a church, their speech level drops to low volume (with the exception of North Americans). When a teacher enters the classroom, whether or not she says anything, even if her mind is on other things, the pupils get ready to take notes. The *ritual sign* of the teacher entering the room, always in the same manner (giving rise to the belief that her intentions are always the same), always provokes the same reactions.

Every society has its rituals, and consequently its ritual gestures and signs. This technique tries to uncover them. The point of uncovering each society's rituals is that they are the *visual expressions* of the oppressions to be found at the heart of a society. Always, without exception, an oppression will produce visible signs, always it will translate itself into forms and movements, always it will leave traces. Just as it is possible to discover and discuss social oppressions in spoken discourse, one can also achieve this end using image techniques.

In the same way as soldiers, tourists and pupils respond mechanically to known stimuli, whatever our profession or social class, we all of us do the same. Which brings us back to the premiss that in all professions, in all social classes, there exist rituals particular to those classes and professions. It is up to us to discover them, to bring them to light and study them.

Social code, ritual and rite

All societies establish norms of behaviour acceptable to all. One cannot indefinitely sustain any form of behaviour which is original in relation to the norm. All societies have systems of social regulation, which bear on everything from relations between parent and child, man and woman, neighbours, work- and play-mates, to acceptable ways of sitting on the ground or travelling on the underground. It is not possible for us to spend our lives in constant apprehension of others, continually inventing what to do in situations we are already acquainted with. In a familiar situation, we respond with a familiar action, we give the expected responses. For instance, when a customer enters a restaurant, the waiter expects him to go and sit on a chair in front of a table. If he is accompanied by a woman, the customer may also be expected to help her into her seat. Why? Absolutely none of this is *necessary*. The man might perfectly well prefer to sit on the table with his feet on the chair, and I see no special reason why he should help his female companion to her seat, and not the other way round. But a social code exists which inhibits the couple from sitting on the floor and picnicking in a restaurant (unless of course it is a Japanese restaurant, in which case the reverse scenario operates!).

The *social code* is what dictates the norms of conduct. I have a friend, for example, who likes to invert the social code .... He does this for fun, by way of pastime, but what alarm and disquiet his behaviour can provoke! And yet all he does is invert the order dictated by the social code, without actually altering it at all in its essentials.

So what does he do? He goes into a restaurant, sits at a table, studies the menu long and hard, asks the waiter a few questions about each dish and finally comes to a decision: 'I'd like a coffee.'

The waiter protests, says that this is not possible, that it is lunchtime and that one cannot sit at a table and just order a coffee, that his function is to serve lunch, if you want coffee you can have it standing at the bar counter, etc. My friend says that he has indeed come for lunch, but would prefer to start with the coffee. What usually happens is that the waiter consults with the proprietor, the other customers wonder about my friend's mental health, and eventually, to avoid complications, the waiter brings the coffee, hoping that my friend will depart as quickly as possible. But when he has finished his coffee, my friend then inquires as to what the waiter has by way of dessert ...

Shock piled on shock ... this man eats his lunch ... backwards! And sure enough, he ends up with an aperitif.

And that's all he does. But it's enough. Enough to disorientate the restaurant's whole system of operation: even the chef has to come out and take a look at this phenomenon. And yet my friend is *changing nothing* in the social code, all he is doing is inverting it.

I used to have another friend, a Brazilian, who, also for fun, loved *to make extrapolations* of social codes. For example, there are many forms of merchandise which can be bought on credit or paid for in instalments. Thus he used to try to apply the same principle to other things. He would go to the cinema and offer to pay for his ticket in small monthly instalments. When greeted with refusal, he would suggest a novel variation: he would pay 60 per cent of the cost of a ticket, go in and see that percentage of the film, and then leave – and when he had the rest of the money he would come back and pay for and watch the remainder of the film ...

If, however, a social code is absolutely necessary and indispensable (a society without any form of social code would be unthinkable), then equally it cannot avoid being to some extent authoritarian.

When a social code does not answer the needs and desires of the people to whom it is addressed, and thus those people see themselves as forced to do things which run counter to their desires, or obliged to abstain from doing things which they want to do, then we can say that the social code has turned into a *ritual*. A ritual is therefore a code which imprisons, which constrains, which is authoritarian, *useless*, or, at worst, necessary *as the vehicle for some form of oppression.*

To give an example which is a good illustration of the difference between the two terms, let us cite an actor, in love with the role of Hamlet, who performs this part every evening with the greatest possible passion and enthusiasm, with huge pleasure and joy. Every day he repeats the same words, every day he does the same move-ments – as if in joyful obeisance to a *theatrical code*, to which the other actors are paying equal homage. And the show is done one, two, maybe three hundred times. Our actor is tired. He comes to the theatre every evening, but he no longer shows the same interest. Every evening he repeats the same words, he executes the same movements, but devoid of life, emptied of passion. Our actor has become mechanised and for him the show has turned into a veritable *ritual*, joylessly to be repeated night after night.

This is what happens in our lives. How many things do we do in obedience to a ritual? How many things do we do, or not do, simply because we haven't the courage to break with an established ritual?

Finally, what do we mean by the word *rite*? A rite is when the whole *social code*, in concert with the *ritual*, draws people into a single group. The *rite* preordains the nature of the public event, and consequently the gulf between *actors* and *spectators*. A rite can be, for example, a mass, the opening of a bank, a military parade ... ritual events which become spectacles.

For us, it is important to separate these concepts, which correspond, in our opinion, to precise moments and particular forms of social interrelation.

The model

The joker asks someone to come into the middle and make a *ritual gesture*, that is, an action which belongs to a ritualised social structure. The rest of the group observe the gesture. When anyone thinks he has worked out which ritual it belongs to, he goes into the middle and 'completes' this gesture with another, equally ritualised. A second person, then a third, then all those who think they've understood the initial gesture, as well as the modified – completed – gesture, also go into the middle and together form a large static image of the ritual suggested by the first gesture.

Obviously the other participants will only be able to understand and complete ritual gestures which belong to a particular society, culture, or historical moment. Sometimes such gestures will be incomprehensible except to a few 'victims'. An example: when doing this exercise in Paris, I frequently see, say, an Arab, a black person, or someone 'different from the norm', copying the gesture of the police officer who bends forward with an outstretched hand. Other Arabs and black people immediately understand and complete the action; it's a policeman asking for identity papers in the Métro or in the street – something which generally happens only to Arabs, black people and 'different' people. This very gesture (the half-bow with outstretched hand) is, however, seen by everybody, every day. But it only makes an impression on those to whom it is directed, those who are oppressed by this gesture.

The same gesture made in other towns, where the persecution of 'different' people is not so acute, will produce no reaction and the participants will not complete it, for they won't understand it.

Completing the ritual gesture is in itself revealing. Take, for example, the ritual gestures of a male customer in a restaurant. He reads the menu, he calls the waiter. The person who comes into the image and sits beside him will reveal their own thoughts; for instance, if it is a woman, how does she carry herself? Like a 'dolly-bird' or like a partner? Is the waiter servile or does he try to maintain his dignity, without lowering himself? Who sits next to them? How do they eat? What are their expressions? Are they alone or in a group? What is the cashier's attitude? Are there other waiters? Are they all equal or is there a hierarchy?

Another *ritual gesture* frequently seen in Europe in this technique is that of the woman, in anger or exasperation, counting how many pills she has left. The 'complementary' action is also revealing. When the man slips into the bed what does he do? Is he worried or tired? Does he read the paper or get dressed again? Does he sleep? Does he go over to the far side of the bed? Does he snore? Does he smile? Does he care? The current state of relations between 'couples' leaps out at one when using this technique.

The dynamisation

This is the same as the dynamisation in the second technique: rhythm, words, movement.

At a sign from the joker, all the members of the single complex image which has been created with the *ritual gesture* as the starting point must make a rhythmic movement suggested by the position they are in. The rhythm enhances our understanding of the image.

At a second signal, all at the same time, the participants say and repeat the same phrase several times. Then the joker interrupts the game and asks each of the participants individually to repeat their phrase, which must belong to the *character* represented in the image and not to the *person* who is performing it. Frequently at this stage, one notices that the original *ritual gesture* has been misinterpreted. In such a case the performers are uttering phrases which have nothing to do with the overall image. But even in this case the image can be revealing: why was it misunderstood? What ambiguity was there in the ritual gesture, such that it could have been misunderstood?

Artistic *error* is completely unlike scientific *error*; an error in a mathematical calculation invalidates the result – in art it can enhance the result. All outcomes, whether intended or not, should be analysed, and lessons should be drawn from them.

Another signal. Each participant starts a movement prolonging the movement implicit in the model. In other words, each person proceeds as if the static image (the model) was a freeze-frame in a film, which now starts running. It is at this moment that the *ritual gesture* is transformed into *ritual*: movements, actions, words, gestures, etc., mechanised, predetermined. A ritual is a system of expected, pre-determined actions and reactions.

8 Ritual

This is a simple and effective technique which is extremely revealing. The construction of the model is already a dynamisation: its own dynamisation. Here is a concrete example.

This took place in Sweden, at Norrköping, during a discussion on the choice of subject-matter. A young woman suggested 'the oppression of women'. Most people went along with this idea, but one woman strongly took issue:

'Why talk about the oppression of women when it doesn't exist here in Sweden? Just because it's the fashion? If the Theatre of the Oppressed is the theatre of the first person plural, if we are supposed to be talking about *us*, then we won't be doing Theatre of the Oppressed because we will be talking about oppressions which don't concern us! By all means, in most countries women are oppressed, like they are in Africa, in Sudan where they even practise infibulation; by all means, women are oppressed even in industrially developed nations like France .... But here in Sweden, we are on an equal par with men, we have the same rights, exactly the same.'

She was so vehement that I was almost convinced. I asked: 'In Sweden do women get the same wage as men for doing the same kind of work?'

She hesitated: 'Well ... not exactly. It works like this: in France *women* earn *less* than men for the same type of work. Here in Sweden, it's different, here *men* earn a little bit *more* than we do ....' Honestly, she did not see her oppression. So then I used the technique of constructing a *ritual*.

I asked for six volunteers, three men and three women. I asked them to construct a model of a flat which could be used by the six. Living room, kitchen, television, bedroom, beds, furniture, WC, etc., to be set out however they liked, to reproduce a typical flat.

187

Then I got them all to go out, except for the first woman. Then I asked her to show me quickly all the movements and gestures she would do ritually from the moment she came home from her work to the moment she went to bed. These gestures and movements had to be done in a demonstrative and non-realistic fashion; that is, they should show, for instance, that she ate and then go on to the next action without going into the details. The whole thing, from her arrival home to her bedtime, had to last three or four minutes; if the time is cut down further than that, the material is not sufficiently revealing.

The first woman suggested the following sequence.

1 She comes in with her bags of shopping.
2 She goes into the kitchen and puts away her purchases.
3 She prepares the meal.
4 She serves it up.
5 She eats in the company of imaginary people (husband, children, etc.).
6 She clears the table and goes back to the kitchen to do the washing-up.
7 She feeds the dog and puts the cat out.
8 She waters the plants.
9 She goes to bed.

The second and third women introduced few changes. They repeated the actions involving the shopping, the fridge, getting the meal ready, laying the table, the washing-up; sometimes they inverted the order of dog and cat, or added duties to do with the children; they might include one or two phone calls from friends; nothing else.

Such was the woman's ritual.

Then it was the men's turn. The first offered the following sequence.

1 He comes in, newspaper in hand.
2 He takes off his shoes and leaves them at the door.
3 He goes to the kitchen to get a glass of whisky (the other two varied this a bit, instead of whisky they went to get a beer or a sandwich . . .).
4 He sits down in front of the television.
5 He goes to the table and eats the meal which magnificently awaits him.

6 He yawns.

7 He gets up, goes to the toilet, then to his room and sleeps like a log!

Such was the man's ritual.

The woman who had said that oppression of her sex did not exist continued to *watch* without *seeing* anything!

'So? Is there oppression or not?' I asked her.

'Why?' she answered.

So then I did a second dynamisation. I asked the six participants to return to the 'flat', and to do the movements they had previously done, but this time all together. They simply had to accelerate the movement, do everything at high speed, as if they were in one of those silent films where everyone seems to be running.

So this was done; the six entered, ran around, repeated the actions they did the first time round. The three women headed for the kitchen, the three men for the television; the three women laid the table; the three men ate and savoured their food; all three women did the washing-up, all three men yawned and went to lie down. All three women continued doing their tasks, dealing with dogs, cats and children, while the men were snoring in their beds...

It was only at this point that the woman finally got to *see* what she had been *watching* without understanding.

Ritual is one form of approach to Forum Theatre, to the theatrical presentation of the Forum Theatre model, an approach to the *staging*, the *setting* of the play.

Ritual is one of the forms (among others) which create the theatrical conditions to ensure that Forum Theatre is *theatre* first and foremost, and not solely *forum*. Very often the ritual contains elements which are causes of the oppression being treated, and, frequently, liberation from the oppression by necessity involves the rupture of its rituals.

Here is another example. A young woman of 25. Her father is an industrialist. He wants to make her go travelling, leave Paris for a year or two, because she is in love with someone whom the father doesn't like (yes, these things still happen today, even in Paris). The father receives the woman in his place of work; he is seated behind a huge 6-foot-wide desk, covered with telephones, books, files, while the 'client' (in the present case the girl) is 2 metres away on a plain little chair. *The ritual* of welcoming the client; the girl comes in, is received by the father's secretary, and then, sitting alone in a corner, disarmed in the face of the imposing telephones, she has to listen to long diatribes from him!

We did a forum on the scene, and all the women spect-actors who came forward were forced to give in – against such a father, it was impossible to do anything, they thought. Until finally a woman spect-actor came up and refused to sit on the chair; she advanced into the room and sat on her father's desk . . . . The ritual broke down. In the chair/desk relationship, there was a terrible paternal oppression. In the relationship of a young girl seated on the desk and disconcerted father seated behind his desk, the father's medieval ideas had no hold on the girl; the father was obliged to look up at his daughter, and his paternal authority could not be maintained in this ridiculous position . . . .

I remember a Chaplin film where Hitler receives Mussolini seated on a little chair, much smaller and lower than his own . . . Visual relationships, image relationships, are also power relationships.

In the setting of a Forum Theatre model, ritual performs a function of enormous importance. But it also serves as an analysis of a given situation. The important thing is always to look for the ritual that reveals the oppression; the ritual of arrival at work, the ritual of the young man and woman in a bar or back at a flat belonging to one of them, the mother's birthday ritual, the police inspector's visit ritual, the ritual of the son asking his father for money, the ritual of the penitent in confession asking forgiveness, etc.

9 Rituals and masks

Rituals determine their masks: *the habit makes the monk!* People doing the same jobs take on the masks prescribed by these jobs; they act in similar ways in the face of the same event, assuming the mask this action gives rise to. Whether trader, labourer, student, actor or whatever, all specialists end up assuming the mask of their speciality.

And we who look on, very often, almost always, we can be *looking without seeing*. Everything seems natural to us, because we are used to watching the same things in the same way. However, it is sometimes enough to change the masks within a particular ritual for its monstrosity to become apparent.

In this technique, described in more detail under 'Games of mask and ritual' elsewhere in this book (pp. 139–48), the same ritual is retained but the young man and the young woman swap masks; the penitent swaps with the confessor, the father with his child, the teacher with her pupil, the worker with the boss, etc.

Equally, one can keep the ritual and change the motivations; or analyse the masks by multiplying the rituals in which the character is participating, so that he can be simultaneously father, child, worker, husband, etc., and thus study all his relations with others.

To sum up, the idea is to dismantle social masks and rituals. During this process, one can lay bare all the oppressive relationships which emerge, and one can study the character of the oppressed/oppressor relationship, that most common of patterns, from a distance, in a social context.

New Image Theatre techniques

Recently* we have been working on certain new Image Theatre techniques, particularly within the framework of an ongoing work-shop called 'The cop in the head'. We set out from the premiss that the oppressions suffered by the citizens of authoritarian societies (such as we are all familiar with) can profoundly damage them. Authoritarianism penetrates even into the individual's unconscious. The cop leaves the barracks (the moral, ideological barracks) and moves into one's head. It is not in the least surprising that in certain extremely repressive and oppressive societies one does not see battalions of armed police and soldiers in the streets, as one does in Chile, Argentina, El Salvador, Guatemala, etc.; they are not necessary – we carry them within us, they are our 'cops in the head'.

These techniques are used mainly to help us understand the true nature of the cop. We are theatre artists, not therapists. Our approach can be explained in the following way: someone recounts a personal experience, where he or she has felt oppressed. This is his or her *particular* case. Instead of investigating the *singularities* of this particular case, we try, using the participation of others, to go from the particular to the *general*, by which we mean the *universality* of particular cases within the same category.

When a person tells us their particular case, using theatre as the medium of expression, it is the group that becomes the protagonist of the session, and not the individual who told the story. If we are

---

* Since the time of writing, this work has been considerably developed, and is the subject of a new book by Boal, *Méthode Boal de théâtre et de thérapie – l'arc-en-ciel du désir* ('The Boal method of theatre and therapy – the rainbow of desires') Paris: Editions Ramsay, 1990. The very title suggests that Boal has moved some distance in his thoughts on therapy in the past few years. *A.J.*

able to perceive within ourselves those oppressive elements present in the particular case recounted to us, we may then be able to perceive the 'cop' in our heads, with the hope of ascertaining how it got in and which 'barracks' it came from.

As with the rest of the Theatre of the Oppressed, these techniques have two main goals: to enhance our ability to know or recognise a given situation, and to help us to rehearse actions which can lead to the breaking of the oppression shown in that situation. *To know and to transform* – that is our goal. To transform something one must know it first. Knowing is already a transformation – a transformation which supplies the means to accomplish the other transformation.

The techniques can also be used in the preparation of a Forum Theatre piece, or in the preparation of any production.

The cop in the head techniques

1 Dissociation – thought, speech, action

Someone gives an image of her oppression. This image can be realistic, symbolic, surrealistic ... whatever; the important thing is that for that person, the image speaks. She can use the bodies of other participants, two, three, four, as many as necessary; equally she can use objects – chairs, tables, sheets, mattresses, pens, paper, anything to hand.

Dynamisation

(1) Over five minutes (which is a long time), all the people in the image must voice their *interior monologues*, at low volume and without stopping. Everything that comes to mind, as *characters*, not as *individuals*, in other words, everything that that body, in that position, could think. The body thinks. There can be a contradiction between the person playing an image and the image he is playing – the idea is to think what the image thinks. For example: if I am put in an image where I am trying to strangle someone, I must express all the thoughts of the person trying to strangle someone, even if I personally am incapable of such an action.

The only rules are that people must not stop the murmured delivery of their thoughts and they must not move, everyone must stay frozen in their positions.

The participants should try not to listen to what others are saying.

In this way, each person starts to descend deep into the *interior monologue* of their character, to root the character in themselves, to bring out all the thoughts which could belong to that character, who, for the moment, is no more than a body thinking out loud (quietly).

(2) In the frozen image, the participants must talk to each other for another five minutes. Interior monologue gives way to *dialogue*. Internal roots give way to social structure. People speak to each other, but no one moves; there will sometimes be a considerable disparity between what people say and the positions they are holding while saying it. There can also be a discrepancy between the monologue and the dialogue, between what people were thinking and what they end up saying. These are alternatives.

(3) Now, without speaking, you put into *action* everything you have thought (monologue) and everything you have said (dialogue). Movements should be done in slow motion, to allow each individual continually to take stock, to think, to change her mind, to hesitate, to have second thoughts, to choose between several alternatives. Extreme slow motion.

2 The analytical image: the multiple mirror of how others see us

The starting point is a scene. One person rehearses, with partners of his choice, a scene of his oppression (an actual, existing oppression, an oppression which is still a source of discomfort, something he would like to change, to transform, but has not yet managed to – a better knowledge of the oppressive situation is required in order to be able to change it). The actors in the scene play it in front of the rest of the group.

The audience group should be seated and relaxed, and should allow their bodies small movements, so as to let themselves be impregnated, whether by the image of the protagonist or that of the main antagonist, or anyone else in the scene (if there are others).

After the scene, any member of the watching group who wants to can come on to the stage and make one image with her own body: how she saw the protagonist or antagonist or other character. This image is not meant to be realistic – one shows what one has felt and how one felt it.

This image should be *analytical* – in other words each participant (active observer, spect-actor rather than spectator) who watched the original scene should lift a detail from it, something which perhaps escaped the notice of others. This detail will be magnified, enlarged in her image – other details, which were for her less important or striking, will not appear in the image she shows. It is an analytical image because each image is the analysis of a single element which previously existed intermingled with many others, dissolved and perhaps disguised. The analytical image reveals this element, brings it into the open, into the full light of day. Normally the protagonist himself is amazed, even if he recognises the hidden element suddenly revealed; which is why it is important to do away with all that is unremarkable to his eyes.

The group should do several analytical images, it should *break down* the original image shown by the protagonist.

With all these images on stage, we already have the model; we have broken down and analysed the scene we started with. We now have on stage several analytical images, some of the protagonist, some of the antagonist(s). This is already an achievement, we could stop there. But now we move on to the dynamisation of the images.

Possible dynamisations

(1) All the images together. The protagonist has the opportunity to see himself in a 'multiple mirror', as seen by the group.

(2) The original actor takes the place of one image of the antagonist and plays the scene against another image of the protagonist (which he has chosen). He can do it several times, each time choosing a different image of the antagonist to replace to 'experience' the fight against an image of the protagonist (i.e. himself). The participants play the image (playing the character of that image, not the people they are themselves).

(3) The other way round – the original actor takes the place of an image of himself (protagonist) and enters into dialogue (plays) either with a single image of the antagonist, or with all the antagonist images at the same time; in the latter case, since all the antagonist images are no more than the analysis of a single character, so each actor playing an antagonist image should behave as if he was simply part of a whole, a whole made up of all the antagonist images on the stage – thus anything said by one person-image is the responsibility of everyone else playing the same character.

(4) All the images together, both those of the protagonist and those of the antagonist(s), engage in simultaneous dialogue, all joining battle at the same time.

(5) The affective magnet: this dynamisation is very delicate.

Having made all the possible images, each image must seek 'its complement', the emotional negative for its positive, or vice versa. The expression 'its complement' is deliberately ambiguous. What is 'its complement'? Each actor (in each image) must try to sense what this complement is, and it won't be the same for everyone; a powerful element of subjectivity intervenes.

It can happen that two images of the antagonist (for instance) choose as their complement the same image of the protagonist. It is up to the actor playing the protagonist-image to choose between the two of them. The one who does not get chosen must go and find another complement.

When couples have been formed, each couple comes back on to the stage on their own and plays the original scene as they remember it, whilst keeping the same image throughout. The image can move in the scene, but without changing its essential nature: if the image is that of a seated man, then it is vital that he remain seated throughout the scene, even if this entails moving around with his chair. If the image is a woman hiding under a table, she must always remain in hiding, though she may move with the table.

The script the actors speak should be the script they remember, as they remember it. Even mistakes, mishearings or misunderstandings, will contribute to a better understanding of the original scene, *as it was experienced by the group* – that particular group, on that particular day.

Each couple must play the same scene, each in their own way, with their recollection of it, while remaining in their images.

(6) Incorporation. This last is a very long dynamisation and one which, if it is to yield results, must be very meticulously executed.

Members of the group make images, but only of the protagonist. These images are multiplied. The antagonists stay on stage in their original incarnations; in other words the same actors who played the scene at the start. A number of images of the protagonist, together. The original protagonist has the right to veto an image if he does not recognise it in himself, unless the other members of the group consider that the rejected image is actually accurate.

The dynamisation begins when the original actor replaces the first of these images he himself has aroused; he moulds himself into that image and when the actor who made the image is happy with the likeness, she goes off. The protagonist, all the while keeping the image he has assumed, plays the scene, or a significant part of the scene, in this position. Then he takes up the exact position of the second image, down to the smallest detail, and replays the scene. Then the same process with all the other images, one after another.

While he is playing he can choose what to do with the image he has at that particular moment. We know that analytical images reveal either 'subversive' or 'submissive' aspects of the protagonist. If the protagonist thinks that the analytical image is one of subversion, he must attempt during the course of the scene to reinforce this character, to develop it. If he thinks that the image is one of submission, in the course of the scene he must shake it off, that is, metamorphose into the opposite of the image as it was when he first took it on. He must end the scene as far as possible from the scene which was the starting point of the exercise. This transformation should be slow, in slow motion, as if the actor was breaking out of a shell, a mask, a suit of armour, to take on the image he desires.

The process of incorporation can thus be a process of rejection. One rejects the unwanted stance of submission, which is impeding the desired action, one eliminates all that, at the same time as reinforcing all the dynamic characteristics, which can help dispose of the oppression present in the original scene.

3 Somatisation

The original scene is played, and then replayed without physical self-censorship; the feelings the script engenders in each character are shown corporeally. The idea is not to illustrate, rather to let come whatever comes.

This is also a dislocation; the text must be the same the first and second times – it should not be altered. But the second time, the physical presentation should correspond mainly to the interior monologue and not to the dialogue.

4 The circuit of rituals

The protagonist makes images of rituals which he goes through in real life; these images are frozen at first, then dynamised with the protagonist present in them. On his exit from the image it freezes again; the other actors stay in position, in the same image, now lacking one figure, that of the protagonist. In each image there will always be one figure lacking – that of the protagonist who looks from a distance at all the rituals in his daily life, especially those linked to the oppression he wishes to speak about.

Dynamisation

The protagonist goes from one ritual to another. Each time he enters into a ritual, the scene comes alive, the actors play. When he leaves, the scene stops.

In each ritual he will inevitably take on the mask which belongs to that ritual. The joker tells him where to go, moves him from one ritual to another, and another, and another, backwards and forwards, in such a way as to be able to study the moments when a mask which might be suitable for one ritual is used by the protagonist in a different ritual. Thus a protagonist will show different rituals, in which he might play the mask of father, teacher, son, boss, lover, spouse, etc. By means of this game of rituals one can pinpoint the moments when, for example, while playing the ritual of lover the protagonist is wearing the mask of boss, or when playing the ritual of spouse he is wearing the mask of son, etc.

5 *The three wishes*

The model: the protagonist shows an image of oppression as it is.

Dynamisation

(1) The protagonist has the right to three wishes (and, subsequently, as many wishes as necessary). She has the right to modify the image three times (and more ...). She is to carry out these wishes in her own order of importance.

Each person she intends to change should offer as much resistance as will challenge the protagonist's power and ability just up to their limits, without overstepping these limits (see the exercise 'Pushing against each other' on p. 65). A resistance which the protagonist will be able to overcome, but not too easily; she should have to use all her strength, and in the act of doing this, she will develop other strengths.

(2) The group analyses what she did first, second, third, etc.; alternatives are suggested.

(3) Try to bring the scene to life (with the actors playing their characters and not themselves), with dialogue and physical actions.

197

6 *The polyvalent image*

The model: an actor models an image of his oppression.

Dynamisation

Each person in the image tries to feel what the image says to him, without worrying about coherence; for the person who made the image, a woman can represent his mother, while the woman in this role can take herself for the Queen of Sheba. They are both right.

When the image is dynamised, everyone should behave as the character they think they are; in this way, completely different styles, epochs and symbols are juxtaposed and mixed up, which can give rise to a non-realist perspective, through which the protagonist can better understand his situation, his oppression.

It is sometimes very difficult to hold it all together, because the progress of the scene can seem too incoherent. But if you persevere, a deep internal coherence can be found, in spite of (or precisely because of) the external incoherence. You have to go beyond the stage where coherence is confused with banality, with commonplaces, stereotypes and clichés – you must look for profound coherence, inside the characters, concealed coherence.

7 *The screen image*

The model: the protagonist constructs an image of her oppression, without worrying about making it comprehensible. It can be symbolic, it can be whatever the protagonist wants.

Dynamisation

This dynamic image is played a number of times. Each time, each participant has the right to replace the oppressed character and, within the dynamic of the image, try to break the oppression she has seen. Each participant should project her own experiences on to the image she has seen, without trying to understand what she has seen. What matters is that she be able to project her own oppressions on to that screen.

Examples

'Four people walking, the fifth person dancing' Four people are walking in step, almost in a military manner; a fifth person prefers to waltz. The four people throw her to the ground. She stands up again, repentant, and joins in with the others. Now five people are marching. What does this say to you? Project whatever you want on to this dynamic image and try to avoid joining in with the four. What would you do in the protagonist's place? Fifteen, twenty answers may emerge, maybe even more. And that is precisely the objective of the Theatre of the Oppressed: to show that there are always ways of breaking oppressions, in all situations.

'Bigger and bigger obstacles' Three obstacles: a chair lying on the floor, a chair standing upright, three chairs on top of each other. Three actors at the far end, watching. The protagonist looks at the first obstacle. A man helps him to surmount it. The protagonist looks at the second obstacle. The man comes and helps him surmount it. The protagonist looks at the third obstacle; the man comes and urges him to sort this one out on his own. The protagonist is disappointed – he could have got over the first two obstacles (for which he had assistance), but not the third, for which he has no assistance. What would you do in his place?

'It's too late' Three tables: one close to the protagonist, one halfway across the room, the other far away. The protagonist runs quickly over to the far table. A person seated behind the table stands up, saying: 'It's too late.' The protagonist goes back to the start, a little saddened, and starts out again, less fast this time, in the direction of the middle table, the seated occupant of which stands and says: 'It's too late.' Completely demoralised, the protagonist goes back to the start and, this time walking rather than running, she slowly goes over to the most accessible table, the nearest one. However, when she finally gets there, the person there draws himself up and says the same thing: 'It's too late.' What would you do in her place?

In this technique it is particularly important not to 'explain' what the image 'means'. It means exactly what it says to each individual and each individual will project on to it what she feels and, in participating, will break her own oppression. The image is no more than an empty structure which one fills according to one's own personal

199

life and experiences. However, for information, I can say that the three people who constructed these images were:

1 a cashier in a bank – she wanted to break the oppression of her work, to change, to escape;
2 a boy who felt that his teachers gave him lots of help when he was in school, when he had the strength to overcome obstacles on his own – but when it came to trying to get a job, no one was there to help him;
3 a girl who was so afraid of everything that she always arrived late; she did the impossible so as not to be on time.

But the origin of these images is not important – what is important is that they can awaken in the group lived experiences. The oppression is pluralised in the multiplicity of the interventions.

8 The image of the image

The best way to explain this technique is by citing an example. A woman called Martine played a scene telling of an episode in her life, involving two men who wouldn't leave her alone. She wants to escape them, they come back, she hasn't the strength to get rid of them. They keep coming back. And she hasn't the strength, or the will, to get rid of them.

We could have played the scene as a forum, replacing Martine and trying possible solutions. Instead, we used the *image of the image* technique. The group was asked to make an image to reflect how the group had experienced the dynamic images which Martine had shown us.

The group made an image: Martine on all fours, the two men sitting on her back.

This image needed to be dynamised. The protagonist was asked to dispose of the oppression in this image (not in the image she had shown us before). In the act of trying to free herself in this image (of the original image) she repeated, in movement, in visual terms, the same stances we had seen in the story told at the beginning. She shook off the two men, and then went back on to all fours; of course the men came back and sat on her.

The image of the image allows us to dispose of certain elements present in the initial story which can get in the way of our understanding. The image of the image creates *metaxis**; Martine played with an image we had created, purified of all material which seemed to us extraneous, and not with the image she had presented to us. But the same person is playing both scenes, and, as long as the image created by the group contains, transubstantiated, the same oppression, then, in trying to break the oppression in this image (of her image), the protagonist will become stronger, will train to break the oppression in her reality. By realising that she had voluntarily chosen to reposition herself on all fours, the actor could become more self-aware, a knowledge of herself which could be a source of strength.

GENERAL REHEARSAL EXERCISES

Exercises with or without script

1 Improvisation

This is the classic exercise which consists of improvising a scene starting from a few basic elements. The participants must believe in and accept whatever facts others may introduce during the course of the improvisation. They must try to complete the improvisation using the new elements invented by their colleagues. It is forbidden to reject any invention. In order to prevent the improvisation dwindling into emotional stasis, to keep it dynamic, it is vital that the actors engage their 'motors'; by 'motor' I mean a *dominant will* (resulting from a struggle between – at the very least – one will and one counter-will) which has the capacity to produce an internal, subjective conflict. It is vital that this dominant will collides with the dominant wills of the other participants, in such a way as to form an external, objective conflict. Finally, it is vital that this conflictual system evolves both quantitatively and qualitatively. It is not enough for a character to hate himself continually and with a rising momentum – he must also change this hatred into blame, or love, or whatever is appropriate. Simple variation of quantity is much less theatrical than the same accompanied by a genuine qualitative variation.

A distinction must also be made between will (which can be the result of psychological whim) and social need. The wills which

---

* *Metaxis*: belonging to two worlds at the same time, the world of reality and the world of fiction.

concern matters of work tend to be those which express, in the domain of individual psychology, a social need. Will is need. Also interesting is the will which runs counter to a need: 'I want (to do) something, but I mustn't.'

Themes for improvisation, particularly when working with popular theatre groups, should be taken from newspaper reports, in order to facilitate ideological and political discussions. This allows the placing of individual problems within a larger context of social, political and economic reality.

An example of an improvisation of this kind (mimed or spoken): 'The Badly Brought Up Monkey'. This is based on a true story (and there are documents to prove it). It was taken from a newspaper story, a method we used often at the Arena Theatre, in order to show that theatre was not aloof, that we could improvise with everyday material. The aim of this kind of improvisation was not to alter the essential elements of the story's development, but to breathe life into bare printed facts, to investigate the characters behind this item of news, to give it a human face. The story went as follows.

A high-ranking army officer is out walking with his worthy wife, their children and their faithful servant. They decide to go to the zoo.

They walk up and down in front of the animals' cages, and their faces show what they are looking at – elephant, lion, crocodile, zebra, birds, fish, rhinoceros, camel, etc.

They have great fun in front of the monkey cage, watching the animals play. Suddenly, high drama – a monkey quite shamelessly starts masturbating in front of the high-ranking officer's worthy lady wife, their worthy children and the faithful family servant. Moral panic. Indecision. Shame. What should he do?

The worthy officer gets out his revolver and shoots (worthily) at the monkey, which immediately dies. Some people are outraged, others applaud. The worthy wife faints, slowly enough to be caught and helped.

The director of the zoo arrives, alerted by the sound of the shot. He feels duty-bound to press charges against the army officer for having shot the masturbating monkey. A policeman notes down the identity of the officer and everybody leaves.

At the trial, the prosecutor defends the monkey and its inalienable right to act according to instinct, and not according to human laws and conventions.

The defence lawyer alleges that the monkey violated the officer's inalienable right to amuse himself in the company of his family on a sunny Sunday afternoon. According to the defence, the monkey did not have the elementary education necessary to belong to a zoo in a civilised city such as our own, with its close links to Christian traditions. He lists the great historic names of the land, the names of scientists and men of letters, members of the Academy, etc., and even of certain exemplary animals, especially those imported from other lands, which are living proof of the advanced nature of civilisation – flamingos, parrots, etc.

The judge decides to acquit the officer, to the cheers of the assembled audience. Further, he inflicts a heavy penalty on the other monkeys in the cage, whom he considers to be accomplices of the murdered monkey, since they did nothing to stop this terrible crime of masturbation. Thus the monkeys are all sentenced to a strict course in good manners, to be strenuously administered by vets well versed in the art of castration.

Smiling and happy, with clear consciences, everyone leaves the trial. Justice has been done.

2 The dark room

In a relatively dark place, an actor sits, with his eyes closed, with a tape-recorder by his side. Another actor, or the director, starts giving him instructions which indicate where he is – in a particular street. The actor must imagine the said street and describe it in minute detail, right down to the clothes he is wearing and the faces of the passers-by. The director might, for instance, order the actor to go into a restaurant – the actor keeps talking, describing the waiters, the chairs, the customers – to sit down, and then to try to steal a briefcase belonging to a large man who is sitting quietly reading his newspaper. This is an imagination exercise which is also intended to release the actor's emotion. Having eaten rapidly and described in detail the smells and tastes of the food, he goes to the toilet, fails to steal the case, pays his bill, and runs out into the street in fear of being accused of the crime he has failed to commit. When the exercise is over, the actor listens back to what he has said and tries to re-create the action and re-live the emotions a second time over.

203

3 One story told by several people

An actor starts a story, which is continued by a second actor, then a third, and so on till the whole group has taken part. At the same time another group of actors can silently act out the story as it is told.

4 Change the story

A play tells a story, i.e. it recounts what happens. But the play also contains in itself the negation of what happens – what doesn't happen. So that the actors may be aware of all the possibilities of what could have happened (and didn't), it is worth rehearsing the scenes of what didn't happen; how the marriage of Hamlet and Ophelia would have gone, how Othello would have pardoned Desdemona, how Oedipus would have understood that it wasn't his fault and would have split up with his mother-wife on friendly terms, how a military government would have decided to liberate its people from imperialism, how the Brazilian people would have been happy under dictatorship, etc.

Imagination has no limits. It is always good for the actor to know what could have happened.

5 One line spoken by several actors

Each actor says one word of a particular line (chosen in advance), trying to give it the same inflection as it would have if the line was being spoken by a single person. To make it easier, the actor can, at the start, say the whole line in her own way, and the others try to imitate her, while each in turn only uttering a single word.

Games of emotional dynamisation

Often in the theatre we talk of 'getting into someone else's skin'. This is an artifice of language. The character, the dramatis persona,* the acting role, does not exist, one cannot get into a character's skin. What does exist is the individual, the *person*. But in every one of us the *person* is not revealed in its totality. Either from choice or as a result of social constraints, the person is reduced and becomes the

---

* The three words in French are '*personnage*' (character), '*personne*' and '*personalité*'. A.J.

204

personality. The personality is only one possible manifestation of the person. The character, the dramatis persona, is another possible manifestation. Both personality and dramatis persona emanate from the same person.

What can the actor do in order to create his character? Forget his own personality (that reduction of his person) for the moment, and plunge into the depths of the character he is playing, to seek out emotional and other elements which can assist in the construction of the character; the character being no more than one possible personality, which the actor can play in the theatre and jettison afterwards.

To help the actor delve into his own person in search of elements which will constitute the character, we suggest various exercises and games.

1 Breaking the oppression

The actor tries to remember a moment in her life where she was the object of a powerful oppression.

Here are two examples. A black actor attending New York University had to pay a visit to her family in Georgia, in the south of the USA, where the level of social oppression against black people is incredible. The young woman was used to New York where the problem is less extreme. One day in Georgia, when buying an ice-cream with her aunt in a drug-store, she was forbidden to eat alongside the other customers; she was allowed to buy the ice-cream, but she had to take it away to eat it. If black people and white people were allowed to mix here, how could they be segregated for other social activities?

In Buenos Aires, a young man remembered having been invited to a party; when his companions realised he was Jewish, they asked him to leave.

The exercise is done in three phases. In the first, the idea is to reproduce the event exactly as it happened, without adding or subtracting anything, and with an abundance of detail. Thus in this first phase of the exercise, in both cases cited, we saw the protagonists try to offer resistance, which was blocked by the other characters present in the scenes.

In the second phase of the exercise, the protagonist does not accept the oppression. We know well enough that wherever there is oppression and whatever its nature, it continues to exist because it has a hold over its victims. If humanity loved liberty more than life, there would be no oppression – the most that could be done to a person would be to kill them. We are oppressed because we tend to make concessions, to accept oppression, in return for the prolonging of our lives.

In this second phase, the scene was replayed and the young black woman did not accept her oppression and wanted to eat her ice-cream on the premises, beside the white people. Immediately the whole apparatus of oppression was turned on her, including the members of her own family. Her father said to her: 'Why do you want to eat your ice-cream here and not back at the house with us?' Her friend whispered: 'It's for your own good – come with us.' But the girl stood her ground, she had decided to stay put and not let herself be oppressed.

Similarly, in the Buenos Aires story, the young man decided to stay at the party till everyone else had gone; the party finished a little early, but there was no oppression.

In the third phase of this exercise, the actors change roles and play their opposites; the black girl played the white girl who had stopped her eating her ice-cream, and vice versa; the young Jew played the part of the person who was most determined to get rid of him, and so on.

Usually some interesting things happen in this exercise. For example, the young Jewish man in his oppressor role was better than all those who had played the part before, because he knew his oppressor very well, much better than actors who had never endured this form of oppression; when a young Catholic man played the Jew, in absolute sincerity, he put up no fight against his oppressors (one might almost have said, he did this better than the Jew himself). In fact, the young Jew was so used to this and other forms of racial oppression that he had developed a number of defence mechanisms, including cynicism; thus when he was thrown out of the party he already knew what to answer back, whereas the young Catholic – when he played the Jew – was completely defenseless, not understanding what was happening. In the second part of the exercise one of the black members of the group, playing a friend of the girl's, ran off when the sheriff threatened him with a gun; but in the third phase, a white man playing the role faced up to the sheriff. The black man explained: 'Fine, because you're white – but even in the context of an exercise we can't forget that he wouldn't have shot at you, but he would have shot at me.'

2 The oppressor's confession

In these exercises the actor who breaks the oppression always has the best part, we are on his side; he is the victim, and not the cause, of this violence. That is why in the last phase of the exercise we ask the actor to remember a moment in his life when he acted not as oppressed but as oppressor.

Emotional warm-up exercises

1 Abstract emotion

This exercise focuses on having no concrete motivation – the actors perform pure emotional gymnastics. At the beginning they are very friendly to each other, smiling and happy, trying to see everybody else's good side. In order to rule out any possibility of motivation, they cannot use words to express themselves, only numbers – 23, 8, 115, etc. Then they start to vary the quantity of this tenderness (quantitative variation), first having a higher opinion of the other people, then a lower opinion, pushing this now qualitative and quantitative variation to the point of hatred, and carrying this hatred to its ultimate level of violence. The only inviolable rules are that the physical safety of the other actors must not be threatened, and that they must not let their attention wander to focus on their own physical self-protection, but must direct all their concentration on to the emotion. Then, gradually, the actors start discovering anew the good sides of their colleagues – all the while speaking only in numbers, never words – and eventually they return to total harmony.

2 Abstract emotion with animals

A variation of the preceding exercise. The actors set out from one emotion to arrive at the opposite emotion, then return to the original emotion – but this time instead of using numbers, they make the noises of whatever animal they choose. This exercise can be done in two ways: (1) the actor acts like an animal; (2) the actor acts like a humanised version of the animal, i.e. without losing her own human characteristics. Either all the actors can imitate the same animal, or else each can imitate the animal of their choice.

3 Abstract emotion, following the master

Five actors on each side. The two facing each other in the middle are the masters of the four in the opposite line. They start a disjointed conversation on any topic using words, numbers, or sounds; the phrases need have no meaning. All the others repeat the gestures, inflections, sounds, body movements and facial expressions of their masters, while the latter must carry their emotion to the extreme, then instantly returning to calm and clarity.

4 Animals or vegetables in emotional situations!

The actor imagines herself as, for instance, a palm-tree on a beach on a summer's day; the weather starts to change, a storm approaches and is unleashed; the joy of summer gives way to the fear of seeing the tree destroyed and carried off by the waves (other actors do the wind). A young rabbit plays with its brothers and sisters, a fox comes along; the rabbit hides until the fox goes away. A fish swims along happily, till it swallows the bait.

In all these animal exercises, the noises must be very expressive, since while human beings use words and concepts to express their emotions, animals use only sounds and no language. This is what gives human self-expression a sensory poverty, in spite of its infinite richness in terms of concepts. Without losing her power to express things in conceptual terms, the actor should also give free rein to her immense sensory possibilities.

5 Ritual in which everyone becomes an animal

The actors carry out any ritual, however conventional – the opening of a bank, a mayor's speech on taking up office, a parents' wedding anniversary, etc. They improvise in dumb-show, and with words. In the course of the ritual, each actor transforms himself into an animal, and continues the ritual in the same manner.

6 Stimulation of the dormant parts of ourselves

This exercise must be done several times, always varying the 'dormant' parts being stimulated. The premise is the notion that each of us is capable of feeling, thinking and being, in ways infinitely more various than we do these things in our daily lives. One day an actor at the Arena played the role of a torturer and became aware, to his utter consternation, that he had experienced real pleasure in the act of torturing. He had never realised that he was capable of doing something so callous. Thus he understood that virtuous behaviour was the result of a free and conscious choice, and not the fruit of an incapacity for wrongdoing. A person may have the capacity for taking pleasure in torturing people, but not do it because he has chosen not to torture people. Human beings must invent themselves in the midst of an infinity of possibilities, instead of passively accepting their roles because they think they could not be other than they are.

Nothing of what is human is barred to anyone. We are all, potentially, good and evil, loving and hating, heterosexual and homosexual, cowardly and brave, etc. We are what we choose to be. The Brazilian fascists are culpable not because of their capacity for making people die of hunger, while they line their pockets, but because they have chosen to pursue this course of action.

A female actor, on discovering the infinite multiplicity of her being, exclaimed: 'Ah, how I would love to be a whore!' Her wish was not to walk the streets, but simply to feel during an exercise everything that could be felt or thought by a whore, which role existed within herself as an 'unchosen' possibility, a 'dormant' possibility. And that is exactly what the exercise consists of – stimulating those latent parts of each of us, the better to understand everything that is inherent in human beings. The actor is not asked to 'alter' her personality, only to sound out her possibilities, and by the same token, those of the characters she is going to play. I remember one actor who chose to obey and be humiliated, a role which he never accepted normally; another chose to become the kind of Nosy Parker who wants to know everything, who asks the most uncalled-for questions, such as wanting to know if such-and-such a couple who are going into a hotel are married or not, who farted, etc. – i.e. a total pain in the neck!

To encourage this total freedom of expression and stimulation of dormant traits, the exercise can be done in a surrealist fashion. The characters have a free choice of the place they are in and they can change it, making two places exist in the same space, etc. Depending on the circumstances, the exact opposite can also be done, carrying out the exercise in a totally realistic fashion.

Ideological warm-up

Theatre is an ideological representation of images of social life. It is important that actors do not become alienated from society at large, however specialised their technique may be. The actor will be presenting to the audience images of the social struggles between bourgeois forces of reaction and the progressive forces of the working classes, whatever the nature of the piece in which this struggle appears. The actor must always be aware of the progressive nature of his mission, its pedagogical and combative character. Theatre is an art and a weapon.

1 Dedication*

The Arena Theatre had a custom of dedicating shows to particular people or events. The significance of this person or event was often enough to stimulate the actor ideologically – a dead comrade, a strike, whatever.

2 Reading newspapers

The reading aloud and discussion of newspaper articles on political and social events, the demystification of the bourgeois press, the presentation of information not contained in the newspapers, by people with special knowledge.

3 The evocation of historic events

Drawing parallels between historic events and the current national situation, by careful choice of material.

4 Lessons

Depending on the nature of the group and its awareness of historical events, lessons or explanations can be a useful stimulant; for instance, explaining the theory of surplus value.

---

* This idea may now sound dated and/or obvious, but we once dedicated a show to Heleni Guariba, a friend of ours who was killed by the police. All of us had a personal relationship with Heleni. We dedicated the show to her, not just to an abstract idea of freedom but to an idea personified, a person who sacrificed her life for freedom. This form of dedication is much more powerful. A.B.

210

Exercises for the preparation of a Forum Theatre model or for the rehearsal of other kinds of theatre

1 Play to the deaf

This is the ultimate exercise for developing what we have earlier referred to as the actor's 'undercurrent'. The actor must stay absolutely faithful to the piece and its rhythm, and think all his lines, trying to bring out all that is contained in the undercurrent, *without speaking a single word or making a sound*. To make this happen he must apply all his concentration. What should be avoided at all costs is that the exercise be allowed to turn into a mime exercise; not a single gesture or movement should be added to help the other actors work out where the dialogue has got to or is heading – this is a workshop exercise, not a game, the actor must be genuinely 'transmitting' at 'undercurrent' level.

When actors do this exercise properly, the results can be sensational. It can happen that spectators come into the room during a silent rehearsal and can immediately take part in a discussion afterwards, without having felt the least sense of a lack of dialogue; as far as they are concerned, they saw some theatre.

In plays conceived according to the 'joker system' (see *The Theatre of the Oppressed*, London: Pluto Press, 1979), the 'Play to the deaf' exercise is vital to ensure that the masks do not become 'clichés', symbols, or signs; the exercise helps to 'Stanislavskify' the masks.

2 Stop! Think!

Our thoughts are in a state of continual flux – we never stop thinking. Communication between actor and audience takes place at two levels, 'wave' and 'undercurrent'. As has been remarked earlier, human beings are capable of transmitting and receiving far more than they are aware of. When two people love each other, each knows what the other is going to say before it is said. Before asking for a wage rise, the worker already knows whether the boss will give it or not. This is perception on the undercurrent level. In the same way, actors communicate to an audience on a conscious level by the words they say, the gestures they make, the movements they do, etc.; but they also communicate at the 'undercurrent' level, by means of the thoughts they 'emit'. When an actor's thoughts are not in accord

211

with his actions – i.e. when there is a clash between wave and undercurrent – the audience/receiver experiences a phenomenon similar to interference on the radio; the audience receives two contradictory messages and it is impossible to register them both. If the actor in the course of his acting thinks about something which has nothing to do with the role he is playing, his thoughts will be transmitted to the spectator just as his voice is.

In the 'Stop! Think!' exercise, at a particular moment the director/joker stops the rehearsal and shouts 'Stop! Think!'; all the actors have to start speaking in an undertone at the same time, letting loose an interior monologue of everything that is in their characters' minds at that particular moment. Thus all the actors talk in a continuous flow, making their thoughts explicit, until the director shouts 'Go on' – at which point the actors pick up the scene exactly where it stopped, without a break. This can be done as many times as necessary in any scene.

Since the characters' thoughts are in continual motion, in direct relation to what is happening on the stage, this exercise can prevent the actors from lapsing into static lakes of emotion such as still sadness, or joy, or any emotional state whatsoever which doesn't have this constant flux of ideas. It can also help to structure a scene around the central action, as long as the thoughts are related to this central action. Furthermore, the exercise helps the actor to prepare subtext.

3 Interrogation

Each actor in turn goes to sit 'in the dock' in front of the rest of the group. In character, they are then interrogated by the group (also in character) about what they think of the other characters, what they think about the events in the play, anything. The exercise is conducted like court proceedings.

Variation

The same exercise, but it is conducted while the scene is playing. So at any point an actor can be questioned mid-action – the scene freezes, the actor answers the question, then the scene picks up immediately where it left off.

Variation

As above, except that the scene does not stop for the questions. The actor has to answer as best he can while continuing to play the scene.

4 The reconstruction of the crime

The actors rehearse a scene in front of the group. Whenever an actor comes to a moment she considers important, she can turn to the audience and speak directly to them, in character, justifying her actions in the scene; i.e. 'I am doing this because of such and such a thing' or 'I am saying this because I feel such and such an emotion'. While the actor is speaking, everyone else in the scene freezes.

This exercise is different to Brecht's 'Street Scene' exercise,* in that here the character speaks in the first person, defending her own behaviour from a subjective standpoint, rather than dispassionately and objectively commenting on her actions in the third person.

5 Analytical rehearsal of motivation

It is often difficult for an actor to master the full complexity of a motivation, just as it can be difficult for a painter to use all the colours in her palette at the same time.

The 'analytical rehearsal of motivation' consists of the separate rehearsal of each of the elements of which the motivation is composed; first the will, then the counter-will, and finally the dominant will. For instance, Hamlet wants to kill himself, but he also wants to live. First rehearse the suicidal will, completely isolating this component of the motivation, and eliminating all desire to carry on living; the same script is used, only everything is now directed by that single will. Then rehearse the scene using only the will to live, eliminating all sign of the death wish.

Finally, rehearse the dominant will, the complete motivation. This helps the actor to deal with each of the individual components and integrate them into one whole. The better the actor can master will and counter-will, the better his interpretation of the dominant will.

* See p. 129, *Brecht on Theatre*, trans. John Willett, Methuen, 1964.

6 Analytical rehearsal of emotion

The same considerations apply to emotions as to motivations – in real life, emotions are never pure, one never feels 'pure hatred', 'pure love', etc. But when creating a character, an actor needs to sample this purity of emotion. Rehearse a scene giving the actors a single pure emotion as the starting point (the two main emotions being love and hate). The actors play the scene first with hate, with a violent and terrible hatred contained in every line and every action. Then they replay the same scene with love alone. Finally, depending on the precise nature of the conflict being shown, choose the most appropriate emotions for each scene: impatience, nervousness, disinterest, fear, or moral traits such as courage, cowardice, meanness, etc.

7 Analytical rehearsal of style

A variation on the preceding exercise, where the actors decide to play the piece in a different genre or style – circus, melodrama, farce, sitcom, documentary, etc.; whether appropriate or not, it is likely to generate new material or other possibilities.

8 Opposite circumstances

The aim of this exercise is to disturb the mechanisation of action and reaction which can occur because the actor knows beforehand what he is going to say, do and hear. The actor gets used to going on stage without even thinking. To avoid this, force the actor to play the scene in circumstances opposite to those he is familiar with. For example, a scene of great violence is to be played in complete calm; the actor must put across the same content using other words; alternatively, change the setting; or play a naturalistic scene which is usually full of props, with words and no objects at all; or even play a Lope de Vega text (for example) in a totally naturalistic fashion, or vice versa. Opposite circumstances can be applied to the setting, the motivations, or the script itself.

9 *Artificial pause*

Repeated delivery of the same words and movements in the course of rehearsals and performances tends to have a hypnotic effect on the actor, whereby his ability to perceive and be aware of what he is saying gradually becomes attenuated; consequently he puts it across in a correspondingly weaker fashion. Rehearsal with artificial pauses entails forbidding the actor to speak immediately, or immediately execute whatever action he has to do; on the contrary, he has to insert an artificial pause of five to ten seconds, or longer. Thus the actor loses the mechanical support which the rhythm of the text and action gave him, he has to forgo the 'structural' security of the piece, and his awareness and sensibility are reawakened. Any kind of thought is allowed to enter or be introduced into the artificial pause.

10 *Self-interrogation*

A variation on the artificial pause technique, in which the actor asks herself questions about what she has heard and what she is going to say or do, and considers the different possibilities. Thus the actor's choice will be determined by doubt, by a whole collection of possibilities and options which will eliminate the danger of 'mechanised' behaviour.

11 *Opposite thought*

This is an artificial pause exercise, in which the actor thinks about doing or saying exactly the opposite of what she is about to do or say in the script. In normal rehearsals, in the act of thinking about what she is going to say, the actor rules out the possibility of not saying it, or the possibility of saying the opposite of what she is going to say, or even of inserting dialectically the opposite of what she is saying into what she actually says.

In rehearsal of the opposite thought (which is also rehearsal of the opposite action), before speaking the actor thinks and feels exactly the opposite of what she will then say; thus her text and action will have all possible nuances of variation. When Romeo tells Juliet that he loves her, he must previously feel deep irritation that she won't let him leave, thus putting his life in danger. Before killing Desdemona, Othello must feel a great urge to make love to her.

215

12 Rehearsal of the cue

The fact of continually hearing another actor say the same words also has a hypnotic effect – one no longer hears, one no longer listens, one no longer understands what the other person is saying. The cue rehearsal exercise consists of inserting an artificial pause before speaking, in the course of which the actor thinks, or speaks, a résumé of what his interlocutor has just said. Thus he incorporates the actions of others within his own action, avoids subjective isolation and integrates himself within the overall conflictual structure.

13 Speed runs

This exercise is also called 'Two kicks', and is modelled on a Brazilian football exercise. None of the players can keep possession of the ball for more than two kicks. They cannot stop the ball, and having touched it twice, they must pass it to their neighbour. This exercise is especially recommended for actors in the Stanislavskian Actors' Studio mould; they push subjectivity to its utter extreme and allow that subjectivity to become reality. And it is this very process which transforms realism into expressionism; reality is seen through someone. Sometimes this kind of actor will pause for ages before saying 'Good morning'. These torrents of subjectivity hinder the structuring of action, since each actor wants to impose his own personal vision on reality. In the speed exercise, by acting fast, with as much emotional violence and as great a clarity of ideas as possible, the actor must work in such a way as to ensure that the action unfolds at high speed.

14 Silence on set – Action!

In this exercise any idea anyone has must be tried in rehearsal without discussion. An actor briefly suggests how a scene might be played and immediately the joker shouts, 'Silence on set – Action!' and without further ado the idea must be tried. No ideas, however wild, are rejected – their validity is immediately tested in action, rather than in discussion.

15 Invisible characters

A scene is played with one or more of the actors invisible – or at least not on stage. Since the other actors cannot see them, this forces them to listen and use their imaginations. Strangely, some actors reach a much clearer perception of their colleagues when they cannot see them. The actors are obliged to imagine the dialogue which is unsaid and the movements which are not made. However, there is a danger, in that actors can imagine the performances of invisible actors to the extent that when those actors are actually present, they project on to them images from their own mind; they end up working in the realm of imagination as opposed to reality. Such actors must understand that the essence of 'theatricality' is interaction.

16 Before and after

This is simply a matter of trying to improvise what could happen before each actor comes on stage and what could happen after they leave; the point of the exercise is to give a continuity to the action and enable the actor to enter the scene 'warmed up'.

17 Transference of emotion

This is a rather mechanical and tiring exercise, but one which can yield good results, particularly if there are inexplicable blocks in the actors' performances. I have already told the story of how an actor used to generate a terrible, deathly shiver on stage when, revolver to his head, he asked himself whether or not he should kill himself. The 'emotion memory' the actor was conjuring up consisted of thinking of how awful it was taking a cold shower in winter. The actor effected an original emotional transference, which overcame the block of his incapacity to feel the imminence of death. Likewise the woman actor who had never known orgasm, who used her summer day on Itapaon beach in Bahia to supply the emotion memory for an experience she had never had. These instances of emotional transference are not dishonest, because they help the actor to feel and express one emotion with another emotion as the starting point; cold water in winter has something of mortality about it, just as an ice-cream on a sunny beach does contain a touch of the orgasmic.

GAMES FOR ACTORS AND NON-ACTORS

18 Slow motion

Of necessity the actor has a subjective point of view when interpreting a part; he sees the whole work and all the other characters from that subjective standpoint. Thus it is a good idea to do the first rehearsals without the actors knowing which parts they are going to play. By contrast, the director must see the whole work in its totality, objectively. This conflict between the actors' subjectivity and the necessary objectivity of the director often stifles the possibility of the actor's creative richness. A scene can require a certain pace or speed which hinders the slow development of a character. The 'slow motion' exercise resolves this problem and gives the actor the time and space he was lacking to achieve all the actions, transitions and movements, he wanted to do; having once done them, it will be easier to condense them. This exercise should be alternated with the 'Speed' exercise (p. 216).

19 Sensory focus

A variation on the 'Slow motion' exercise. The actor tries to open his senses to all external stimulants, entering into sensory, sensual and even sexual contact with the outside world. There are people who make love mechanically, without the slightest hint of sensuality. The actor, by contrast, should be able to deliver even a mathematical formula sensually, i.e. 'aesthetically'.

20 Low volume

Sometimes an actor can lose some of the power of her thought or emotion in a particular scene because of the physical effort required to vocalise a sound, or make a move, or exaggerate an expression (for instance, when performing in the open air in front of thousands of people, with dogs or other animals wandering around). Turning down the volume can be a useful way to revitalise such scenes, so that the actor can concentrate all her energy on the part and not have to worry about her vocal power; in this way, the actor hears herself and gets a better grasp of what she is doing.

21 Exaggeration

The actors exaggerate everything – emotions, movements, conflicts, etc. – without deviating from the substance of the original piece, but going far beyond the normal limits of acceptability. The idea is not to replace one thing with something else, but to exaggerate; when hating, exaggerate the hatred; when loving, exaggerate the depth of the love; when crying, exaggerate the tears, etc. In trying to find the right setting for the microscope, the wise man does not increase the magnification bit by bit, but rather starts from the other end and works his way downwards. Similarly, the right level for a performance can be found after first having made it too big.

22 Free-style rehearsal

The actors are free to do whatever they like, to change their moves, script, everything; the only rule is that they mustn't physically endanger others (so that they may also do what they want). This exercise is based on the fact that a large proportion of artistic creation is rational, but by no means all. There is always the unexpected, an actor who lets himself be carried away by the moment, by irrational and unplanned sensations. This free rehearsal can give rise to numerous nuances. When an actor is not sure what her colleagues are going to do, it can act as a stimulus to creativity and observation. Like the preceding exercise, this can be dangerous if undertaken before establishing the fundamental, rational premisses on which the piece rests.

23 Reconnaissance

A single actor does all the actions and says all the lines, not in the present – there and then – but in a vision of what she will think in the future; 'I will say this, then I'll do that, but not now.' First we reconnoitre the paths to be trod; we do nothing, we simply identify what we are going to do.

24 Caricature

An exercise which can be done in two ways: either the actor himself ridicules his performance, or one of his colleagues does it. Bergson said that people laugh at their own automatism, their own rigidity. When you do a caricature of someone, laughter is provoked by the revelation of the surprising in the automated behaviour of the person being caricatured. If the actor is able to see, via the caricature, what is automated in his own performance, he will easily be able to modify or revitalise that performance.

25 Swapping characters

In order to gain a better understanding of the characters, revolve the actors and their roles in the course of a rehearsal (preferably swapping within a single relationship – husband/wife, father/son, boss/worker, etc.). The actors do not need to know each others' parts by heart, it is enough for them to give a general idea, the rough content of the role.

26 Need versus will

It is often the case that the 'will' of a character is none other than the expression in individual terms of a social need. The social need becomes flesh and is individualised in a 'psychology'. The important thing is the character's social function and not his idiosyncrasy. The Pope 'wants' Galileo to respond to the accusations of the Inquisition only because he is Pope. The genocidal war against the heroic Vietnamese people was led by three presidents – Kennedy, Johnson and Nixon. Three psychological characters, but a single social function, president of a misanthropic imperialism. The character 'believes' in the action which, as a matter of 'duty', he must carry out. But it can also happen that the individual will enter into conflict with the social necessity. In this exercise, the actor tries to feel, understand and demonstrate that all his actions are predetermined in relation to what he can or cannot 'want'. The exercise works on the opposition between 'will' and 'duty', between the 'I want' and the 'I should'. Do it, even if you don't want to.

27 The rhythm of scenes

In the course of a rehearsal with the script, the actors invent a rhythm they feel matches each scene, and they start playing the scene with that rhythm. The rhythm changes when the content of the scene changes. The idea is not to sing or chant the script, but to speak it with rhythm. This is an exercise which helps the integration of the group and the objective structuring of the 'subjectivities' (of each actor and each part).

28 Holy theatre

Play a scene as if it were a mass, with great piety; each detail acquires importance, becomes magnificent. This is the perfect antithesis to the *'laissez-faire'* of the 'free-style rehearsal'.

29 Analogy

To give their imaginations freer rein, the actors decide to improvise a scene analogous to the one they are working on. For instance, if they are rehearsing a scene of fascist repression by the Brazilian police against the people, what better than to do an 'analogous' improvisation on the Nazi repression of the Jews, or Governor Wallace's police against the blacks in Alabama?

The tick-tock sequence

These games serve mainly to develop the actor's agility, his capacity for rapid changes of emotion or character, giving him a greater physical, mental and emotional suppleness, along with greater awareness and concentration. The more difficult the conditions the actor works in, the richer his ultimate creation. These sessions are vital for shows which use the 'joker system'.

1 Plain tick-tock

All the actors against the wall. The director, or an actor, says a line from the script and gives indications on how the scene should be played: hideous caricature, with exaggerated love, etc. Immediately all the actors who are in the scene which contains this line rush to the positions they normally occupy when this line is said. Thus the starting point for their action is this line and the suggested playing style. A few minutes later, a second actor says a line, with another style. The action of the scene is immediately interrupted and is speedily replaced by the second scene requested; the actors take up the positions they occupy when this second line is spoken, and so on with other lines and other subjects.

221

2 Tick-tock-tag

Exactly the same, except that the actors who are in the first scene
but not the second, continue to perform it at the same time as the
second scene is being played. Sometimes some of the actors in the
first scene also have something to do in the second – so those who
remain in the first scene do the 'Invisible characters' exercise (p.
217). After a few minutes, a third actor delivers a third line and a
third theme: all the actors who are in that scene immediately start
playing the scene as requested by the third actor, starting from the
line indicated. The actors who are in the first or second scenes but
not the third, continue in their respective scenes, with invisible
characters if necessary. Thus three scenes will be being performed
in three different ways. You take this up to a maximum of five scenes.
When a scene reaches its end, the actors move on to the next scene.
If they reach the end of the final scene of the play, they start again
with the opening scene. Once a scene has been started, the actors are
not all allowed to move on to the next scene suggested; there must
be at least one actor per scene (all the others being invisible
characters). In the end, there will be five simultaneous scenes.

3 Tick-tock-tag in the hot seat

In this variation all the starting-point lines must correspond to scenes
in which one actor has an important role. This serves to concentrate
the effectiveness of the exercise on a particular actor who is having
difficulties.

4 Tick-tock-tag ping-pong

This is a variation which increases the difficulties. In the preceding
exercises the actors move from one scene to the other without ever
going backwards in chronology. In the ping-pong variation, if the
actor has no lines and no actions in the main scene – the last scene –
he must play ping-pong on one of the scenes in which the character
he is playing has an important line or role; so while playing his part
in the latter scene, the actor must remain conscious of both scenes.
All the scenes are performed in the same acting area. This exercise
is a constant game of ping-pong of actors through the scenes. Each
actor, when he jumps from one scene to the other, must immediately
go to the heart of the proposed subject: love, hate, etc. The actor

thus ends up having five scenes to play and five ways of doing them. These jumps must be as light as a ping-pong ball.

And if liked, to increase the concentration requirement still further add a piece of music which has nothing whatsoever to do with the scenes!

4

FORUM THEATRE: DOUBTS AND CERTAINTIES

Forum Theatre is still in its infancy, and much research and experimentation will be required before this new form reaches its full maturity; at present we are still at the stage of exploration, of finding and opening up new ways of working

This particularly applies to the Forum Theatre 'show'. In Latin America, I never took part in a 'show'; all the Forum Theatre sessions were organised by a core group of people of homogenous social origin, whose common interest was the resolution of relatively immediate problems. The Latin American experience had led me to construct a model ideal for Latin America, or at least for the particular experiments I had taken part in. The development of Forum Theatre in numerous directions in Europe inevitably entails a reconsideration of all the forms, structures, techniques, methods and processes of this kind of theatre. Everything is once again open to question.

Only the fundamental principles of the Theatre of the Oppressed are excluded from this re-evaluation, because they are what defines Forum Theatre as Theatre of the Oppressed – its intention to transform the spectator into the protagonist of the theatrical action and, by this transformation, to try to change society rather than contenting ourselves with interpreting it.

Now in all this fresh discussion and re-experimentation around the multiple forms and fashions of practising Forum Theatre, how many doubts and how many certainties come to light? Notwithstanding these doubts and certainties, I think I can suggest some twenty fundamental topics, to which we could usefully apply ourselves.

TWENTY FUNDAMENTAL TOPICS

1 Oppression or aggression?

Let us imagine the following situation: a man is in a gas chamber. He has a few minutes left before his death. The executioner opens the cyanide capsule. Elsewhere, another man is tied up, with his eyes blindfolded, in front of the firing squad. A few seconds more and the officer will shout: 'Fire!'

Can one make a Forum Theatre scene starting from such givens? Can a spect-actor shout 'Stop!' and replace the protagonist to try to find a solution? I think not.

Certainly, these are extreme cases. But groups do often prepare forum pieces which present this kind of situation, with a degree of plot development such that the possible options are limited or non-existent and that there is nothing more one can do. In such cases – when the spect-actors are disarmed on being confronted with the model – the effect is negative in all respects. This is fatality or impossibility! And our goal with Forum Theatre is to make breaches, to open up paths of liberation, not drive people up against a wall of resignation.

For example, I remember a Forum Theatre scene in which a girl was raped in the underground, at midnight, by four armed individuals, when waiting alone on a deserted platform. Obviously in this case, apart from physical self-defence, there was not a great deal the girl could have done. And all the spect-actors' interventions highlighted the inadequacy of the model, in which the only real prospect was inevitable catastrophe. I remember another model where a woman was beaten up by her husband, at their home and without a single witness. Or again the case of the man seized by three armed policemen in the street.

In all these situations there is nothing, or almost nothing, anyone can do to bring the piece to a different ending. The girl can run and call the station-master. The woman can scream. The man can call for help. Then what? These stories are about physical aggression, pure physical aggression, and thus any solutions can only be in the realm of the physical. Which is to say that if the three people had learnt karate or ju-jitsu, then, sure, they could have broken the oppression.

Cases like these are of no use for Forum Theatre shows because they do not present *oppression* against which one can struggle but *aggression* which one cannot evade.

225

Let us be clear about the concepts: we use the word 'aggression' to designate the last level of oppression. 'Oppression' is not an exclusively physical phenomenon, to be resolved in physical terms. Oppression is very often interiorised; *the oppressed can still liberate themselves*. Victims of aggression, if they are physically strong, can return the aggression – one possibility, that's all.

Consequently, when the model presents an aggression, the only answer is resignation because all the possible courses of action depend exclusively on physical strength. What is even more pernicious is that this totally demobilises the spect-actor. And in situations like this I believe it is best to go back, pick up the story again at an earlier point in time, and find out at what point the oppressed still had a choice of several solutions (before the scenario wends its way to an aggressive end). Take, for instance, the girl who went into the underground all on her own – what might she have done before the point at which she found herself alone on the platform? Why was she alone? Could she not have awaited the arrival of the train near the station-master (if there was such)? Could she not have insisted on being accompanied by a friend? Or, why hadn't she bought one of those tear-gas canisters designed for handbags? Or even, why didn't she stay over at her friend's place?

Similarly, the woman attacked by her husband, physically incapable of defending herself – why hadn't she left him earlier? Why had she stayed at home that night? Why didn't she call someone?

As for the man picked up by the police, what tactical errors had he committed to let himself be taken by surprise? What precautions should he have taken?

To summarise, if everything is impossible, if the situation is blocked, it only remains for the audience to become *witnesses* to the tragedy. The Polish director, Grotowski, said somewhere that the audience should be witnesses to an event, and by way of example he cited a scene which had made a great impression on him: it was a film which showed a Buddhist monk in Vietnam immolating himself by fire. The crackling of the flames merged with the death-rattle of his breath. A very powerful image which lends itself perfectly to a theatre where the spectator is a *witness*. But in the Theatre of the Oppressed, far from being a witness, the spect-actor is, or must do his utmost to become, the *protagonist* of the dramatic action. Consequently this image of a monk fated to die, an image of a man who cannot be saved, is unusable and the scene does not lend itself to an exercise of real action, which is the objective of all the forms of the Theatre of the Oppressed.

To make a good Forum Theatre piece with the monk scene, one would have to show the moment at which, having doused himself with petrol, the monk is still holding the box of matches in his hand, and the match has not been lit. At this key moment, when the thing has not yet been set in motion, an excellent forum could be done! But when the body is burning, nothing more can be done.

I also remember a book by a Jewish doctor describing the Nazi atrocities and the progressive restrictions imposed on the Jews. First, the carrying of the star of David – why not, some said, if we're proud of it? Then the prohibition on following professions such as doctor and lawyer – why not, they said, since we can do other jobs and, by giving way on this point, we will calm the enemy down? Then the obligation to live together, in ghettos – why not? – and finally the transportation to concentration camps and death. At no point in the book does this doctor make excuses for the Nazis having been the executioners of his race. And yet he, as a Jew, asked himself: in the gas chamber there was nothing more we could do, but before that, could we not have done something? This is a feasible subject for Forum Theatre – was it not possible to do something before? Who could have done it? Why didn't everyone do it? In the event of the same thing happening again, what could one do? (Of course many Jews did take positive actions when they realised the danger they were in – actions which ranged from emigration to armed resistance – though this is often ignored in histories describing the period.)

My conclusion is that Forum Theatre is always possible when alternatives exist. In the opposite case it becomes fatalist theatre.

2 The style of the model

When the central problem is concrete, generally the model tends towards selective realism. I would even go as far as to say that the majority of forum shows I have seen have been produced in this style. But this is absolutely not obligatory.

The most important thing, over and above anything else, is that Forum Theatre should be good theatre; that the model in itself offers a source of aesthetic pleasure. Before the 'forum' part begins, the show itself must be watchable and well constructed.

My own preference is that the model be developed by means of the various Image Theatre processes, especially the sequences of techniques which end in the construction of the 'ritual' concretising the subject being treated. It may be that the ritual in question is rich, theatrical and stimulating: for example, the mother's birthday ritual cited earlier (p. 144). Here are 'possible' theatrical elements, which can help to 'reify', or 'visualise', the relations between the characters.

By contrast, other rituals may have no hint of the theatrical, or the stimulating, about them. And the danger of a poor production is that it can seduce the audience into a spoken participation, into having *verbal* discussions about possible solutions, instead of doing it *theatrically*. In such cases, in my view it is best not to try to 'stage' or make use of the 'ritual' in its literal form, but by recourse to other Image Theatre techniques to find images which, however symbolic or surreal, can concretise the subject in a theatrical form, at the same time enriching it.

To give an example of this approach, in a show produced by French-language teachers in the course of their annual congress (Strasbourg 1979) and directed by Richard Monod and Jean-Pierre Ryngaert, there was a scene which depicted a government inspection of teachers. However, in theatrical terms, the ritual element of this kind of examination is poor. Two people seated side by side at the same table. So what did the teachers do? They remained faithful to the text used in such circumstances, but the scenic action they presented was the ritual of confession. The teacher knelt in front of a confessor. The point of this was not just to add a touch of theatre, but to highlight one of the fundamental characteristics of 'the inspection' – its 'confessional' aspect, the similarity between the teacher-inspector relationship and the worshipper-confessor relationship. The inspector-confessor had the power to absolve or condemn the teacher-worshipper. This is what we call 'extrapolated ritual'.

In the same show, another ritual also unfolded around a table; this was the giving of marks. This too was represented in a symbolic fashion, in the form of a pyramid with the headmaster at the top, then the maths teacher (highly placed in the hierarchy), then lower down, in fact right at the bottom, in this case under the table, all the other teachers who repeated in chorus the marks and criticisms doled out by the maths teacher. This is what we call a 'metaphoric ritual'.

In my view, the style is of little importance – one should use the style which is most appropriate to the content. Three forms of ritual are possible: (1) the realistic ritual, (2) the extrapolated ritual, (3) the

metaphoric ritual. The former remark also applies to the staging –
and I would say the same *vis-à-vis* the dramaturgy, but that would lead
us on to another topic: 'Can a Forum Theatre show be Chekhovian?',
which remains to be seen.

On another training course, a group of teachers suggested a scene
which at first seemed to offer limited theatrical potential. A young
woman nurse is arguing with four of her colleagues, seeking support
in her stand on nurses' rights against the head of the staff. One after
the other, they refuse, citing different reasons. The first because she
wants to keep her reputation and not get mixed up in battles; the
second because being a nurse is for her almost a religion; the third
out of fear that in demanding their rights, she would lose her job; the
fourth because the union this, the union that – union was the only
word she knew.

In the staging of this scene, the actors opted for a symbolic
representation: actor 1 put a bag over her head and hid in the darkest
corner of the room; actor 2 dressed up as a nun; actor 3 busied herself
with scrubbing the floor; actor 4 blocked her ears so she couldn't
hear. In the following scene, the head of the staff was seated on a
chair, on top of a huge table, with two secretaries protecting her from
the young nurse, who was making her request on her knees. *The
images* here contained a significance which was easily understood in
the debate, in the forum.

3 Do the problems have to be urgent or not? Should they be simple or complex?

One day, one of my pupils at Censie suggested doing a Forum
Theatre scene on her own situation, her problems. She was tired, she
told me, of so many forums about concrete, urgent problems – wages,
strikes, oppressed women, factory work, rates of production, etc. She
offered her own problem. She was young, living alone in a huge flat;
her separated and re-married parents each lived in their own places.
In a kind of way, she wanted to reconstitute a family. She had invited
some friends to live with her. They had come, a couple, plus a male
friend and another female friend. But her companions did not fulfil
the required functions of father and mother. When she wanted them
there, they were out; when she wanted to be alone, they were there.
Ultimately she wanted to get married to set up her own 'family home'
and she was giving serious thought to monogamy … while at the

same time she was attracted to her actual polygamous situation. She wanted contradictory things, she wanted everything at the same time.

We did not do that forum; as with the rest of her life, she wanted at the same time as not wanting... .

Some time later, I proposed this subject to another group. I should say that in the process I learnt an enormous amount about the Parisian youth of today. But I should also say that in this case the lack of precision in the model led to a lack of precision in the forum. The model did not throw a clear enough light on the problems and the oppressions, and the forum didn't get very far, though in theatrical terms it was very lively.

This is open country. When one has a problem which is clear, concrete, urgent, logically the debate should lead to solutions which are just as clear, concrete and urgent. A woolly subject will lead to woolliness – I think.

It is possible that, on the contrary, a lack of precision may only be apparent and the forum may serve to *analyse* a situation without *synthesising* possible solutions.

4 Do we have to arrive at a solution or not?

I believe it is more important to achieve a good debate than a good solution. Because, in my view, the thing which incites the spect-actors into entering into the game is the discussion and not the solution which may or may not be found.

Even if one does reach a solution, it may be good for the person who has proposed it, or good within the confines of the debate, but not necessarily useful or applicable for all the participants in the forum.

Certainly, one almost always learns something useful in a forum debate. I remember, for example, a show about the power of the medical profession. A sick person, the victim of a road accident, was taken to hospital where he was put through a whole series of hoops and hurdles before he could get to find out exactly what was wrong with him. From room to room and operating table to operating table, he was subjected to examinations and analyses of all kinds, and obliged to swallow various pills and be injected with various substances, without anyone telling him why.

The spect-actors tried a number of arguments on stage to obtain information, to force explanations. Till a woman appeared who, by a stroke of luck, was a nurse. Taking the role of the protagonist, she asked to sign a discharge form. She informed us that in French hospitals the law permits patients, whatever their state of health, to leave the hospital if they sign a document by which they take charge of themselves and discharge the hospital and the doctors of all responsibility.

Well, this was a useful piece of information which neither we nor the audience knew. And it's good to know for the future. But already, even before we were aware of this fact, we were all actively participating in the search for solutions, arguments, steps to take, if the situation should ever arise.

Debate, the conflict of ideas, dialectics, argument and counter-argument – all this stimulates, arouses, enriches, prepares the spectator for action in real life. Thus, when the model is not *urgent*, that is to say when it is not about having to act in reality immediately on leaving the show, finding a solution is not of prime importance.

Sometimes a forum can have the function of 'previewing' a solution which will automatically be tried on leaving the show. Take, for example, the case of a forum the purpose of which was to *form* a group of residents from an area to go in a delegation and register a complaint at the town hall, or to demand some right or other. In this case, the process is not simply a matter of providing a *stimulant for autonomous activity* but rather of developing a concrete, detailed plan of campaign, a strategy and tactics for an imminent action. Who will do the talking? What arguments will they put forward? What can they expect from the other side? Thus, in this case, it is absolutely vital not only to arrive at a generic solution, but to detail the concrete plans for the action which is to be taken.

5 Does the model of the future action need to be depicted or not?

I think that in the preceding case it is necessary to depict the model of the future action, since this action will be experienced in reality in the immediate future. This kind of depiction can function as a *dress rehearsal* of the actual act.

I also believe that in a Forum Theatre show, such a representation can help condense the results of the said forum. In all debate a portion escapes the audience's memory. A representation can help to summarise it.

However, certain precautions should be taken. If the model of future action is suitable for all those present, its representation will serve as fresh and final stimulus for the real action. In the opposite

case, one runs the risk of presenting an 'evangelist' model, rec-
ommending actions which are impossible to realise in practice. A
precaution to take, a danger to avoid.

6 Model or anti-model? Error or doubt?

Perhaps the term 'model' already contains the connotation of path to
follow. In fact, I have no hesitation in repeating that a piece of Forum
Theatre must always present doubt and not certainty, must always
be an *anti-model* and not a *model*. An anti-model to debate and not
a model to follow.

There is another word which can, in some instances, influence or
manipulate the audience (when the desired effect is exactly the
opposite) – the word *error*. If we inform our spect-actors that the
protagonist of our anti-model has committed an error, this implies
that we think the protagonist has taken the wrong approach. However,
this is for the spect-actor to say, not for us. Consequently, the right
way of expressing this is to say that in the *anti-model*, we have
doubts about the way the oppressed protagonist behaved.

7 The conduct of the joker

During the two-week Theatre of the Oppressed encounter in 1979
(La Quinzaine du Théâtre de l'Opprimé au Théâtre Présent), we had
the chance to observe at least ten jokers in action. Each had their
own personality and behaved differently in front of the audience.
Nevertheless, from our observation, we can conclude that there are
some rules for jokers which are almost obligatory.

1 Jokers must avoid all actions which could manipulate or influence
the audience. They must not draw conclusions which are not self-
evident. They must always open the possible conclusions to debate,
stating them in an interrogative rather than an affirmative form, in
such a way that the audience can answer 'Yes' or 'No', 'We said
this and not that', instead of being confronted with the joker's own
personal interpretation of events.

2 Jokers personally decide nothing. They spell out the rules of the
game, but in complete acceptance from the outset that the audience
may alter them, if it is deemed necessary for the study of the
proposed subject.

3 The joker must constantly be relaying doubts back to the audience
so that it is they who make the decisions. Does this particular

solution work or not? Is this right or wrong?

And this principle applies most of all in relation to the spect-actors' interventions. Often a spect-actor will say 'Stop!' before the preceding spect-actor has finished their own intervention. The joker must than tactfully persuade the newly intervening spect-actor to exercise patience, while also trying to sense what the audience wants; they may well have already understood the intervention and want to move on. Another delicate situation, which the joker must be able to refer back to the audience, is the evaluation of whether or not the spect-actor/protagonist has won. In the event of a spect-actor victory (and only then), anyone is free to replace the oppressors. Once again, the decision rests with the audience.

4 Jokers must watch out for all 'magic' solutions. They can interrupt the spect-actor/protagonist's action if they consider this action to be magic, not *ruling* that it is magic, but rather asking the audience to decide.

Another memory: we did a Forum Theatre show for the lawyer's union. At a certain point, a spect-actor (a judge) mounted the stage with the intention of dismantling the court, and 'destroying' the files on the accused, who had been caught red-handed. As I was the joker, I interrupted the scene with a cry of 'Stop, that's magic!' But the audience, which was made up entirely of judges and attorneys, immediately opposed this; no, this was not magic, they themselves believed it, for them it was the only solution – all the more so since this was exactly what they had done two or three weeks earlier, in analogous circumstances, in a Paris court of law. For me it was magic, while for them – and they were all personally involved – it was real, it was possible. I immediately took a step back and let the scene follow its course.

Sometimes the solutions proposed are at the opposite end of the spectrum to *magic*, they are *inadequate*. In these cases, the joker must try to push the spect-actors into finding more active solutions. The magic solution is cheating, but the inadequate solution is demobilising.

However, we should take note of the fact that when the audience shouts that such-and-such a solution is not magic, that the solution is possible, *that shout is the beginning of a process of self-motivation* on the spect-actor's part, it is the stimulus for a real action.

5 The physical stance of the joker is extremely important. Some jokers are tempted to mix with the audience, to sit with other spect-actors; this can be completely demobilising. Others, by their demeanour, allow their own doubts, their own indecision or timidity, to show through. Now everything that happens on stage, by which I mean all the *images* produced by the body or by objects, is *significant*. If the joker on stage is tired or confused, he or she will transmit a tired and disorientated image to the audience. But beware – being dynamic does not mean seeking to influence the outcome!

6 Finally, as I have already said, the joker must be Socratic – dialectically – and, by means of questions, by means of doubts, must help the spectators to gather their thoughts, to prepare their actions. *Maieutics* – the joker is a midwife. But a *maieutics* of body and spirit, not simply a cerebral *maieutics*. The joker must assist the birth of all ideas, of all actions.

8 Theatricality or reflection?

Beyond the conduct of the joker, there is the conduct of the event itself. Ultimately, should the presentation of a forum tend towards the theatrical? Should one seek to produce an event which is good theatre, even after the presentation of the anti-model, or should one, on the contrary, aim to stimulate reflection, argument, action?

I think that this depends on the objectives of the show and the conditions in which it is being enacted. It depends on the number of participants and on concrete givens, such as place, subject-matter, nature of the stage, etc.

Normally, in a theatre, there is an almost inevitable tendency towards theatricality. I even know one group who have introduced elements of spectacle into forum; for example, a gong, like a bell in a boxing match, giving notice of the beginning or end of a new spect-actor's intervention. Another group limits the duration of each intervention, to force everyone to think quickly (and also to achieve dramatic effects of 'rhythm'). In the end, I think that the presence of a large audience – in Porto and Stockholm I did forums for audiences of over 1,000 people and at Sant'Arcangelo di Romagna, 3,000 people – makes the theatrical nature of the show almost inevitable. It is also in the latter type of situation that exhibitionists are at their most numerous – spect-actors tempted to lead the performance towards burlesque or vaudeville. All such excesses are to be avoided

... but I still believe in the power of forum as stimulus and activator, even in these extreme cases.

When dealing with smaller audiences, of motivated people, reflection gains the upper hand, and the search for solutions can be more fruitful; especially if the forum is to be followed by a real action.

9 The staging

Very often the groups who practise Forum Theatre are poor groups, with limited economic resources. Generally speaking, sets are limited to tables, chairs, and nothing else. This should be taken as contingency, rather than choice. Ideally the set should be as fully developed as possible, with as minute detail and as much complexity as is necessary. The same goes for the *costumes*. The characters should be recognisable by the *clothes* they wear and the *objects* they use. Very often, oppression is reflected in clothes, in things. Objects and dress should be real, charged, clear, stimulating. The more care is taken over the aesthetics of the show, the more it will stimulate, and the more the audience will take part. How wonderful it is to see a spect-actor come on stage and dress for the part, before she starts to act! The spect-actor feels more protected, feels more one of the dramatis personae (without ceasing to be a person). A spect-actor in her character's costume is much freer, much more creative.

This also applies to the other elements of the staging. Ultimately the *anti-model* is a piece of theatre just like any other, with the single difference that it is not evangelical, it carries no message, no words of wisdom, just doubts and anxieties which will stimulate judgement and action on the part of the assembled audience. Which is why if one can use music, it should be used a lot; if one can use dance, there should be as much dancing as possible! If one can play with colours, why limit oneself to black and white?

Yet another important thing – blocking, movements on stage. Every movement of every actor is significant. The stage business and the actor's playing styles together endow each moment with dynamic images which carry meaning. Movement cannot be arbitrary, it must have a content. The distance between two people is important in terms of the ideas it conveys, rather than as a matter of centimetres and metres.

In Rio de Janeiro, a Forum Theatre piece involved a young man who loved music and dancing. And yet, on stage, he didn't dance and not a note of music was heard. The fact that he loved music and

235

dancing was not articulated 'aesthetically' to the spect-actors, but verbally. Besides, this was not one of the essential elements of the problem. When, on its second showing, music and movement were introduced into the model, the spect-actors were much more stimulated and participated with much greater enthusiasm.

10 The function of the warm-up

In all the forum shows I have taken part in, there has always been an element of 'warming-up' of spect-actors. Generally this is done in one of two possible ways.

(1) Over ten or fifteen minutes, the joker explains Theatre of the Oppressed, recounts some experiences of forum shows or Invisible Theatre, and fixes the rules of the game which is to follow.

Then he proposes some exercises, starting with the simplest, the least off-putting, those that arouse the least resistance. For example, in Egypt, touching exercises provoked a very powerful resistance; which, by contrast, was far from the case with magistrates in Paris! It all depends on the culture, the country, the region, the moment.

After the exercises, we move on to Image Theatre. Here the spect-actors begin to work aesthetically, and to suggest subject-matter for images themselves.

Then finally the group presents the anti-model, and from that starting point comes the forum.

(2) I have in the past used, and seen others use, other less effective processes – starting immediately with exercises, with an explanation *a posteriori*. In these cases, I have noticed that a portion of the audience feels manipulated and reacts negatively. By contrast when the explanation comes first, the joker almost always ends up winning over the audience, and gaining their acquiescence and their confidence.

Which doesn't mean that the warm-up is absolutely indispensable. I believe it prepares the spect-actors for action. In any case, the thing which will best prepare them is really the subject-matter and the play itself. The case of Het Trojaan Paard, a Belgian group from Antwerp, is significant; they have performed the same show, about the woman who is 'a leader at work, a slave in the home', in a hundred towns in Belgium and Holland (the group speak Flemish), without ever doing the slightest preliminary warm-up. They just explain what is going to happen. And the show is so evocative and so galvanising that all the spect-actors always want to take part.

11 The function of the actor

Forum Theatre demands a different style of acting. In certain African countries the people measure the talents of singers by the extent to which they can seduce their audiences into singing along with them. That is what should happen with good Forum Theatre actors. In their performances there must not be the slightest trace of the narcissism so commonly found in *closed* theatre shows. Because the presentation of the anti-model should, by contrast, principally express doubt; each action should contain its own negation; each phrase should leave open the possibility of saying the opposite of what is being said; each *yes* allows for an imagined *no*, or a *perhaps*.

During the forum proper, actors must be extremely dialectical. When they take up a counter-stance against a spect-actor/protagonist who wants to break the oppression, they must be honest and show that the oppression is not so easily defeated. They must show the difficulties which will appear, while retaining a manner which encourages the spect-actor to break the oppression. Which means that while still countering every phrase and action, they should awaken in the spect-actor other stances, other approaches. While impeding the attempt to break the oppression, they should rouse the spect-actor to achieve it.

If the actor is too firm, it can discourage or, worse still, frighten the spect-actor. If the actor is too soft and vulnerable, with no counter-arguments or counter-actions, it can mislead the spect-actor into believing that the problem posed by the play is easier to resolve than he or she thought.

In Berlin, at the Hochschüle der Kunst, a forum showed a young man trying to convince his family to give him a certain sum of money a month. In order to achieve this, he had to undergo endless rituals, family conversations and reunions, discussions about the war, about the past, about members of the family who had disappeared, etc. The actors were so enthusiastic that every spect-actor who came forward was subjected to an avalanche of arguments, to such an extent that very soon the whole audience was up in arms and shouted in unison 'Stop – that's magic!', concluding that no family could be as fear-somely exasperating as that.

I repeat, the actors must be dialectical, must know how to give and take, how to hold back and lead on, how to be creative. They must feel no fear (which is common with professional actors) of losing their place, of standing aside. A great magician is someone who not only knows how to do magic, but also how to teach tricks to others. A great footballer loses no status by teaching someone else how to shoot with both feet.

One learns by teaching others. Pedagogy is transitive. Or it isn't pedagogy.

12 The repeated scene

Once the anti-model has been shown and the debate is under way, it is often the case that several spect-actors, one after another, want to break the same oppression. This means that the same scene will be shown several times. The only thing to be careful of is letting the show (however well constructed it may be) become monotonous. So, a word of advice: on each repetition the actors should accelerate the rhythm, so as to avoid showing exactly the same scene several times, or any more than necessary. Excessive repetition can diminish the audience's interest, enthusiasm and creativity.

13 Macrocosm and microcosm

In a good Forum Theatre show, the actors must be very much in tune with each other and ready for every eventuality. It can happen that the solution desired or suggested by a spect-actor may be unachievable within the 'microcosmic' world of the anti-model. To find the solution it is necessary to look elsewhere. How?

In Turin a young couple were searching for a flat. A letting agent asked them for their papers, their wage slips, asked them what their resources were, and so on. Then a man came in who wanted to rent the same flat as the venue for occasional liaisons with his mistress. He could have gone to a hotel, but he preferred the comfort of a flat. The agent, in view of the man's economic status, decided in his favour, instead of offering the flat to the young couple who really needed it. What was the solution? The young people broke into the 'flat' and occupied it. And what was the agent's next move? Calling the police.

However, in the anti-model there was no scene with the police. The agent dialled a telephone number and immediately an actor off stage answered; he turned himself into a police inspector. The other actors, assisted by a few spect-actors, immediately improvised the police station. The inspector decided to intervene, arresting the couple and sending them to the police station. There, the young man rang his lawyer. In the microcosm of the anti-model, of course there was no lawyer. No problem – an actor answered and once again, with the help of a few spect-actors, all in character, a lawyer's office sprang up. And now it was the lawyer's turn – he phoned the young people's parents. Actors and spect-actors improvised homes, families, parents and grandparents, uncles and aunts and neighbours. In a matter of minutes the whole room was involved in a huge scene in which almost everybody had a part.

This goes to show that the anti-model presents only a microcosm – but that that microcosm fits into the macrocosm of the whole of the society under examination. The whole of society can be involved and can enter into a Forum Theatre show, whatever the dimensions of the anti-model.

14 How to replace a character without transforming it into another

A spect-actor can sometimes replace an actor and modify the character in such a way that the solution becomes completely magic. The spect-actor must respect the 'givens' of the problem.

If the spect-actor replaces the actor and exactly follows the behaviour of the character in the anti-model, clearly he or she won't greatly change anything in either the action or the course of events. However, it is equally clear that something must change. An *individual* is replacing another *individual*, a spect-actor is replacing a character, a human being is replacing another human being. Something changes. What can one change and what can one not change?

First: one cannot change the given social circumstances of the problem. One cannot alter the familial relationships between characters, the ages, the economic status, etc., which condition their actions. If these factors are adjusted, the solutions will be of no use because they will apply to cases which have nothing to do with those proposed in the anti-model.

Second: one cannot change the character's motivation. For example, in Norrköping one anti-model showed a young working woman who was forced to abandon her job in order to follow her husband to his new place of work in another town. Her central motivation in taking this course of action was to hang on to her husband. A woman spect-actor was the first to come on stage, and the first thing she did was to say to hell with her husband! Obviously, she was changing an essential 'given' of the situation. If the woman in the anti-model had detested her husband, his transfer to another town would have been a solution, not a problem. But she loved him.

Thus, what can be changed is the characteristics of the motivation: how to do what one has to do. Which is where the problem resides.

15 What is a 'good' oppression?

It is not uncommon during the preparation of a forum to hear a group discussing what constitutes a good or bad oppression, which oppressions are important, which are minor. My feeling is that all oppressions are of equal importance ... to the people who are being subjected to them.

There is always someone suffering more than us, though that is not an argument which should prevent us speaking about our own oppressions, even if they seem minimal in comparison with those inflicted on, for example, the Cambodian refugees on the Thai border, the unarmed victims of armed groups of soldiers or smugglers. Our oppressions are infinitesimal compared with those of the Hindu untouchables, pariahs of a caste-oriented society. But when we are suffering, our oppressions weigh heavily enough on us. The purpose of the Theatre of the Oppressed is to help us to free ourselves!

Equally, I believe that one should not subordinate oppressions, ranking one below another.

Of course there are some oppressions which are more savage than others; of course some oppressions bear down on a great number of people with more cruelty than others. But I believe the struggle against one oppression to be indissociable from the struggle against all oppressions, secondary as they may be.

Thus I believe that we should not hierarchise different kinds of suffering; we should consult our audience and use all oppressions for the construction of Forum Theatre anti-models, as long as these oppressions are real oppressions, experienced by the forum participants, who must have a genuine desire to free themselves.

16 Who can replace whom?

For a Forum Theatre showing to qualify as true Theatre of the Oppressed, only spect-actors who are victims of the same oppression as the character (by identity or by analogy) can replace the oppressed protagonist to find new approaches or new forms of liberation. This attempt to find solutions does not only have a meaning in the context of the play; the spect-actors (who are as oppressed as the protagonist) will at the same time be training for self-defensive action in their real lives.

If a spect-actor who is not experiencing the same oppression wants to replace the oppressed protagonist, we manifestly fall into theatre of advice; one person showing another what to do – the old evangelical theatre.

But there is yet another possibility, which can be at once different and stimulating. At Stockholm, for example, during the Soder Festival, a group showed a forum anti-model on the relations between men and women. I remember a young girl telling me something which amazed me:

I am afraid to tell a man that I fancy him.

Why? Because you are afraid that he might say he doesn't fancy you?

No, it's much more complicated. I am afraid that he might say that he *does* fancy me.

So where's the problem?

It's even more complicated than that. I am afraid that he might say yes, but that in his heart of hearts this might not be true – that he might be saying yes because he doesn't dare say no ...

As you see, the problem was far from simple. ... Anyway, as I am not in the habit of hierarchising oppressions, I accepted the idea of doing a forum on this subject without hesitation. The show took place in the street, on a Friday – for those who don't know Sweden, I should explain that on Friday evening after ten o'clock half the population is completely drunk! This added more spice to the show!

The first scene went off without any problems, the second likewise. In the third scene, which contained this very dialogue with the indecisive girl, a male member of the audience shouted 'Stop!' We assumed he wanted to replace the young man, but he took the place of the girl to show how, in his view, girls should behave in such situations. I was going to stop him – I was the joker – but before I did so, as always, I consulted the audience. The whole audience shouted to let him go on. And the man, happy as Punch(!), began to give lessons in good behaviour to the women in the audience. They listened and plotted their revenge. So when he thought that he was about to retire victorious, several women spect-actors, in quick succession, with a shout of 'Stop!', hurried to take the place of ... the young man! So on stage a man was showing women how he thought they should behave, while the women were playing the role of the man and showing men how they should act.

The result was extraordinary, because men and women, playing the roles of their 'adversary', were showing theatrically (aesthetically and not merely verbally) what they thought of each other; they were trying to correct one another, to demonstrate what oppressed them in their interlocutor's behaviour. And it is worth saying in passing that their performances, in terms of authenticity and experience, were neither exaggerated nor for a single moment caricatured! However, generally speaking one should steer clear of the non-oppressed person (who is very often in fact the oppressor, as in the foregoing example) who claims the right to give lessons or show tactics to the oppressed themselves.

This episode also taught me something else; the Theatre of the Oppressed does have its rules, and these must be respected. But if, by chance, the audience at a particular moment and for a particular reason decides to change these rules, then you change them. Nevertheless the only rules which the Theatre of the Oppressed cannot alter are its two fundamental principles: spect-actors must be the protagonists of the dramatic action and these spect-actors must prepare themselves to be the protagonists of their own lives. That is the most important thing.

17 How should an anti-model be rehearsed?

An anti-model, like any other play, can be rehearsed in different ways. However, I suggest the method which seems to me to have always yielded the best results, and which can equally well be used in the form of 'improvisation' for the dramaturgic construction. It involves a process of analytical exercises on motivation and style, before attacking 'synthetic' rehearsals which combine these parts into a whole.

Having established the 'embryo' of the piece (or having mapped out the piece of its entirety), the actors should analytically rehearse the same text a number of times. Thus a first rehearsal forces them to 'analyse', by which I mean to separate, to individualise, motivations. For example, 'hate'; all the actors in all their scenes, in all the situations they encounter, must think exclusively in terms of hate; then immediately afterwards they must analyse everything from the opposite angle and rehearse scenes and situations with, for example, 'love' as the sole motivation.

This rehearsal of the isolated, purified motivation first of all helps the actor to discover nuances which may not have been obvious in the test, and make them rise to the surface and be thought and felt; secondly, in the case of the embryo of a piece (not the fully fledged play), it helps the actor to invent, to create words and actions to be integrated into the definitive text. Lastly, it helps the actor prepare responses to the future interventions of spect-actors.

Whenever any actor discovers or suspects that in their character or in a scene, a certain emotion or motivation is not sufficiently foregrounded, then an analytical rehearsal of that emotion or motivation should be set in motion. For example, performing the scene with the greatest possible indifference, then the greatest possible anxiety, then irony, distrust, fear, courage – in any manner which may assist the actors, by means of analysis, or concentration on a *single* emotion, a single motivation, in the gradual construction of their characters and the scenes they are involved in.

Then the piece can be rehearsed a number of times with an 'artificial pause', with each actor waiting a few seconds before saying their lines, and during these pauses trying to concentrate on the conflicts they're involved in. One can also do a 'pause for the opposite thought', during which the actor thinks the opposite of what they're going to say. Or even silent rehearsals, where the script is thought, interiorised, but not spoken.

So these are a few of the exercises which help develop motivations. And the same applies to questions of style – the text should be rehearsed in ways which display all its possibilities, all its facets: in cowboy western style, as comedy, tragedy, circus, opera, silent film, horror film, etc. At each rehearsal the actors can either read the same, previously set, script, but with a different style each time, or equally, if the group is starting from an embryo, they can introduce new lines and new actions, to arrive at the definitive script.

These rehearsals are useful as a way of arming the actors with a sort of painter's palette containing all the possible colours of their character; little by little they paint the character in. This last part of the process should be done during synthetic rehearsals, when all the scripts, all the actions, all the new forms of expression to be used on stage have been incorporated.

18 Can a forum change themes?

Yes, sometimes, as, for instance, happened in Rio in December 1979. The theme was simple: a lift had crashed in Copacabana, in one of those high-rise blocks of flats, which respect no architectural norm and whose existence is governed only by the law of profit. The residents, who were affected by the accident, wanted to institute proceedings against the construction company. A meeting was arranged, and this meeting was the forum.

But during the debate, the participants displayed such violence and exasperation that it was impossible to reach agreement, either on how to set proceedings in motion or even on the need for everyone to have their say and express their feelings.

In the end the theme of the forum was: how to organise a forum!

19 Can people remain 'spectators' in a Forum Theatre session?

No!

As a rule I never give peremptory answers, but in this case I answer blithely: No! In a Forum Theatre session no one can remain a 'spectator' in the negative sense of the word. It's impossible. In Forum Theatre, all the spect-actors know that they can stop the show whenever they want. They know that they can shout 'Stop!' and voice their opinion in a democratic, theatrical, concrete way, on stage. Even if they stay on the sidelines, even if they watch from a distance, even if they choose to say nothing, that choice is already a form of participation. In order to say nothing, the spect-actor must decide to say nothing – which is already acting.

Generally, everybody has something to say, and everybody ends up speaking, by entering into the game, especially if there is the motivation, the desire to express their opinion, their theory, their inclination, their wishes – and this expression is the scene. The keener the desire to take action, the more the spect-actors hurry on to the stage.

One more example, from Perugia, a little Italian city in Umbria, the first case of 'vertical' participation! Let me explain. I worked with a group of women, Le Passere, for three days. In the afternoons we worked on little scenes, with practically no script, just mimed, and in the evenings we would play these scenes in forum on the small medieval squares in the town. Small welcoming squares, surrounded by houses three or four storeys high, peppered with windows which gave directly on to the square. In the course of one of these evenings, I noticed that the windows were bulging with spectators, mainly women, who wanted to see the show. So I shouted to them to come down, to 'facilitate' their participation. A good number of these balcony spectators descended. The others pretended not to have understood or not to have heard. I persisted, then gave up; they stayed comfortably parked in their armchairs.

The show began, as always, with exercises. Up above, the women (most of whom were quite old) split their sides laughing. Then came the animals game, the images of the family and the ritual of coming home from work. At this point the women started barracking – what the intervening male spect-actors were showing down there on the square was untrue, it bore no resemblance to what they did when they came home. The wives on the balconies heaped abuse on these husbands who, on stage, were exemplary husbands; they made supper, took care of the children, saw to the cats, the dogs, they laid the table ... this was too much! So from above one heard cries of: '*Macalzone!* Liar! You're not like that here, you've never been in a kitchen in your life. Lazy buggers!'

The volubility of the Italians is such that in a few moments the whole place was in uproar, with horizontal shouting (from the participants in the audience in the street) and vertical shouting (women spect-actors in action, even though they were still settled at their windows). Attacks and reproaches flew in all directions till the husbands, who had shown these beautiful images of themselves, left the stage in shame ...

No one in that square had remained a 'spectator'; they had all been spect-actors, sitting, standing, far away, close by, up above and down below ...

20 When does a session of the Theatre of the Oppressed end?

Never – since the objective of the Theatre of the Oppressed is not to close a cycle, to generate a catharsis, or to end a development. On the contrary, its objective is to encourage autonomous activity, to set a process in motion, to stimulate transformative creativity, to change spectators into protagonists. And it is for precisely these reasons that the Theatre of the Oppressed should be the initiator of changes the culmination of which is not the aesthetic phenomenon but real life.

This is theoretically what should happen, and it is what has happened in practice.

Let us look at an example of Forum Theatre. The oppressed creates an anti-model, made up of images from his or her real life. In other words, an oppressive reality shown in images. These images possess two essential characteristics – being images of the real, and being real themselves. The fact of being represented makes them exist. Thus, starting from the creation of the anti-model, we can observe both the existence of a real oppression, and real images of that oppression. As if there were two worlds, the world of the reality from which the oppressed has drawn to create images, and the world of the images themselves.

Or to simplify: if I take a photo of Maria, Maria is a real being, but the photo, which is her image, that photo is also real. If I draw Maria or if I sculpt her, or if, inspired by her, I write a poem or novel, I am creating images of Maria, images which are real, like Maria.

By extension: the oppressed person responsible for the creation of the anti-model (a dynamic collection of images) and all the oppressed people who identify with him or her (by absolute identity or by analogy) are the privileged of this new form of theatre. They participate simultaneously in these two worlds, the world of the reality and the world of images made real. People who do not identify themselves with the oppressed who have created these images can also gain from them, but at a distance – they will never be able to apply to their real lives experiences realised in an imaginary life. As for the oppressed, they will be able to practise, to train for action, they will be able to act within the imaginary life of the theatre forum, so that afterwards, catalysed, they can immediately apply this new energy to their real lives, since these oppressed are part of both worlds.

Let us pause to stress this fundamental point. The oppressed act as subject in both these worlds. In their fight against the oppression of the imaginary world, they are practising and fortifying themselves in preparation for the future fight they will undertake against the real oppressions, and not simply against the real images of these oppressions.

In truth, a session of Theatre of the Oppressed has no end, because everything which happens in it must extend into life. Theatre shall never end! The Theatre of the Oppressed is located precisely on the frontier between fiction and reality – and this border must be crossed.

If the show starts in fiction, its objective is to become integrated into reality, into life.

Now, in 1992, when so many certainties have become so many doubts, when so many dreams have withered on exposure to sunlight, and so many hopes have become as many deceptions – now that we are living through times and situations of great perplexity, full of doubts and uncertainties, now more than ever I believe it is time for a theatre which, at its best, will ask the right questions at the right times. Let us be democratic and ask our audiences to tell us their desires, and let us show them alternatives. Let us hope that one day – please, not too far in the future – we'll be able to convince or force our governments, our leaders, to do the same: to ask their audiences – US – what they should do, so as to make this world a place to live and be happy in – yes, it is possible – rather than just a vast market in which we sell our goods and our souls.

Let's hope.
Let's work for it!